The Politics of
Black Citizenship

RACE IN THE ATLANTIC WORLD, 1700–1900
Published in Cooperation with the Library Company of Philadelphia's Program in African American History

SERIES EDITORS

Richard S. Newman, Rochester Institute of Technology
Patrick Rael, Bowdoin College
Manisha Sinha, University of Massachusetts, Amherst

ADVISORY BOARD

Edward Baptist, Cornell University
Christopher Brown, Columbia University
Vincent Carretta, University of Maryland
Laurent Dubois, Duke University
Erica Armstrong Dunbar, University of Delaware
  and the Library Company of Philadelphia
Douglas Egerton, LeMoyne College
Leslie Harris, Emory University
Joanne Pope Melish, University of Kentucky
Sue Peabody, Washington State University, Vancouver
Erik Seeman, State University of New York, Buffalo
John Stauffer, Harvard University

The Politics of Black Citizenship

FREE AFRICAN AMERICANS
IN THE MID-ATLANTIC
BORDERLAND, 1817–1863

Andrew K. Diemer

The University of Georgia Press
ATHENS

Paperback edition, 2019
© 2016 by the University of Georgia Press
Athens, Georgia 30602
www.ugapress.org
All rights reserved
Set in 10.8/13 Garamond Premier Pro by Kaelin Chappell Broaddus

Most University of Georgia Press titles are
available from popular e-book vendors.

Printed digitally

The Library of Congress has cataloged the hardcover
edition of this book as follows:
Names: Diemer, Andrew K., author.
Title: The Politics of Black Citizenship : Free African Americans in the Mid-Atlantic Borderland, 1817-1863 / Andrew K. Diemer.
Description: Athens, Georgia : The University of Georgia Press, 2016. |
Series: Race in the Atlantic world, 1700–1900 | Includes bibliographical references and index.
Identifiers: LCCN 2015036979 | ISBN 9780820349374 (hardcover : alk. paper) | ISBN 9780820349367 (e-book)
Subjects: LCSH: Free African Americans—Civil rights—Atlantic Coast (Middle Atlantic States)—History—19th century—Case studies. | Free African Americans—Maryland—Baltimore—History—19th century. | Free African Americans—Pennsylvania—Philadelphia—History—19th century. | African Americans—Segregation—Maryland—Baltimore—History—19th century. | African Americans—Segregation—Pennsylvania—Philadelphia—History—19th century. | Baltimore (Md.)—Race relations—History—19th century. | Philadelphia—Race relations—History—19th century.
Classification: LCC E185.18 D54 2016 | DDC 323.1198/07307409034—dc23
LC record available at http://lccn.loc.gov/2015036979

Paperback ISBN 978-0-8203-5550-4

FOR *Gretchen*

Africans have made fortunes for thousands, who are yet unwilling to part with their services; but the free must be sent away, and those who remain must be slaves? I have no doubt that there are many good men who do not see as I do; and who are for sending us to Liberia, but they have not duly considered the subject—they are not men of colour. This land which we have watered with our tears and our blood, is now our mother country and we are well satisfied to stay where wisdom abounds, and the gospel is free.

—RICHARD ALLEN, *Freedom's Journal*, November 2, 1827

CONTENTS

Acknowledgments xi
Abbreviations xiii
Introduction *1*

PART I: COLONIZATION AND AFRICAN AMERICAN IDENTITY

CHAPTER 1. The Dialectic of Colonization *11*
CHAPTER 2. America, Africa, Haiti *31*

PART II: BLACK POLITICS ON THE BORDER

CHAPTER 3. Interstate Diplomacy and Fugitive Slaves *49*
CHAPTER 4. Black Citizenship in the Age of Nat Turner *63*

PART III: THE POLITICS OF BLACK MORAL REFORM

CHAPTER 5. Black Citizenship and Reform *83*
CHAPTER 6. White Immigrants, Black Natives *112*

PART IV: THE FUGITIVE SLAVE LAW AND THE COMING OF THE CIVIL WAR

CHAPTER 7. The Tumultuous Politics of the Early 1850s *137*
CHAPTER 8. African Americans and "Political Insubordination" *161*
CHAPTER 9. The End of the Border: Black Citizenship, Secession, and the Civil War *184*

Notes *195*
Bibliography *223*
Index *245*

ACKNOWLEDGMENTS

I have been living with this book for what seems like a long time. It is a relief to finally get a chance to thank the people and institutions who have helped me along the way.

The research and writing of this book were made possible by fellowships from a number of institutions. Temple University provided a generous University Fellowship that funded my early research. The Albert M. Greenfield Foundation funded a semester of research at the Library Company of Philadelphia and the Pennsylvania Historical Society. The Center for Humanities at Temple also provided funds for a semester of research and writing, and the Maryland Historical Society provided a Lord Baltimore Fellowship. Thanks to the research staff at the Charles M. Blockson Collection, the Free Library of Philadelphia, the Friends Historical Library at Swarthmore College, the Historical Society of Pennsylvania, the Library of Congress, the Library Company of Philadelphia, and the Maryland Historical Society.

I have received extensive support from Towson University. Terry Cooney, dean of the College of Liberal Arts (and a historian himself) has been unfailingly supportive, and Ronn Pineo, chair of the Department of History, has been generous and kind. My colleagues in the department have taught me more than they know about balancing the many responsibilities of academic life. My students have kept me learning along with them, even if they have not realized it. All have been patient with me as I traverse the mid-Atlantic borderland between Philadelphia and Baltimore several times a week (though generally at a faster rate than the individuals discussed in this book).

I began this project with a short research paper in a graduate seminar taught by Professor Wilbert Jenkins. I thank him for starting me down this road and for awakening in me a love for African American history. Many other people have also offered advice on various parts of this manuscript, and I am grateful to all of those who offered feedback. I have taken many suggestions, and I will surely regret not taking more. As is customary, none of them bear any blame for the flaws that remain. Thanks to Beth Bailey, Corey Brooks, Marc Egnal, Kelly Gray, Craig Hammond, Scott Hancock, Matt Johnson, Christian Koot, Peter

Logan, Kate Masur, Joanne Melish, Abigail Perkiss, Larry Peskin, Paul Polgar, Patrick Rael, Kelly Shannon, Bryant Simon, Beverly Tomek, Jennifer van Horn, and Donn Worgs. Special thanks to Nic Wood, who read a late draft of this manuscript and offered some crucial guidance. The anonymous readers for the University of Georgia Press provided me with startlingly extensive feedback on various versions of this manuscript. I cannot thank them enough. Also, thank you to Walter Biggins at the University of Georgia Press for his patience and thoughtfulness, and to Ellen Goldlust for her heroic work copyediting this book.

Rich Newman has been a friend and advocate. He was kind enough to read a seminar paper from a graduate student he did not know, and he has been unfailingly supportive of me and this project ever since. Drew Isenberg helped to get me thinking about borderlands, though it took me a long time to really understand just how central the concept would be to this project. I hope he approves. David Waldstreicher has helped me at every stage of this process. He has been willing to offer hard criticism when necessary and been generous with praise. Above all, perhaps, he has been an example of someone who cares passionately and intensely about history.

I cannot imagine this book without the guidance and support of Elizabeth Varon. She has been a model mentor, allowing me to find my own way but always seeming to recognize what was best in my work, often before I did. She is an amazing scholar and teacher, but above all she is a good and a kind person. I am glad to know her.

Surely any first-time author owes a debt of gratitude to those who set him on the road to this profession. I had the benefit of several fine history teachers in high school, particularly Joel Chesler, who cares so passionately about his students. At Williams College I had the honor of studying nineteenth-century history with two amazing teachers and scholars, Robert Dalzell and Charles Dew.

My parents have been patient and supportive all the way through, including dropping everything on short notice to babysit. They have even refrained from asking about the progress of this book as often as I know they would have liked.

My children, Marcus, Anna, and Katherine, have been a source of unbelievable joy and only a little frustration. They have not read any of this book yet, but it is exciting that they are growing up near where much of it takes place—playing baseball across the street from Mother Bethel, walking past William Still's house on a regular basis, going to school on Lombard Street near the heart of antebellum black Philadelphia. This is their history.

Finally, I cannot express all that I owe to Gretchen. I can only say thank you.

ABBREVIATIONS

ACS Papers	American Colonization Society Papers, Microfilm Edition
ARCJ	*Washington African Repository and Colonial Journal*
BGDA	*Baltimore Gazette and Daily Advertiser*
BL	*Boston Liberator*
BP	*Baltimore Patriot*
BS	*Baltimore Sun*
CA	*New York Colored American*
CR	*Philadelphia Christian Recorder*
FDP	*Rochester Frederick Douglass' Paper*
FJ	*New York Freedom's Journal*
GUE	*Baltimore Genius of Universal Emancipation*
GUEBC	*Baltimore Genius of Universal Emancipation and Baltimore Courier*
MG	*Annapolis Maryland Gazette*
NASS	*New York National Anti-Slavery Standard*
NE	*Washington National Era*
NG	*Philadelphia National Gazette*
NS	*Rochester North Star*
NWR	*Baltimore Niles Weekly Register*
PADA	*Philadelphia Poulson's American Daily Advertiser*
PAS Papers	Pennsylvania Abolition Society Papers, Microfilm Edition
PF	*Philadelphia Pennsylvania Freeman*
PI	*Philadelphia Pennsylvania Inquirer*
PL	*Philadelphia Public Ledger*
USG	*Philadelphia United States Gazette*

*The Politics of
Black Citizenship*

INTRODUCTION

In February 1826, a crowded stagecoach headed for Harrisburg, Pennsylvania. Riding in this car was one remarkable man who struck up a conversation with his fellow passengers as they rattled along their way. He explained that he was bound for the state capital to fight against a bill that was then before the legislature, a bill intended to aid slaveholders in their efforts to recover fugitives fleeing across the border into Pennsylvania. Legislators, looking to assuage the concerns of antislavery constituents, had coupled this measure with provisions intended to make it more difficult for kidnappers to seize free blacks in the state and sell them into slavery, though the details remained uncertain. If he could not prevent the passage of the bill itself, the man hoped at least to shape these details, for he knew from experience that free blacks in Pennsylvania were always in danger. Twenty years earlier, he had been the victim of just such a plot. By the time of his attempted kidnapping, however, even the constable enlisted to serve the warrant knew that Richard Allen was no fugitive slave.[1]

The intervening years had only solidified Allen's status as the most respected and influential African American in Philadelphia and perhaps in the United States. Allen had made his name as a church leader, but he had almost immediately become a political leader as well and been among the most prominent voices challenging the institution of slavery and defending the rights of free African Americans.[2] This new fugitive slave bill especially worried Allen because it had been drafted at the request of a delegation from the state of Maryland. Slaveholders of Maryland had long worried that the border with Pennsylvania undermined the stability of slavery in their state, and the Maryland legislature had sent delegates to neighboring states to argue for more favorable legislation.

Pennsylvania legislators had defended their support of the fugitive bill by arguing that it fulfilled their constitutional obligation to return fugitives; they also pointed to its antikidnapping provisions as a defense for legally free blacks. Free black leaders in Philadelphia, however, recognized that the influence of the

The Reverend Richard Allen, 1823. Courtesy of the Library Company of Philadelphia.

Maryland delegates could be countered only by a strenuous effort to mobilize the opposition of those Pennsylvanians who looked favorably on the rights of African Americans. Allen and others helped to stir up what one commenter referred to privately as a "hurricane" of opposition to the bill. They warned that large numbers of free blacks would be kidnapped under the legislation, but it is clear that in fighting for greater protection for free blacks, Allen was also hoping to make it more difficult for masters to recover their absconded "property." He had initially worked through white allies from afar, appealing to them both in person and in print. Ultimately, Allen had determined that he could best influence the legislation in person, and he set off for the capital.[3]

Much to his dismay, Jonathan Roberts, a former U.S. senator, found himself sharing a car with Allen. In February 1826, Roberts was a Pennsylvania state legislator returning from his home outside of Philadelphia to the capital.[4] He may have recognized Allen (whom Roberts later described to his wife as "your Black Methodist bishop Richard Allen"), but Allen seems not at first to have recognized Roberts. Discovering the identity of his fellow passenger, however, Allen began to press Roberts on the issue of the fugitive bill. Roberts, who supported the bill, was evasive and "successfully resisted his efforts without departing from civility." Roberts was clearly contemptuous of Allen ("Like his people generally," wrote Roberts, "he abuses the language unmercifully and seems to be sen-

Alexander Rider, "Kidnapping," engraving in Jesse Torrey, *Portraiture of Domestic Slavery* (Philadelphia, 1817). Courtesy of the Library Company of Philadelphia.

sible of no deficiency"), yet the legislator obviously felt the need to conceal his contempt.[5] He might have wanted to avoid making a scene in a crowded stagecoach, but he also recognized that Allen could not be easily dismissed. Many white Philadelphians sympathized with Allen and with his concerns. Roberts needed to be publicly respectful of Allen, even if in private he was much more in agreement with the slaveholding commissioners from Maryland.

Allen's plan to personally lobby against the fugitive bill came to naught, since the final bill was passed before he (or indeed Roberts) reached Harrisburg. In a larger sense, however, the efforts of Allen and other free blacks succeeded. The final version of the bill, as Roberts admitted, had been "modified however to be very useless."[6] The concerns of the defenders of black rights had helped to produce a bill that not only failed to facilitate the easy flow of fugitives back to the South but also would eventually be seen as a legislative bulwark against the claims of southern masters.[7] Allen and his allies among Philadelphia's free blacks recognized that even though their political rights were circumscribed, they were not without political power and influence. They understood that in 1826, white Pennsylvanians were not prepared to deny their constitutional responsibility to return fugitive slaves or to accept free blacks as full and equal citizens. By helping to shift the terms of the debate, however—for example, by emphasizing the dangers of kidnapping—free blacks marshaled what sympathy did exist for the defense of black rights and took advantage of the limited notion of black citizenship that many white Pennsylvanians did endorse.

The following year and less than one hundred miles to the south, William Watkins was engaged in a different sort of black politics. Watkins, a leader among Baltimore's growing free black population, was concerned not with the practical consequences of denying free blacks the protection of the law but rather with the broader notion that African Americans could never be granted their "unalienable rights" in this "the land of our birth." His particular target was the American Colonization Society (ACS), which sought to encourage the removal of free African Americans from the United States and their settlement in a colony in West Africa. The ACS had been founded a decade earlier, but interest in colonization had recently surged. Ezekiel Chambers, a senator from Maryland and one of the commissioners who had petitioned Pennsylvania for a stronger fugitive slave law, introduced a memorial on the floor of the U.S. Senate calling for congressional support for colonization.[8]

Writing under the pseudonym "A Colored Baltimorean" in *Freedom's Journal*, a black-edited newspaper based in New York, Watkins made the case against African colonization. He addressed his letter to the supporters of colonization, the supposed "wisest and most philanthropic men in the country." How, asked Watkins, could free African Americans, the object of colonization "philanthropy," trust an organization when so many of its members were slaveholders? As he pointed out, "A philanthropic slaveholder is as great a solecism as a sober drunkard." Such men, he argued, could not be trusted.[9]

Yet Watkins's opposition to the ACS was not simply about trust. He also objected to the "anti-christian doctrine" that black men could never acquire citizenship rights in the United States, "that if we desire the privileges of freemen, we must seek them elsewhere." Watkins noted that the leaders of the ACS would not permit American free blacks to acquire those privileges in Haiti as a consequence of "its proximity to this country." Only across the Atlantic, "on the burning sands of Africa," could blacks become full citizens. Nor, Watkins noted, was this denial of citizenship a response to some criminal act; it was simply a response to the "darker hue" of African Americans. Watkins "one of those coloured sons of the Union," objected to the notion that free African Americans could never truly be men in their native land.[10]

Black Philadelphians and black Baltimoreans sought to advance the cause of black citizenship using a variety of means within a political system that for the most part formally excluded them. Allen's and Watkins's efforts suggest some of the ways that the debate over the political and legal status of free African Americans was woven into nineteenth-century American politics. This book examines the politics of black citizenship in these two cities and in the larger mid-Atlantic region, illuminating the role that free African Americans played in antebellum politics and documenting the complexity of the struggle for black citizenship. The book begins with the vigorous response of free African Americans to the ACS, especially its argument that free blacks had no place in their native United States, and ends with two related events—black troops' participation in the Civil War, which profoundly shifted the basis of black claims on American citizenship, and the collapse of the mid-Atlantic borderland, which meant that Maryland slave owners found their ability to recover fugitives profoundly constrained even before the state officially embraced emancipation in 1864.

Baltimore and Philadelphia loomed large in the antebellum politics of black citizenship. They possessed more free black residents than anywhere else in the United States, and the percentages of African Americans in the population of these two cities dwarfed those of other northern cities.[11] For this reason alone, debates about the political and legal status of African Americans in these two cities had profound importance. Moreover, this importance was magnified by the fact that these two commercial centers were also centers of print culture, meaning that such debates played out in books, pamphlets, and newspapers and were reprinted in publications across the nation and beyond.

Even more important, Baltimore and Philadelphia served as twin anchors of a larger region, cut in two by the legal boundary between slavery and freedom, in which free African Americans were a large and visible presence. The cities are just one hundred miles apart, and the area between them was home to large numbers of free African Americans. Canals, steamships, and railroads increasingly linked the two commercial centers, facilitating travel between them. The promoters of this transportation revolution may not have intended to help African Americans move from slave states to free states, but fugitive slaves took advantage of these changes. Indeed, the most famous fugitive to pass through this borderland, Frederick Douglass, traveled the newly completed Philadelphia, Baltimore, and Wilmington Railroad on his passage north.[12] Movement across the legal border between the slave state of Maryland and the free state of Pennsylvania as well as concerns about the consequences of that movement generated political debate, not just in Baltimore and Philadelphia but in the state capitals of Annapolis and Harrisburg and throughout the nation. Perhaps more than any other part of the United States, this mid-Atlantic border region forced Americans to ask difficult questions about the place of free blacks in the United States.[13]

This book recovers the dynamism and political engagement of free blacks across this border region. A generation of scholarship on the free black communities of the North has helped us to appreciate the importance of the black institutions built in this period, yet this work has tended to depict the antebellum decades as a period of withdrawal, a time when African American communities turned inward in response to rising white prejudice.[14] But the struggle for black citizenship rights forced engagement with the world of white politics and remained critical to free blacks in this border region. "Although what they built was for many purposes a world apart," notes historian Stephen Kantrowitz, "it did not represent a full-scale or principled withdrawal from the wider world. Even if they had wished to forge such an enclave, they could not create walls that slavery and prejudice were bound to respect." Free blacks certainly learned that many whites were unreliable allies, but white allies, even tepid ones, were necessary nonetheless.[15]

Free blacks living in the Philadelphia/Baltimore borderlands recognized the tenuousness of their legal protections and therefore understood the necessity of political engagement. This area became the center of the politics of black citizenship. Though historians have long recognized its importance, the border between the free and slave states has been the subject of renewed attention in recent years, inspired in part by the burgeoning scholarship on other sorts of borderlands. This scholarship has shown that the spaces between empires and nation-states have never corresponded neatly to the lines drawn on maps; instead, in borderlands we find that authority is uncertain and power is contested. As two of the leading historians of borderlands have put it, "Borderlands history is at its core about the negotiation of power." This idea includes negotiation between states, of course, but borderlands have also often opened up opportunities for nonstate actors, even those who have in other ways been denied influence over the state.[16]

This book does not provide a comprehensive examination of this mid-Atlantic borderland but instead focuses on the politically charged question of black citizenship. The volume emphasizes the extent to which this particular border region became a place of political conflict. This is not to deny that forces within this border region worked to promote cooperation and comity.[17] Certainly black Pennsylvanians lamented the willingness of many of their white neighbors to accommodate slave holding Marylanders, but this only meant that the political divisions provoked by the border and by the issue of black citizenship did not run neatly along that border. Black Philadelphians appealed to white allies who were unwilling to support full black citizenship, but who nevertheless were uncomfortable with the idea of denying all citizenship rights to black Pennsylvanians. Similarly black Baltimoreans reached out to whites on their side of the border who had even less enthusiasm for black citizenship but who for a variety of reasons opposed the harsh proposals of many slaveholding Marylanders.[18] Such appeals to white allies did not preclude a willingness to resort to extralegal measures when necessary. Rather free African Americans saw their fight for citizenship rights as central to their strategies of self-defense—that is, as an effort to shape the political context in which specific incidents of violence and active resistance took place.

This long fight for black citizenship took two distinct though related forms. First, African Americans advocated on behalf of specific, limited citizenship rights. While almost every African American believed that free blacks were entitled to broad equality, for practical purposes many black activists focused on specific citizenship rights, especially those necessary for the defense of free blacks from kidnapping or reenslavement. These leaders recognized that some of these limited citizenship rights could be won in the short term even if broad political and legal equality remained an elusive longer-term goal. This dimension of the struggle for black citizenship reflects the complexity of early nineteenth-century notions of citizenship in general. While the right to vote was certainly one for which free blacks fought, it was not the *sine qua non* of citizenship. Notions of citizenship, though often invoked, remained underdeveloped, rooted in membership not merely in the nation but also in states and localities.[19] African Americans recognized that although few whites supported full and equal black citizenship, many believed that free blacks were entitled to some citizenship rights and that a "colored citizen" of the United States existed in certain contexts.

Second, to advance their claims on the rights of citizenship, free blacks found that they needed to convince whites of the validity of African American claims on the United States, the land of their birth.[20] For many whites, however, people of African descent were incapable of being American citizens because they were racially inferior. Black activists certainly hoped to change these people's minds but also recognized that doing so would be extremely difficult and perhaps impossible. These activists focused instead on whites who offered more tentative, hesitant justification for their opposition to African American citizenship. These whites generally saw free blacks as inferior to whites, as somehow degraded, but believed that this condition was temporary. Whatever the nature of African American inferiority, these whites insisted that blacks could never be granted the rights of full U.S. citizenship and that African Americans, even those born in the United States, maintained some deeper connection to Africa—they were "aliens in the land of their birth." Free blacks stressed their birth on American soil and their contributions to the country's history, hoping that by asserting their Americanness, they might recover what they saw as their birthright.[21]

This book follows the fight for black citizenship rights, its victories and its failures, from the early to mid-nineteenth century. It generally proceeds in chronological fashion, but some chapters emphasize different yet interdependent elements of the fight—the pursuit of specific citizenship rights and the struggle to establish the Americanness of African Americans. The book thus illuminates the ways in which this fight took place at the local, state, and national levels.[22] Two factors that played a leading role in catalyzing debates over black citizenship were not unique to the mid-Atlantic borderland but were especially critical here. First, the efforts to control the movement of black bodies across the legal boundary between Pennsylvania and Maryland (that is, to recover fugitive slaves and to prevent the kidnapping of free blacks) gave the sometimes abstract notion of black citizenship a particular immediacy. Second, debates about African colonization were especially prevalent in the mid-Atlantic borderland and often forced to the surface otherwise latent disagreements concerning black citizenship rights.[23]

In emphasizing the local and state context of African American politics, this book contends that free blacks remained vital participants in American politics in the decades preceding the Civil War and that the issue of black citizenship remained critical largely as a result of the work of African Americans themselves. While historians have generally come to recognize that slave resistance, including slave flight, played a vital role in the events leading to the Civil War, free blacks have played a relatively small part in much of the recent political history of the late antebellum period.[24] By illuminating African Americans' fierce struggles for the rights of citizenship in the mid-Atlantic borderland, this book shows free African Americans as vital political actors.

PART I

*Colonization and
African American Identity*

CHAPTER I

The Dialectic of Colonization

In December 1816, *Poulson's American Daily Advertiser*, a Philadelphia publication that was one of the most widely read American newspapers of its time, began publishing a series of pieces laying out the case for African colonization. The first article was a brief notice of a meeting of citizens in Princeton, New Jersey, who asked the New Jersey legislature to promote "some plan of colonizing the *Free Blacks*," though few details were given. Weeks later, a writer using the pen name "Argus" argued that colonization offered a "mode of getting rid of this *National evil*." The writer scoffed at the notion that "the Middle and Northern States are to afford Asylums for those freed negroes." Next came a long piece emphasizing the potential for colonization to redeem Africa. A free black transported back to "the abode of his fathers" would become "the instrument of introducing amongst his savage brethren the blessings of civilization," chief among them, the Gospel.[1]

Poulson's and other U.S. papers also began reporting on the formation of a new national organization promoting the colonization of free blacks. At the group's December 21, 1816, meeting, Kentucky congressman Henry Clay reiterated some of the themes that had characterized earlier discussions of colonization: it would help civilize Africa and provide some atonement for the wrongs that had been done to the continent via the slave trade. In addition, colonization would remove free blacks, a benefit both to them and to white Americans. Clay also noted that the organization would not "deliberate upon or consider at all, any question of emancipation, or that was connected to the abolition of slavery." John Randolph of Roanoke, Virginia, insisted that slaveholders would support the colonization society's efforts, since the presence of free blacks was widely considered to pose one of the greatest dangers to the security of slave property. The official resolution adopted by this meeting made clear the emphasis on the removal of free blacks and civilizing of Africa, though the question of blacks who were still enslaved went unmentioned.[2]

On January 10, 1817, *Poulson's* printed an account of a meeting of free blacks in Georgetown in the District of Columbia. This group rejected African colonization and instead advocated the creation of a settlement for free blacks along the Mississippi, within the boundaries of what the writers termed their "beloved union." Before long, black Philadelphians had weighed in on this matter as well. At a January meeting attended by an estimated crowd of three thousand at Mother Bethel African Methodist Episcopal Church, "the large assemblage remained in almost breathless and fixed attention during the reading of the resolutions and other business of the meeting." When participants were asked who supported the notion of colonization, "you might have heard a pin drop, so profound was the silence." But when the attendees were asked who opposed colonization, "One *long, loud*, aye TREMENDOUS NO, from this vast audience, seemed as if it would bring down the walls of the building."[3]

It is unsurprising that the mid-Atlantic borderland loomed so large in the early debates about African colonization. In the late eighteenth and early nineteenth centuries, both Baltimore and Philadelphia saw dramatic growth in the number of free blacks, and this growth promised to continue, rendering debates about colonization particularly resonant. In addition, the nature of colonization made black citizenship especially important to those debates. Historians have long noted that one of the great strengths of the American Colonization Society (ACS) was the ambiguity surrounding its purpose.[4] Those who sought to end slavery could support African colonization, as could those who wished to strengthen it. The ACS attracted those who desired the civilizing of Africa and those who wished to purify the United States, those who sought to benefit American free blacks and those who despised them. Such a coalition would necessarily be fraught with tension. What is less obvious is what held together such a coalition. The colonization of free African Americans was not a self-evident solution to the perceived problems its supporters ultimately hoped it would address. Appealing to such profoundly divergent audiences posed a significant challenge to colonization's promoters. Critical to making this case was an argument about the nature of the American nation and an attempt to exclude free blacks from membership in that nation. Colonizationists coupled their efforts to physically remove free blacks from the United States with a rhetorical effort to define African Americans as outside of the nation's boundaries.

Free black opponents of colonization, especially but by no means only those from Philadelphia, recognized this argument as the glue holding together the colonizationist coalition. The effort to refute this argument, to assert the right of African Americans to be citizens in the land of their birth, decisively turned many free blacks against the ACS. Black opponents of colonization recognized that whatever the intentions of white colonizationists, the movement's rhetoric undermined black citizenship rights in the United States. Opposition to the ACS helped bring calls for black citizenship to the forefront of black politics. Free blacks demanded American citizenship both as their birthright and as something they had earned; they insisted that they were and had always been Americans.

African Colonization, the Black Atlantic, and Early American Politics

In 1816, the project of African colonization seemed promising. It had significant support among prominent free black leaders and fit neatly into the prevailing internationalist black diasporic consciousness. At the same time, white politicians saw colonization as potentially useful both as a practical means of removing some of a troublesome free black population and as a rhetorical means of assuaging some of the political tensions created by slavery.

The ACS's argument rested on the related concepts of nationalism and consent. The organization's founders pointed to this historical moment, in the wake of the war with Great Britain, as allowing Americans finally to turn their attention to strengthening and perfecting their nation. The preamble to the ACS Constitution, passed unanimously at its December 1816 organizational meeting, made this sentiment clear. While noting that Americans had always been troubled by the "situation of the free people of Colour," the document declared that the events surrounding the founding of the United States and "the subsequent great convulsions of Europe" had prevented the new nation from addressing the problem.[5]

The ACS positioned itself as a part of a resurgent American nationalism. Clay took the chair at the group's organizational meeting, and the rhetoric of his American System echoed the language used to describe the colonization of free blacks. Colonizationists, like Clay's brand of economic nationalists, made the case that the power of the federal government should be wielded to serve the national interest. Supporters saw colonizationism and economic nationalism as ambitious projects that would strengthen the bonds of union. According to its advocates, colonization was not a sectional undertaking for the benefit of one group of Americans at the expense of another but rather an effort to promote the good of the nation.

From the start, colonizationists paid careful attention to the importance of symbols in expressing this national purpose. Crucial to the portrayal of the ACS as a national institution was its membership. It drew its support from leading men of all sections, including three of the men (Clay, Andrew Jackson and William Crawford, slaveholders all) who would seek the presidency in 1824 as well as northern philanthropists such as Philadelphia's Richard Rush and Robert Ralston. Not only was the society founded in the nation's capital, but from the start it held its annual meetings in the U.S. House Chamber. Perhaps just as important, the ACS chose as its first president Bushrod Washington, a Supreme Court justice and nephew of the first president (and resident of Mount Vernon) whose stature transcended the sectional and the partisan. Washington's imprimatur brought immediate national credibility to the ACS. For good measure, the organization's first annual report also included a copy of an 1811 letter written by Thomas Jefferson in which he supported the idea of colonizing free blacks.[6]

Northern supporters of colonization not only fully embraced the patriotic depiction of colonization but also attempted to portray the ACS as a part of God's providential design for the American nation, which included both the redemption of Africa and the removal of an unwanted free black population from the United States. This argument helped to depoliticize colonization and make an enormous undertaking seem possible.[7]

The second concept on which the ACS rested was related to but distinct from the first. The word *consent* was ubiquitous in the printed discourse of colonization, and the propagandists of the ACS generally italicized the word to emphasize its importance to their project. Colonizationists stressed that any eventual emancipation of slaves could occur only with their owners' consent. Charles Fenton Mercer of Virginia, a driving force behind the early colonization movement, claimed at the organizational meeting that slaveholders generally wanted to emancipate their chattel but refused to do so primarily because of the continued presence of free blacks. Therefore, rather than forcing the actions of slaveholders, colonization would provide them with a liberty which was currently denied them. Clay reiterated Mercer's point that the society did not intend to "encroach" on the rights of property holders, though he took issue with Mercer's contention that slaveholders wanted to emancipate their slaves: Clay said that he did not intend to emancipate his slaves even if they would be removed to Africa.[8]

The ACS also argued that any slaves who remained behind would have consented to their status, thereby securing slaveholders' property. In the words of John Randolph, free blacks "serve to excite in their fellow beings a feeling of discontent" that undermined what would otherwise be the consensual relationship of master and slave.[9]

If the political viability of colonization depended on the consent of slaveholders, it also proclaimed the importance of the consent of free blacks, who had ample reason to fear that forced deportation lay behind the sometimes benevolent exterior of colonization rhetoric. Immediately after insisting that he had no intention of freeing his slaves, Clay added that "it was equally remote from the intention of the society that any sort of coercion should be employed in regard to the free people of color who were the objects of these proceedings." The ACS's founders resolved that colonization of slaves could only be carried out "with their consent."[10]

Colonizationists emphasized consent with the goal of appealing to free blacks as well as to white northerners. Many northerners not only hoped that colonization would promote emancipation but also believed that whether or not it had any impact on slavery, the removal of free blacks from the United States would genuinely benefit them. Some historians have emphasized northern racism as the impetus for the support of colonization, but the motives of many northern supporters of the ACS were more complex. Ralston, for example, had also been instrumental in raising funds to build an independent black church in 1791. Appeals directed to him and other Philadelphia colonizationists reinforced the sense that free blacks were a particularly degraded—though not necessarily inherently inferior—people. These appeals often decried the racial prejudice that helped to produce these conditions but suggested that this prejudice was insurmountable. As a result, supporters of colonization contended, free blacks would voluntarily agree to leave the United States. Northern newspapers printed numerous articles expressing great optimism at the prospect of Christianizing Africa combined with a seemingly sincere desire to remove blacks from the oppression of white prejudice.[11]

African colonization was not a new idea at this time. Both white and black Americans had periodically discussed the idea of establishing a settlement on the west coast of Africa, taking the British colony of Sierra Leone as a model and focus. By the mid-1810s, the emigrationist idea was being advanced most vigorously by Paul Cuffe, a black Quaker ship captain from Massachusetts. His father had been a slave, born in what is now Ghana and later emancipated by his Quaker master, and his mother was a Wampanoag from Martha's Vineyard. Cuffe's father established himself as a prosperous businessman and settled his family in a small Quaker community in southeastern New England. Paul followed in his father's footsteps and by 1800 had become a successful merchant and ship captain. He promoted education for people of color, establishing a school for all children, regardless of race, on his property.[12]

Cuffe saw African colonization as a means of promoting a larger, more cosmopolitan black Atlantic community that would span national boundaries. He sought not to remove African Americans from the United States but rather to promote Christianity and civilization in Africa, especially as a means of undermining the slave trade. In a June 1813 memorial to Congress, Cuffe noted that several respectable families from Baltimore, Philadelphia, New York, and Boston were eager to go "to Africa for a Temporary residence" to promote the "Civilization of Africa." Historian Floyd Miller argues that by late 1816, Cuffe had come to believe that colonization would undermine not only the slave trade but slavery itself and that a colony needed to be established in Africa to accept large numbers of African Americans (presumably freed slaves). Nevertheless, he continued to support the idea that blacks should also remain a part of the United States. In fact, he also advocated the establishment of a colony for free blacks in the western United States.[13]

Cuffe found supporters among Philadelphia's black elite, including perhaps the city's most respected African American, James Forten. Forten was born free in Philadelphia in 1766 to a family whose members had resided in the colony of Pennsylvania for almost a century. He became one of the city's leading sail makers and one of the country's wealthiest black men. In addition, Forten stood in the crowd, listening as the Declaration of Independence was read aloud for the first time, and he went on to serve in the American Revolution aboard the *Royal Louis*, captained by Stephen Decatur. In short, Forten had distinguished himself as a patriot and had good reason to consider himself an American.[14]

The African Institution of Philadelphia, of which Forten was president, supported the idea of a colony of free American blacks in West Africa by providing financial assistance to prospective emigrants. Though he personally had no interest in settling in Africa, Forten saw colonization as a means of promoting commercial ties that would benefit both Africa and African-descended peoples in America. And like Cuffe, Forten believed that some of those who traveled to Africa would not stay permanently. In October 1815, he asked Cuffe who would bear the financial burden for the return of who did not find the African "climet" agreeable. Forten and most black supporters saw colonization as a way to bring Africa and the United States closer together, not a way to permanently remove free blacks from the country.[15]

The published rhetoric of black freedom celebrations and other pamphlets produced in Philadelphia from 1808 to 1817 show that the city's African Americans embraced a cosmopolitan and often Anglophilic worldview.[16] Subsequently, however, African Americans emphasized their birth on American soil, a shift that emerged out of the opposition to the ACS but developed alongside the older internationalist theme.

Some champions of African Americans as native-born Americans had also been exemplars of the internationalist mode. Absalom Jones, the black pastor of Philadelphia's African Episcopal Church of St. Thomas, delivered a January 1, 1808, sermon that typifies the internationalist theme. Jones celebrated the end of the slave trade by comparing African Americans' trials to those of the Jews enslaved in Egypt, focusing on the role of God in securing the liberties of his children: "He *came down* into the British Parliament.... He *came down* into the Congress of the United States." Jones thus celebrated an international movement as well as a broader Christian worldview. In addition, though Jones appealed to the U.S. government to emancipate the remaining slaves, he based this appeal not on the country's founding principles but on the will of God. Finally, Jones was just as concerned that the end of the slave trade should bring the Gospel to "our African brethren" as he was that it should produce the end of slavery in America.[17]

Other prominent black leaders echoed Jones's internationalist rhetoric. Russell Parrott delivered and published three orations between 1812 and 1816. In the first, Parrott espoused a transnational and divinely inspired tradition of abolitionist agitation, listing as the heroes of this movement not only Americans John Woolman, Anthony Benezet, and Benjamin Rush but also British abolitionists Granville Sharp, Thomas Clarkson, and William Wilberforce. Parrott closed by noting that African Americans would prove themselves loyal defenders of the United States if called on to do so, but he declared his appreciation for the state of Pennsylvania, not for the nation as a whole. His 1814 address built on its predecessor, tracing the bonds that slavery had created among Europe, Africa, and the United States. Abolition, according to Parrott, would spread civilization and the Gospel throughout the world. Two years later, Parrott explicitly defended "our degraded race from the foul aspersions which malevolence and interest have cast upon us." Though he referred to the United States as "my native land," he also asserted the humanity of "the oppressed of every colour, and of every clime." In all three orations, Parrott lauded the United States not for its exceptionalism but for its participation in an international effort to end the slave trade. In such pieces, abolitionism emerges as an Atlantic alternative to a specifically American claim on liberty.[18]

Sermons of thanksgiving for the end of the slave trade were not the only works of political protest published by free blacks in these years. In response to a proposed ban on the immigration of free blacks to Pennsylvania, Forten published a "Series of Letters by a Man of Color." He opened by quoting the Declaration of Independence but noted that its principles were not distinctly American but rather universal: "The idea embraces the Indian and the European, the Savage and the Saint, the Peruvian and the Laplander, the White man and the African." To defend black rights, he called not on the United States but on the state of Pennsylvania and its proud tradition as the asylum for African Americans. At the same time, though, he laments the betrayal of this tradition, noting the fact that black Philadelphians "dare not to be seen after twelve o'clock in the day" on the Fourth of July.[19]

The late eighteenth and early nineteenth centuries also witnessed the rise of an ideological connection to Africa among many African-descended Americans. Earlier generations of African Americans had maintained specific ethnic identities derived from their own memories or from traditions passed down to them. As historian James Sidbury has shown, prominent black writers and activists in the second half of the eighteenth century increasingly identified themselves as "African," invoking a shared identity with those throughout the black diaspora that drew together people of vastly different ethnicities. By identifying their institutions as "African," blacks in the United States asserted their distinctiveness and linked themselves with an international "African" identity. This sense of ideological connection to Africa made many African Americans open to overtures of African colonizationists, at least initially.[20]

Free Blacks and the ACS

Despite the hopes of black and white supporters and despite the seemingly complementary international and African orientation of much of early nineteenth-century black rhetoric, African colonization, especially as championed by the ACS, was profoundly unpopular among free African Americans. This opposition served as a crucible of black protest that resulted in a commitment among black writers and orators to celebrate the Americanness of black Americans, which they frequently rooted in birth on American soil. Some speakers and authors continued to draw on the international rhetoric of the early nineteenth century, but they more frequently described African Americans as native-born Americans.

Some of the resistance to the ACS flowed from the inherent tensions between white and black supporters of colonization. Robert Finley, a white northern evangelical and early supporter of colonization, contacted Cuffe in January 1817 and found him receptive to the idea of working with the ACS. Cuffe recognized that the support of the national government would be crucial to the success of any effort to establish a colony in Africa and hoped that colonization might undermine the African slave trade. Cuffe may not have recognized the conflicting motives among colonizationists or understood that many white colonizationists rejected the proposed connection between colonization and emancipation. In addition, his dealings with Finley may have led Cuffe to hope that the supporters of emancipation would ultimately win out over their opponents within the ACS.[21]

But black Philadelphians overwhelmingly opposed the ACS, a development that Forten and Cuffe could not have found entirely surprising. Six months earlier, Cuffe had learned that a significant number of black Philadelphians were skeptical of plans to colonize Africa even as members of the black elite worked with Cuffe toward precisely that goal. When black Philadelphians met in January 1817 to discuss the ACS, Forten, Parrott, and other men who had previously promoted colonization now took the lead in the public opposition to the ACS. Although the published account of the meeting described participants' unanimous opposition to colonization, Forten, who chaired the gathering, later wrote to Cuffe that he was sympathetic to the plan and that he had freely expressed his opinion before acquiescing in the majority's opinion.[22]

Black Philadelphians were troubled not simply by the idea of African colonization but also by the words that framed the idea. To a certain extent, black leaders backed away from a sincere support for colonization when it became clear that they would not control the process.[23] Forten's letter to Cuffe indicates some discrepancy between the Philadelphian's private sentiments and public words, but his private words cannot simply be taken at face value since they were written to a friend (and business partner) who was passionately committed to the endeavor. Forten ascribed the opposition of many black Philadelphians to the mistaken belief that free blacks would be compelled to go to Africa, another assertion that must be regarded warily: black Philadelphians had reason to be wary about coercion despite white colonizationists' insistence that the "consent" of free blacks would be defended.[24]

The resolutions passed by the anticolonization meeting show that the men who participated in the protest against the ACS were not simply resistant to the idea of moving to Africa or to some vague and perhaps mistaken sense that they would be coerced into moving there. They were specifically addressing the arguments that appeared in the ACS's public discourse. In addition, they did not merely talk privately about this opposition but instead sought to counter the discourse of the ACS. Though opponents lacked the institutional and financial resources possessed by the colonizationists, the resolutions passed by the Philadelphia meeting found their way into newspapers across the nation, including some in the Upper South states of Virginia and Kentucky.[25]

The protesters asserted their continuing connection to the United States, describing the "contemplated measure" of colonization as an effort "to exile us from the land of our nativity." Their statement of their opposition to colonization echoed down through the nineteenth century.

> Whereas our ancestors (not of choice) were the first successful cultivators of the wilds of America, we their descendants feel ourselves entitled to participate in the blessings of her luxuriant soil, which their blood and sweat manured; and that any measure or system of measures, having a tendency to banish us from her bosom, would not only be cruel, but in direct violation of those principles, which have been the boast of this republic.

These black Philadelphians countered colonizationists' claims that free blacks would surely wish to return to "the land of their fathers" (or often simply "their native land") with the unequivocal statement that the United States was their native land. After this opening salvo, attendees systematically rejected other aspects of the ACS's rhetoric. In response to the implication that free blacks constituted "a dangerous and useless part of the community," the meeting noted that many free blacks had served their country in the recent war. Moreover, free black Philadelphians stated their refusal to abandon their enslaved brethren, to whom they were bound by "consanguinity" as well as by "suffering" and "wrong." This resolution spoke directly to northerners who hoped that colonization would promote emancipation, insisting that colonization was intended to strengthen slavery.[26]

The protesters next denounced the ACS not simply for its desire to remove free blacks but for its intent to do so without preparing them for "the savage wilds of Africa." This resolution further tied free American blacks to the United States and differentiated them from and intimated their superiority to residents of Africa, since colonizers would bring to Africa "arts," and "science," and "a proper knowledge of government." The protesters also connected themselves to white Americans by referencing their shared Christian faith—they trusted in "the justice of God" to dictate what was best for his children. This resolution also served as a rejoinder to white colonizationists' claims that Providence dictated the removal of free blacks from the United States. Finally, the meeting resolved that a committee should be formed to inform Joseph Hopkinson, the Federalist congressman from Philadelphia, of the meeting's sentiments.[27] Thus, the meeting's participants did not merely denounce the idea of colonization but specifically responded to arguments offered in favor of the concept, presented a portrait of free blacks at odds with that put forth by the ACS, and stated their plan for political action. That is, they constructed an argument about what was and should be the place of African Americans in the United States, not just a statement on African colonization.

These resolutions reflect the two strains of argument prevalent in African American rhetoric of the era, the more recent nationalist conception that African Americans were first and foremost Americans by virtue of their nativity, and the older cosmopolitan and international political culture that saw blacks in the United States as part of a larger Atlantic world.[28] This internationalism is evident in Forten's private correspondence with Cuffe. Forten wrote that he believed that free blacks "will never become a people until they come out from amongst the white people." By using *they*, Forten reinforces the idea that he is not advocating the removal of all free blacks from the United States (certainly he was not planning to go). He does not deny his own Americanness and suggests that by becoming a people outside of the United States, free blacks might strengthen black Americans' claims to membership in the United States. At the very least, he leaves open the possibility of an international identity, not bound to Africa, for American free blacks.[29]

The cosmopolitanism that led some of the Philadelphia elite to look more favorably on colonization in 1817 seems to have been linked to their status. Historian Richard S. Newman has suggested that "as wealthy and respected men, [Richard] Allen, Forten and Cuffe could go back and forth among continents." These men and other elite black Philadelphians participated in an international network through commercial contacts, through religious and reform print, and through private correspondence with British abolitionists. That participation may well have promoted confidence in the proposition that movement across the Atlantic could go in both directions. This cosmopolitan worldview would have required a leap of faith, especially for the city's ordinary free blacks, who were not accustomed to transatlantic commerce and communication and who might have preferred more immediate local and national connections.[30]

In addition, African Americans' embrace of birthright citizenship owed at least some debt to the relatively close ties between African Americans and Federalist politics. By the early nineteenth century, white abolition was mainly associated with the Federalist Party, especially in Philadelphia. Perhaps even more important, Federalists were far more likely to support the rights of free blacks than were their Jeffersonian opponents.[31] Black Philadelphians' shift from an internationalist to a nationalist focus seems to echo the Federalist political culture: by the late eighteenth century, many Federalists had moved away from cosmopolitanism and toward a more nativist stance, most famously demonstrated by the Alien Acts of 1798 but also on display in Washington's 1797 Farewell Address. Seth Cotlar has argued that this Federalist "cultural offensive" attempted to define America as "a community of blood" while depicting radical "cosmopolitan universalism" as a foreign import. This revised understanding of the nature of the United States and its embrace by free blacks' political allies can at least partly explain their embrace of nativity-grounded definitions of citizenship.[32]

However, this rhetorical strategy did not simply or primarily represent a borrowing from white Federalism. It also constituted an attempt to exploit a fundamental tension in the way Americans conceived of citizenship. Rogers M. Smith has argued that although Americans commonly spoke and thought of their citizenship in universalist terms, whether liberal or republican, those traditions coexisted with ascriptive civic ideologies. According to Smith, American citizenship laws were always the result of a mix of these three traditions. If Americans wanted to think of their natural rights as universal, not linked specifically to their nation, what made Americans distinct? Smith holds that ascriptive understandings of citizenship, among them a continuing belief in the importance of birthright, were far more important than has been commonly recognized.[33] While those who sought to lead the United States advanced an ascriptive version of civic identity for their own purposes, African Americans recognized in this conflict over citizenship a tremendous opportunity to argue for their own right to be included in the nation as full citizens. While white Federalists used this sort of understanding of citizenship to narrow the realm of political participation, free black Philadelphians used it as a powerful argument for an expansion of the citizenry.

Whatever their opinion of these black claims on American citizenship, white colonizationists recognized that free blacks would have an important say in the success or failure of African colonization. Following the January protest meeting, Finley traveled to Philadelphia to meet with the leaders of the black opposition to colonization. While he privately sought to assuage their worries, Finley also endeavored to shape the public perception of black attitudes toward colonization. In a letter first published by the *National Intelligencer* and subsequently reprinted in other papers, Finley attributed free black opposition to colonization to the work of an anonymous circular printed in Washington and sent to black leaders throughout the North. Finley claimed that although the circular had stirred up fears among free blacks, he had spoken to their leaders and had convinced them that their worries were unfounded. According to Finley, eight of the eleven men with whom he met "gave their opinion in favor of an establishment in *Africa*." Finley's account differs significantly from Forten's more complex depiction of continuing black support for colonization.[34]

Finley continued to place his hopes in the "enlightened" black elite, but it was becoming clear that the distance between the black elite and the black masses was not as great as he imagined. The "circular" to which Finley referred bears a remarkable similarity to the printed rhetoric of the Philadelphia anti-colonization meeting. Rather than ignoring the ACS's protestations that it will only act with the consent of free blacks, the author expresses his concern that "divers white persons, currently unknown to your memorialists, and without authority of law [are] devising ways and means for the transportation of your memorialists beyond the seas." Whatever the ACS's intentions, a colonization endeavor could "pass easily from *persuasion to force*." The author also repeatedly refers to the United States as African Americans' "native country," the birthplace not only of the current generation but also of their parents. The continuity between the Washington circular and the Philadelphia meeting suggests that opposition to the ACS arose not from the irrational fears of the black lower classes but from a concerted effort to counter the rhetoric of colonization. This effort brought together free blacks with varying attitudes toward Africa and a larger Atlantic world.[35]

As the ACS's national leaders sought to assuage the fears of both free blacks and slaveholders, supporters of colonization in Baltimore assembled on July 8, 1817, to discuss the formation of a local ACS auxiliary. Published reports of this meeting describe a stirring speech by Francis Scott Key of the national society. He asked his listeners to look forward to a day when the new colony would proclaim the greatness of its founders, and "when it was asked what nation had been the parent of such multiplied blessings, the natives would reply, pointing to the emblem of our sovereignty, the nation with the star spangled banner." Local colonization societies, like the ACS, basked in the glow of postwar nationalism.[36]

Free blacks outnumbered the enslaved in Baltimore but nevertheless experienced profound consequences as a result of the continued existence of slavery. Historians have described Baltimore as offering a sort of "quasi-freedom" in which slavery continued to control free blacks while urban life provided opportunities that provided the enslaved with greater agency in their own lives. Baltimore lacked the sort of prosperous free black upper class found in Philadelphia, and in general free blacks in the Maryland city were far less likely to own property.[37]

Other conditions may also have deterred the emergence of a broad-based opposition to colonization in Maryland in the 1810s. Baltimore suffered economically more than any other city on the eastern seaboard in the wake of the War of 1812. The city had been particularly dependent on the West Indies trade, which never fully recovered after the war. Furthermore, vicious antiblack riots had erupted in Baltimore in 1812 when the city's free African American population was suspected of harboring pro-British sentiment. Black residences were destroyed, and the Sharp Street Methodist Church was saved only through fierce resistance by free blacks. The riots showed the danger that even perceived political allegiances might pose for Baltimore's African Americans.[38]

Nevertheless, the ACS and its local auxiliary did not go unchallenged in Baltimore. Most prominent among the critics was Hezekiah Niles, white publisher and editor of the widely read *Niles Weekly Register*. While Niles admitted the "degeneracy" and "brutality" of free blacks, he argued that colonization was at best a distraction from attempts to address this condition, which he blamed at least in part on laws prohibiting the education of African Americans. His central critique was that African colonization was utterly impractical. Niles published a series of letters in which Colonel J. E. Howard, head of the Baltimore ACS, challenged the newspaperman's position on this point. Howard disputed Niles's calculations of the costs of colonization and suggested that an African colony would in large part pay for itself, as, he claimed, had other colonies founded by European powers. Niles remained unconvinced and called for policies to encourage emancipation, a topic that Baltimore colonizationists sought to avoid. Niles's prescription for the "problem" of free blacks involved settling them in nonslaveholding states, where "a gradual change of *complexion* would be effected" by mixture with whites." Even Niles recognized that leaving free blacks among those who were enslaved was an untenable situation.[39]

On that point, he and Howard agreed. The ACS head asserted that "in a free representative government," all people "should possess alike, personal and political liberty." Since, he argued "it was utterly impossible, that the negroes should, even whilst amongst us, be admitted to a full, free, and equal participation in those rights and privileges," they would always constitute a marginalized class of noncitizens that posed a grave threat to the republic. Supporters of colonization also cited the lack of political rights as a reason that free blacks would want to emigrate. The African colony, according to the viewpoint of the founders of the Baltimore auxiliary, would provide a place where free blacks "might enjoy the inestimable blessings of entire *political* in addition to their *personal* liberties."[40]

On one hand, anxieties concerning the place of free blacks were nothing new in a society that had for more than a century been struggling to draw clear lines between free persons and slaves. On the other hand, Howard's emphasis on the lack of political rights as necessitating the removal of free blacks is noteworthy. He does not argue that violence will result from the influence of free blacks on the enslaved but believes that free blacks will never be content with the denial of their political rights. In private, Baltimore colonizationists coupled anxieties about free blacks' status as men but not citizens with worries about the danger they posed as fomenters of slave rebellion. In public, however, emphasis on the political status of free blacks enabled colonizationists to appeal both to slaveholders and to those who frowned on slavery.[41]

The founding of the Baltimore auxiliary seems to have combined with conditions in southeastern Pennsylvania to lead to a renewed discussion of colonization in Philadelphia. The city's black population continued to grow, mostly as a consequence of the immigration of free blacks, especially from the states to the immediate south. The end of the War of 1812 had brought hard times to Philadelphia, and blacks were the hardest hit. For the first time in the city's history, black Philadelphians made up a disproportionate percentage of those admitted to almshouses. Black imprisonment also was growing, especially as a result of an increase in crimes against property. These economic conditions only confirmed what many white Philadelphians already believed: the black population needed to be controlled.[42]

Philadelphia's defenders of colonization made the case for the need to reduce the black population and attempted to refute the claims that free blacks would be coerced into emigrating to Africa, presenting the ACS as a force for emancipation. They depicted African colonization as a reenactment of the white colonization of America while scoffing at the dangers faced by African colonists: "When our ancestors were first thrown upon this coast they were abandoned by their mother country to the mercy of savages." On August 12, 1817, a group of white Philadelphians met to discuss their support for the colonization movement and to form a local ACS auxiliary. They met at the State House (later known as Independence Hall), following in the footsteps of the national society in linking the project of colonization with symbols of the American Revolution.[43]

Black Philadelphians again responded swiftly. On August 10, two days before the formation of the local auxiliary, free black Philadelphians met "for the purpose of taking into consideration the plan of colonizing the free people of color." Forten again chaired the gathering, while Parrott served as the secretary. Whereas the January meeting had addressed the general proposition of colonization and the particular arguments made by the ACS, this meeting focused on supporters of colonization in Philadelphia. The document produced by the meeting takes a less strident tone, most likely as a result of its intended audience. Supporters of colonization in Philadelphia clearly were not the same as the national organization's leaders, whose opposition to slavery was dubious at best. Many of the Philadelphia colonizationists not only opposed slavery but had actively supported the free black community.[44]

In addressing this audience, Philadelphia's free black leaders sought to express their concerns "HUMBLY and RESPECTFULLY." They did not back down from their assertion that they did not wish to leave "our present homes," but they replaced their previous insistence on their right to American citizenship with a more measured challenge to the colonizationists' depictions of free black misery. The Philadelphians wanted to stay at least in part because of the relatively good conditions they enjoyed. Considering that some of those colonizationists they sought to convince had been involved in benevolent efforts that had helped to produce those conditions, this is a call for continuity rather than the radical shift toward colonization. Their only request was that they "shall be permitted to share the protection of the excellent laws, and just government, which we now enjoy in common with every individual of the community." Moreover, they also argued that conditions in Philadelphia were improving, an explicit challenge to colonizationists' claims that free blacks could find better lives only outside of the United States.[45]

The second part of the address emphasized free blacks' connections to the enslaved, again providing a somewhat flattering picture of the emancipationist efforts already under way, in large part led by white Philadelphians. The black leaders contended that such endeavors would ultimately lead to the extinction of slavery, while colonization might lead to the emancipation of some slaves but would separate families, abandon the unprepared to suffer in Africa, and deprive emancipated blacks of the "consolation of our past sufferings"—that is, the right to enjoy opportunities in America. Most important, those slaves who remained in the United States would be more securely enslaved. This rhetorical shift demonstrated not a retreat from the early demands for American citizenship but rather a tactical move to attack the ACS coalition where blacks might have the greatest influence. Henry Clay might not have cared what free black Philadelphians thought about colonization, but many Philadelphia colonizationists (or potential colonizationists) did, and Clay was indeed concerned about what they thought.[46] Holding together a national coalition in favor of African colonization would demand a great deal of political maneuvering and would only become more difficult.

The Missouri Crisis and African Colonization

The issues at stake in the debates over colonization, the future of slavery, and the status of free blacks in a slaveholding republic soon rose to national prominence. On February 13, 1819, James Tallmadge, a Republican congressman from New York, introduced an amendment to the bill for Missouri statehood. It called for the restriction of slavery as a condition for statehood, prohibiting the introduction of new slaves and providing for the emancipation of all children of slaves born in the state when they reached age twenty-one. This measure inaugurated what one historian has called "probably the most candid discussion of slavery ever held in Congress." At issue were two crucial questions: whether the federal government had the constitutional authority to restrict slavery in

Missouri, and if so, whether doing so was appropriate. Debate was fierce, and southern congressmen almost immediately warned that the discussion of slavery restriction, especially before an audience that contained African Americans, was akin to inciting servile rebellion. Edward Colston of Virginia accused one of his colleagues of "speaking to the galleries" and in so doing sinking to the level of "Arbuthnot and Ambrister," two Englishmen executed by General Andrew Jackson for attempting to arm and lead Indians and fugitive slaves to fight against the United States. As a traitor in the U.S. Congress, Tallmadge "deserves no better fate."[47]

The debate initially attracted little attention outside the halls of Congress, but as the movement for slavery restriction gathered momentum throughout the North, northern congressmen who had opposed the measure began to feel intense pressure from their constituents. Prominent Philadelphians met in November to draft a resolution to Congress opposing the extension of slavery, and a large public meeting unanimously passed the measure. When Congress returned to Washington in December 1819, the fight over restriction took center stage, receiving high-profile newspaper coverage. The debate shattered any impression that there was a national consensus on slavery.[48]

Philadelphia-area congressmen played a prominent role in the debate and in the Missouri Compromise that eventually resulted. Some of the strongest voices in favor of the restriction of slavery belonged to Philadelphians. Congressman Joseph Hemphill delivered an impassioned argument for the Tallmadge amendment that the *Franklin Gazette* termed "unanswerable." A few days later, John Sergeant delivered a tour de force defense of restriction that even his opponents appreciated for its eloquence.[49]

Not all of the local congressmen, however, firmly defended restriction, and congressional leaders hoping to find northerners to support "compromise" looked to Pennsylvania. Clay himself appealed to "the unambitious Pennsylvania, the keystone of the federal arch," to join with him to fight any attempt to disturb the union. Jonathan Roberts, a Republican senator from just outside Philadelphia, became a key swing vote in the effort to secure a compromise. Roberts had initially opposed the Tallmadge amendment but had later softened his position, most likely in response at least in part to the outrage expressed by many of his constituents. He disliked the attitude of many of the southern opponents of restriction but ultimately supported the compromise, apparently swayed by his fear that northern Federalists were using the slavery issue to revive their moribund party. Roberts's decision to suppress concerns regarding slavery to preserve party unity foreshadowed party politics for the rest of the antebellum period.[50]

Black Philadelphians sought to use the Missouri debates as evidence for the insincerity of supposedly antislavery supporters of African colonization. In the midst of the Missouri debates, a number of Upper South congressmen had argued that expanding slavery into the West and the subsequent traffic of slaves out of Maryland and other eastern states would enable the ultimate extinction of slavery in the Border South. This idea at least implicitly conflicted with the colonizationist vision for emancipation.[51] Philadelphia's free blacks met again on November 16, 1819, with Forten again in the chair, and again expressed their opposition to African colonization. This time, the proposed extension of slavery into Missouri had provided them with further evidence that the supporters of the ACS were not genuinely interested in undermining slavery. Though the remonstrance did not mention anyone by name, prominent supporters of colonization had in fact come out publicly against slavery restriction. Not only had Clay taken the lead in promoting the Missouri Compromise in the House but Robert Goodloe Harper spoke in favor of an antirestriction resolution in the Maryland House. Others later took up the link between slavery restriction and colonization, though not always in the way that black Philadelphians had hoped. In an antirestriction meeting later in November, prominent white Philadelphians denounced efforts to spread slavery into Missouri, in part by claiming that an extension of slavery would increase the value of bondspeople, therefore undermining any attempt to use colonization to promote emancipation. These restriction supporters did not reject colonization but did recognize the genuine conflict between the spread of slavery and the sort of consensual emancipation that the ACS claimed to advocate. New York's John Taylor subsequently took this argument to the floor of the U.S. House.[52]

Black Philadelphians' opposition to slavery extension was recognized by their foes as well as by their allies. The pro-slavery *St. Louis Enquirer* expressed hope that the fanaticism supposedly evidenced by free blacks' activism would undermine any effort to prevent the admission of Missouri as a slave state.[53] Whether or not it had an effect on the immediate debate over the admission of Missouri, their attempt to use free black political protest to tar the entire slavery restriction movement foreshadowed a looming crisis.

Congress averted that crisis for a time but did so at a significant cost to the citizenship rights of free blacks. The votes of Roberts and other northerners combined with overwhelming support from southern representatives to pass the compromise measure, which linked the admission of Missouri and Maine, retaining the balance of power between free and slave states. It also restricted slavery west of Missouri and north of the new state's southern border. But the new Missouri Constitution provoked another crisis when it prohibited the legislature from passing any emancipation act and excluded free blacks from the state. These measures proved profoundly disturbing, not only to northerners who had supported the first compromise but also to some southerners. Harper, for example, privately considered the Missouri Constitution to be in conflict with the U.S. Constitution. Clay engineered another compromise that was so vaguely worded that both sides could see it as a victory, yet as historian Robert Forbes has noted, in practical terms this second Missouri Compromise served as an argument that free blacks were not American citizens.[54] Free blacks, however, refused to relinquish the rights that they had come to see as their birthright.

If free blacks were among the first to connect colonization to the Missouri question, many more would follow. In Baltimore, Niles had already contended that the extension of slavery further reduced the feasibility of colonization as a means of emancipation. A meeting of prominent white Philadelphians, including a number of supporters of the ACS as well as members of the Pennsylvania Abolition Society, opposed to the extension of slavery into Missouri, resolved that the expansion of slavery would promote a clandestine slave trade and would render any effort at colonization impossible except as a means of removing the "vicious and burdensome part of the black population." Perhaps unsurprisingly, even in the North the ACS increasingly emphasized the danger presented by free blacks and sought to portray colonization as a means of combating the widely unpopular slave trade rather than the more accepted institution of slavery itself. The argument that an increase in the value of slaves would diminish the likelihood of voluntary manumission had an undeniable logic.[55]

This reasoning was especially clear in Maryland, in what was already becoming the Border South. Slavery's opponents might have hoped that a shift away from a slave-based economy would lead to the emancipation of the enslaved, but far too often, as astute observers like Niles noted, Maryland masters found a ready market for their excess slave labor. Even as postrevolutionary economic transformations spurred the growth of the free black population, far more enslaved Marylanders were pulled into what Ira Berlin has called a "Second Middle Passage," transported south and west into the new heartland of slavery.[56]

By 1820, African colonization had spurred free blacks to assert their American birthright with a vehemence that had never before been seen. Unsurprisingly, the mid-Atlantic borderland, with its substantial free black population and its robust colonization movement, witnessed the most vigorous assertions of black citizenship rights. Supporters of colonization had hoped that the international orientation of American free blacks and their growing identification with the

African continent would lead them to embrace colonization. For many free blacks, however, the language of the chief advocates of colonization and the political context of that language led not necessarily to a rejection of an international identity but rather to an emphasis on their connection to the United States, their Americanness.

CHAPTER 2

America, Africa, Haiti

On New Year's Day 1823, Jeremiah Gloucester delivered an oration that tells us a great deal about how free African Americans negotiated complex questions of identity in the early republic. The eldest son of John Gloucester Sr., founder of Philadelphia's First African Presbyterian Church, Jeremiah ultimately succeeded his father in the pulpit.[1] The occasion, the anniversary of the abolition of the slave trade, had traditionally encouraged an international perspective among both white and black orators. Though such speeches had customarily pointed to the Anglo-American tradition of international antislavery, Gloucester's history of the antislavery movement focused largely on America. He listed the dates on which various states had outlawed the slave trade, noting that they did so before the British. Discussing the international fight against slavery, he pointed particularly to the martyrs who had helped found Haiti. He highlighted the idea that the actions of the Haitian revolutionaries mattered beyond the borders of the new nation. "Their views," he insisted, "no doubt extended to all who were bleeding under the yoke of bondage" throughout the world. Going further, he contended that the Haitians had "proclaimed the imprescribable rights of man."[2]

Even in a speech that culminated in a call for "patriotism itself [to] be lost in universal philanthropy," Gloucester stressed his connection to the United States: "We love this country but we do detest the principle of holding slaves." Perhaps somewhat surprisingly, however, he attributed this hatred not to the inhumanity of slavery or to its violation of the rights of men but rather to the fact that "it tolls the death bell of this republic." He then denounced the American Colonization Society (ACS) on the grounds that the recent expansion of slavery into Missouri had demonstrated that white Americans were not genuinely interested in using colonization to end slavery. Rather, the ACS's plans merely represented a way to remove free blacks and thus strengthen the institution of slavery. He lauded colonization's potential to evangelize and civilize Africa

The Reverend Jeremiah Gloucester, 1828. Courtesy of the Library Company of Philadelphia.

but doubted the ACS's ability to accomplish this goal. Gloucester refused to renounce his claim to be an American citizen and called on his listeners to "defend the rights and liberties which you enjoy in this city."[3] The oration maintains a strong sense of the cosmopolitanism of black identity but does so alongside specific claims on American nationality, especially in the sections dealing with colonization and the challenges to free black rights. Gloucester identified with both the United States of his birth and the Africa of his forefathers.

In the early 1820s, this already complex interaction was further complicated by African Americans' growing interest in Haiti as a destination for black emigrants from the United States. At the same time, supporters of African colonization sought to answer the criticisms leveled by their opponents, emphasizing the civilizing, Christianizing mission of colonization and depicting it as a means of combating the international slave trade. For many African Americans, though, Haiti presented an opportunity to embrace a transnational black identity while rejecting all that was objectionable about African colonization.[4] Whether as a symbol of black success or as a destination for black emigration, Haiti would help to reshape black identity and would be used as an argument for black citizenship in the United States, not as an opportunity to reject American citizenship.

Free Blacks, Haiti, and African Colonization

Despite their growing tendency to celebrate their American birthright, many African Americans continued to see themselves as a part of a larger transnational black diaspora.[5] In some cases, this connection was merely ideological, but increasing numbers of African Americans left behind their native United States. Their choices, their accounts of their experiences, and the debate about their actions had profound consequences not just for emigrants but also for free African Americans who remained in the United States.

Though many African Americans had rejected the ACS in favor of increasing assertions of their Americanness, Paul Cuffe's vision of a transatlantic black diaspora, connecting African-descended people with Africans, retained a great deal of appeal. On February 6, 1820, the Reverend Daniel Coker and about ninety other African Americans set sail from New York to Africa aboard the *Elizabeth*. Coker had been an influential leader in Baltimore's black community and had helped Richard Allen found the African Methodist Episcopal General Convention in 1816. Coker had initially been considered to become the conference's first bishop (possibly as part of a dual bishopric) but stepped aside for Allen. In addition, Coker was an early antislavery pamphleteer. In 1820, however, Coker, with the ACS's support, chose to leave the United States.[6]

Coker also may have had personal reasons for his departure. Despite his stature within the church, at an April 1818 meeting of the African Methodist Episcopal Conference, charges were brought against Coker. The nature of these charges is unclear, but Coker was found guilty and expelled from the conference for a year. Though he was subsequently reinstated, he was admitted to the pulpit "at the discretion of the Elder." There is no hard evidence that his punishment led to his decision to leave the United States, however, Coker wrote back to "my dear African Brethren in America" and alluded to the religious divisions that existed in the United States when he insisted that in Africa, those divisions needed to be set aside. It seems likely that Africa offered Coker a refuge from black politics as well as from white prejudice.[7]

Coker not only saw colonization as a means of civilizing and evangelizing Africa but also saw Africa as a place of opportunity for the oppressed black people of the United States. In his journal, which the ACS published, Coker celebrated the new African settlement as a place where "you can do much better than you can possibly do in America" and marveled at the sight of an all-black grand jury. Yet Coker saw the colony primarily as a way to "civilize" Africans by incorporating them into a wider Atlantic world. Coker also served as a middleman between the white agents of the ACS and the black settlers, a role that soon produced conflict because the black settlers sought to escape white dominance and resented Coker's cozy relationship with the ACS.[8]

Though some free blacks followed in Coker's footsteps and embraced the opportunities offered by the ACS, African American resistance continued to present problems for the organization. As it struggled to appeal to free blacks and at the same time soothe suspicious southern slaveholders, the ACS increasingly emphasized the importance of African colonization to undermining the international slave trade. Supporters of the ACS continued to insist that the group's efforts were part of a solution to "a vast and increasing evil" (though they conveniently neglected to specify whether the "evil" was slavery or free blacks). And by focusing on the fight against the slave trade, which the United States had already outlawed, the group avoided the controversy that accompanied attempts to strike against domestic slavery itself.[9]

The capture of illegal slave ships also spurred the ACS to emphasize its role in ending the slave trade. Colonizationists used the prospect that Africans freed from such ships would nevertheless be auctioned off into slavery to raise funds both from private sources and from the federal government. By depicting colonization as a means of fighting the slave trade, ACS leaders hoped to give the federal government additional latitude to support colonization under the Slave Trade Act of 1819.[10]

This debate came to Baltimore in August 1822, when a Columbian privateer, the *General Paez*, sailed into the harbor. It had intercepted a Spanish slaver not far from Cuba and had taken on forty-two slaves, including fourteen Africans. Though it was unclear what these men thought (none of them spoke much English or Spanish), local antislavery activists and colonizationists sought to claim authority over them through the ACS. ACS supporters saw an opportunity to enlist the federal government's power to promote colonization. Ten of the men eventually were reunited with their families as part of a commercial venture linking Baltimore merchants and West Africa.

The possibility of using African colonization to undermine the slave trade seems to have softened some black leaders' opposition to the ACS. In April 1823, while the ACS struggled to gain legal control over these Africans, Richard Allen presided over a prayer service at the departure from Baltimore of a ship carrying black settlers to West Africa. Nevertheless, most free blacks remained wary of African colonization.[11]

If free black suspicion of the ACS posed one threat to African colonization, an alternate destination in the Caribbean presented another. Superficially, the two plans were similar in that they promised to remove some of the free black population beyond the boundaries of the United States. However, Haiti was the ultimate symbol of black rebellion and seemed to pose a much more immediate threat to slavery than did a colony in West Africa.[12] Emigration from the United States to Haiti had the potential to establish links between the two nations, an idea that excited African Americans and disturbed many whites, including advocates of African colonization.

Interest in the emigration of black Pennsylvanians to the West Indies dated back to the late eighteenth century, when the Pennsylvania Abolition Society had explored the possibility of colonizing free blacks in Saint-Domingue. Prince Saunders, an American-born free black, later became an advocate of Haitian emigration, settling in Haiti himself for a time. In 1818, Saunders addressed many of the black Philadelphians who had so forcefully opposed African colonization, hoping to convince them that Haiti offered a superior alternative. Indeed, interest in Haiti flourished among black Philadelphians as well as among their Baltimore counterparts, who established an organization to promote Haitian emigration.[13]

Political instability in Haiti had sidetracked these plans, but Jean-Pierre Boyer unified the nation under his control in 1820 and renewed his predecessors' efforts to recruit settlers from the United States. In March 1824, Loring Dewey, a Presbyterian pastor and white agent of the ACS from New York, contacted Boyer to determine or allow American free blacks to determine the suitability of Haiti for American settlement. He also sought to determine whether Boyer would provide financial and legal support for such settlement and asked about the religious and political rights that emigrants could expect. Boyer responded by sending an agent, Jonathan Granville, to the United States with funds to charter ships for American settlers. Granville also attempted to convince free blacks of the virtues of the Haitian republic as a destination.[14]

Many black Philadelphians who had vehemently opposed African colonization (especially under the auspices of the ACS) were cautiously optimistic about emigration to Haiti. This optimism was aided by the fact that many *gens de couleur* (people of color) who had fled from Saint-Domingue to Charleston after the Haitian Revolution had moved on to Philadelphia in the wake of the backlash against the 1822 Vesey conspiracy. For these men and women, the appeal of a stable Haiti outweighed any attachments to their adopted home. But the idea of Haitian emigration also proved popular among the same leaders who had invoked African Americans' ties to their native soil in denouncing the ACS—most prominently, Richard Allen and James Forten.[15]

Allen became the foremost African American advocate of Haitian emigration. In August 1824, black Philadelphians organized a society to promote Haitian emigration. According to newspaper reports, "A very large number of coloured people" in Philadelphia were "solicitous to embark for Hayti." Allen personally contacted Boyer, and by the following month, some sixty free blacks had sailed for Haiti, with hundreds more hoping to follow.[16]

While Allen certainly hoped to expand the African Methodist Episcopal Church into the Caribbean, he was not simply (or primarily) interested in Haiti for evangelical purposes. Allen hoped that Haitian emigration would promote black citizenship, not only among the emigrants themselves but also among those who remained behind in the United States. Allen saw Haiti as a "safety valve" that would reduce the pressure building up in Philadelphia and other eastern cities, just as some nineteenth-century Americans saw the West as a safety valve for white Americans. Black poverty reinforced for many whites the inferiority of African Americans and bolstered arguments against black citizenship. By alleviating black poverty, Allen hoped to undermine these arguments. Furthermore, because Haitian emigration was led by blacks and the destination was a nearby black republic rather than a distant and poorly understood continent, many free blacks saw Haitian emigration as a part of the fight against slavery and as the antithesis of African colonization, at least as promoted by the ACS.[17]

Allen nevertheless had concerns about the new Haitian republic and American emigrants' place in it. Saunders had spoken at Allen's church in 1818, trumpeting the Haitian Revolution as uniting political liberties and Christian reform. This depiction of Haiti as a land open not only to black politics but also to Allen's brand of Christian reform likely helped to make the idea of emigrating there so appealing to Allen. The minister sought assurances from Boyer that American emigrants' religious liberties would be protected. Allen's concerns in this area provide insight into how he and many other Americans (black and white) understood citizenship. Religious and political liberties could not be separated, and for many American Protestants, Catholicism loomed as a threat to both. Boyer and his emissaries insisted that emigrants would have the right to practice their religion freely, though Boyer added the proviso that they would also not be permitted to "seek to make proselytes, or trouble those who profess another faith than their own." Even if Allen did not see emigration as simply an opportunity to attempt to convert Catholic Haitians, it is unclear that Boyer would allow the church leader and others to achieve all their goals in the island nation.[18]

The concerns of less prominent free blacks are somewhat more difficult to surmise, but Allen apparently was not the only potential emigrant to express concern about religious liberties. Granville singled out black Methodists as a "class of lunatics," though he offered public reassurances that religious practices would be protected.[19] Many advocates of Haitian emigration also carefully avoided challenging African Americans' claims to American citizenship.

Benjamin Lundy, a white advocate of Haitian emigration, thus forcefully stated, "I am decidedly of the opinion, that the country in which a man is born is his rightful home."[20] While the ACS often claimed that Africa was the true home of black Americans, emigrationists shied away from these sort of claims while touting Haiti as a land of opportunity for African Americans.

Lundy was an early supporter of Haitian emigration in Baltimore, where he had recently relocated his antislavery newspaper, the *Genius of Universal Emancipation*. In July 1824, the paper reported, a "most respectable" group of men met to form the Baltimore Emigration Society; in September, Granville addressed both this group and "a numerous meeting of the respectable people of color" on the subject of Haitian emigration. Granville evidently provided satisfactory answers to their questions, because attendees formed a committee to coordinate the emigration of interested individuals.[21]

The idea of Haitian emigration created considerable excitement as well as considerable concern. ACS leaders quickly saw the new project as a threat. In the summer of 1824, the ACS sent two representatives with instructions to promote the society in the Northeast. In Philadelphia, the agents found that talk of Haiti completely overwhelmed interest in African colonization, and they did not even attempt a collection. Though ACS's annual report portrayed interest in Haiti as just one more obstacle the society had overcome, the idea seriously undermined the ACS's ability to develop support in the major northern cities.[22]

Though Dewey had been associated with the ACS when he made his initial overtures to Boyer, society leaders insisted that the Haitian and African projects must not be combined, in part because of fears that a connection with Haiti would further undermine southern support for the ACS. In June 1824, Robert Goodloe Harper, a Maryland Federalist and an ACS vice president, wrote to Dewey not only to express concerns that Haitian emigration would not contribute to the Christianization of Africa but also to raise the "still more immediate and formidable objection" regarding "the alarms and apprehensions of the southern states . . . which would be excited in the highest degree, by seeing the negro population of the islands in the neighborhood thus increased." The ACS's secretary, the Reverend Ralph Gurley, eventually implied in print that Haitian emigration allowed runaway slaves to escape their masters.[23]

The same characteristics of Haitian emigration that appealed to free blacks made Haiti dangerous to the ACS and its efforts to build a national coalition in support of colonization. Though Haiti certainly presented the possibility of escape from American oppression, it also promised a continuing connection to the United States and to the struggle against slavery. Haitian emigration promised citizenship not by removal from the United States but by promoting a larger conception of citizenship. The relationship between free blacks in the United States and American emigrants to Haiti would be ongoing, whether that relationship concerned the church, commerce, or the international politics of antislavery. While many slaveholders were suspicious of the ACS as a front for antislavery evangelicals, the kind of international black community Haitian emigration could create obviously posed a much more pressing sort of threat. Slaveholders simply could not tolerate a direct connection between Haiti—long an exemplar of southerners' worst fears—and American free blacks.

By the middle of 1825, opponents of Haitian emigration had new evidence to support their efforts to dissuade potential emigrants: "Emigrants Returning," announced an August 1825 headline in the *Genius of Universal Emancipation*. The headline accompanied a sarcastic letter in which Dewey made light of claims that these returns meant the failure of Haitian emigration:

> *Surely*, if all the emigrants from Europe to this country, *are delighted*, and all from the *old* to the *new* western states, are never homesick and *never sigh* to return to their native vales, the emigration to Hayti ought to be stopped.[24]

But emigrants were returning, though in small numbers at first. The two sides in the Haitian emigration battle embarked on a propaganda war, with defenders minimizing the phenomenon or depicting the returnees as lazy and servile. The government of Haiti took this line, at times employing language disturbingly close to that of the American slaveholders or perhaps more negrophobic colonizationists. Granville claimed that those who were unsatisfied had come expecting an easy life of gentility "with the old coats and boots of their masters." If they wished "to return to the broom and the shoe brush," good riddance to them.[25]

Critics, in contrast, portrayed emigration as a cruel hoax that tricked gullible free blacks into settling in a land of "political and religious tyranny." The *Richmond Enquirer* and other newspapers printed letters written by returnees taking pains to note their respectability and intelligence and depicting Haiti as a land of suffering. Lundy responded by declaring that such negative accounts of Haiti were manufactured by slaveholders' agents and spread by "foreign" newspaper editors seeking to make a profit.[26]

At base, emigrants' experiences seem to have reinforced their cultural ties to the United States. Many returnees hesitated to criticize conditions in Haiti to avoid giving slavery's defenders further ammunition with which to argue that blacks were better off and happier as slaves. Yet many emigrants also clearly had found Haiti profoundly different, politically and culturally, from their native land. Some of these differences were celebrated, but others seemed troubling, and these differences likely contributed significantly to the decision to return to the United States.

Religious differences seem to have played a particularly important role. Critics of Haitian emigration believed that emphasizing the lack of religious liberty and the prominence of the established Catholic Church would deter black emigration. Yet religious conflict also arose among supporters of emigration. In 1824, Methodist missionaries in Port-au-Prince petitioned President Boyer for support since they had encountered both crowd violence and official restrictions on their right to meet publicly.[27]

Some American emigrants also seem to have felt alienated by political conditions and by their inability to speak French. One returned emigrant reportedly told a Baltimore colonizationist that "language, religion and even notions of civil liberty" prevented the "amalgamation" of Americans into Haitian society. Emigrants also found significant ongoing political turmoil.[28]

The ACS made the cultural clashes in Haiti a central element of arguments in favor of African colonization. The *African Repository* printed a letter from a supporter who had visited Haiti and believed that American emigrants would be far better off as part of a new settlement in West Africa where they would "have their own manners, customs, language and religion" than as settlers attempting to fit into a strange, unfamiliar culture.[29]

Though this argument proved persuasive in some cases, for far more free African Americans, the cultural strangeness of Haiti reinforced their connection to the United States. While lamenting the sums spent on plans for emigration to both "Hayti and Africa," the editors of *Freedom's Journal* declared, "We feel ourselves to be true Americans."[30] Interest in Haitian emigration persisted, and Haiti remained a powerful symbol of black resistance to slavery, yet most African Americans continued to emphasize their ties to the land of their birth.

Haiti, African Colonization, and American Politics

Relatively few African Americans emigrated to Haiti in the 1820s, but Haiti loomed large in debates about the future of American slavery and the status of free African Americans. Despite the best efforts of leading colonizationists, supposed links between Haiti and African colonization threatened the ACS's efforts to secure political support. Colonizationists sought to contrast the conditions in Haiti with the supposedly superior settlement in Liberia, but many African Americans instead held up Haiti as a symbol of black achievement while continuing to assert their connection to the United States.

At the same time, the ACS was reeling from domestic threats and from a bloody revolt in its colony in Africa. The organization's new secretary, Ralph Gurley, sought to reshape the group into a disciplined, national entity capable of achieving its ambitious goals. Central to Gurley's mission was the creation of the *African Repository and Colonial Journal*, with the first issue printed in March 1825. Gurley used the *African Repository* to trumpet the success and happiness of African colonists and to publicize the society's support from white Americans throughout the United States. Gurley also encouraged clergymen to devote Independence Day sermons to the theme of colonization, asking that collections be taken up to support the ACS. Though the ACS had always attempted to link the patriotic with the sacred, never before had this connection been so explicit. Through the use of the Fourth of July, Gurley hoped to overcome perceptions that colonization was a sectional rather than national undertaking.[31]

These changes did not, however, increase the ACS's appeal among free blacks, who continued to favor Haitian emigration over African colonization. Allen forwarded to Lundy letters depicting Haiti in a favorable light and refuting doubts about the suitability of Haiti as a place for African Americans. Lundy printed the letters along with essays celebrating emigration as a crucial weapon in the war against slavery.[32]

On August 15, 1825, Baltimore's free blacks celebrated their own Independence Day with a gathering in honor of the recent French acknowledgment of Haitian independence. William Watkins, a free black teacher and leading opponent of African colonization, addressed the crowd. Born around 1800 to a father who though illiterate had been one of the founding trustees of the Sharp Street Methodist Church, Watkins went on to become one of the most respected black men in Baltimore. He had initially been apprenticed as a shoemaker but eventually felt called to serve as a pastor and teacher and ultimately emerged as a community leader and as an abolitionist.[33]

In his address, Watkins declared Haitian independence an unparalleled event of "momentous importance." He described how a newly freed slave would be able to travel to a land where he was considered a brother and citizen, an implicit endorsement of Haitian emigration. Watkins suggested that Haiti's recognition by a European power would only increase the island nation's attraction for oppressed African Americans, but he also framed Haiti's struggle for recognition as part of the larger struggle against American slavery. However, Watkins also believed that despite their special connection to Haiti, African Americans also retained an attachment to the "land of our birth," and he pointed to the significant progress occurring in the United States. Watkins depicted Haiti not as a home for African Americans but as a focal point for a broader, cosmopolitan identity. In general, the embrace of Haiti provided free blacks with a way to reassert the international identity that had become so problematic in the wake of the founding of the ACS. Two days later, black Baltimoreans held a second celebration, reasserting this cosmopolitanism. However, although participants referred to themselves as "Sons of Africa," their final toast of the night was to "their Excellencies Presidents Adams, Boyer and [Simón] Bolivar," all of them in the Americas.[34] Colonizationists used Independence Day to make the case that free blacks were not and could not be Americans; Watkins used Haitian independence as an opportunity to invoke a broader, more inclusive notion of black identity that celebrated Haiti alongside Americanness.

As free blacks struggled with the question of Haitian emigration, Haiti was suddenly pushed into the national spotlight. A letter, likely written by Henry Clay, appeared in the *Philadelphia Democratic Press* advocating American participation in a proposed meeting of representatives of newly independent Latin American nations. In April 1825, the *National Journal* published an article outlining a proposed meeting to be held in Panama that October. Items to be considered by this Panama Congress included possible military operations to promote the liberation of Cuba and Puerto Rico, efforts to prevent future European colonization in the Western Hemisphere, promotion of trade, and the possible recognition of the Republic of Haiti.[35]

Martin Van Buren, who had supported Crawford in the presidential election but had subsequently moved into the Jackson camp, identified the Panama congress as an issue that could be used to unite the sort of national political party he hoped to build. In March 1826, Senator Robert Y. Hayne of South Carolina protested to his colleagues about the plan to send a U.S. delegation to the Panama Congress. His critique began with constitutional principles and a call for a return to George Washington's advice to avoid entangling alliances, but he quickly turned to the issue of slavery, a question Hayne described as "not even open to discussion, either here or elsewhere." He warned that the Panama Congress posed a danger to the institution of slavery and was particularly concerned about the recognition of Haitian independence. His suspicions were heightened by the appointment of Philadelphia congressman John Sergeant as one of the commissioners.

> We are to send, it seems, an honest and respectable man, but a distinguished advocate of the *Missouri Restriction*—an acknowledged abolitionist—to plead the cause of the South at the Congress of Panama. Our policy with regard to Hayti is plain. We can never acknowledge her independence.

Hayne alleged that the entangling alliances of the Panama Congress were simply an international extension of the "restriction and monopoly" of the domestic "American System."[36]

Hayne's position was perhaps unsurprising, but Philadelphia's Joseph Hemphill also opposed the Panama mission in Congress, not only because he feared entangling the United States in the matters of foreign governments but also because he believed that the Panama mission posed a threat to slavery. Though he personally opposed it, "the more I see and become acquainted with southern gentlemen, the more I am convinced of the inutility of propositions from non-slaveholding states on the subject of emancipation. They are only calculated to produce irritation without the prospect of accomplishing good." Though Hemphill had championed slavery restriction in the Missouri debates and continued to advocate internal improvements, he had become a Jackson supporter after the 1824 election, and Jackson had announced that he considered the Panama Congress "useless and dangerous."[37] Like Van Buren, Hemphill seems to have recognized the danger that agitation on the slavery issue posed to a national Jackson coalition.

Clay had been a staunch supporter of the Latin American revolutions and as secretary of state under President Adams advocated American participation in the Panama Congress. Clay remained a leading advocate of the ACS and was interested in Haiti not as a destination for free blacks but as a trading partner for the United States. In this way, Hayne was not far off the mark in linking the domestic economic development of the American System with the efforts of the Panama Congress to promote trade among the nations of the hemisphere. Clay had recognized the potency of these fears and had tried to head them off. His agent in Haiti had been attempting to prevent Haitian ships from attempting to enter southern ports and had also suggested that any Haitian ambassador should "be such in colour as not to offend the prejudices of our Country." Nevertheless, opponents of the Adams administration firmly opposed the Panama mission and frankly admitted that Haiti and the threat it posed to southern slavery motivated that opposition. Commercial ties with such a nation could not be tolerated, insisted southern congressmen; official diplomatic relations were out of the question. Despite the Panama Congress's popularity among many throughout the North (especially Pennsylvania, where the legislature passed a resolution in its support), appropriations for the mission remained mired in Congress until May 1826; the meeting adjourned before American representatives could arrive.[38]

Though critics of the Panama Congress did not say so, African colonization also constituted an important part of the American System. In Philadelphia and Baltimore, many of the same men who actively promoted internal improvements and a tariff to protect nascent American industries were also active in the ACS. Such men hoped that African colonization would ultimately promote economic diversification in the South as well as prevent the sectional tensions that often inhibited active government support of industry and economic development. The American System and African colonization faced similar obstacles in obtaining public support. Both struggled to defend themselves as national in character and faced charges that they favored the interests of one region over another. Federal support for either invariably faced constitutional challenges and raised the specter of an increasingly powerful central government. For this reason, advocates of both movements had to walk a dangerous tightrope between consent and coercion. Just as colonizationists had from the beginning emphasized the consensual nature of their project, advocates for the use of the federal government to support economic development through internal improvements, a protective tariff, or the national bank needed to allay fears that they sought to promote the power of government to coerce its citizens. Clay took to the floor of the House in 1824 to defend the proposed protective tariff in terms that bore a striking resemblance to his earlier defense of the ACS. Not only was the tariff in the national interest, but no man would be forced to pay: it would be assessed "voluntarily," not "by compulsion."[39]

These perceived connections could pose problems for advocates of colonization, who sought to present the idea as above partisan or sectional interests. One Philadelphia agent of the ACS complained to the parent society that Pennsylvanians saw the ACS as "a political engine" because of its support from Clay and opposition from Jackson: "partizans of the Gen view us with some suspicion." In South Carolina, Robert Turnbull published a series of pamphlets in which he insisted that colonization, the tariff, and internal improvements were all part of a larger effort to subjugate the South through the power of the federal government.[40]

The specter of Haiti augmented fears about the security of slavery. Advocates of African colonization not only tried to prevent Haitian emigration from drawing off support but also desperately tried to differentiate the two projects to assuage sectional tensions over slavery and open up the Caribbean to American manufacturers. Free blacks sought to use Haitian emigration to do the opposite—that is, to create a transnational black community that would become a weapon in the war against slavery.

Events in Baltimore only increased fears among slavery's defenders, intimating that the supposed gradual and consensual antislavery of colonization might become something more active and threatening. Daniel Raymond, a noted political economist, twice ran for a seat in the Maryland legislature on an antislavery platform. Raymond had been active in the Antislavery Society of Maryland and had served as secretary of the Baltimore Emigration Society. Though an advocate of Haitian emigration (and ambivalent about African colonization), Raymond insisted that neither plan could end slavery on its own. He rejected the idea that slavery could be ended consensually, as the ACS proposed, but insisted that the government of Maryland needed to take an active role, setting a date after which all slaves would be emancipated. He sought to appeal to Baltimore's nonslaveholding whites on both moral and economic grounds, insisting that the persistence of slavery did not serve their interests.[41]

As an economist, Raymond staunchly backed a protective tariff, further linking political antislavery with the supporters of the American System. Comparisons of the prosperous free states with the economically backward slave states were a staple of his campaign rhetoric. Lundy's *Genius of Universal Emancipation* celebrated Raymond's opposition to slavery and provided a forum for his economic ideas, but his opponents also noted these links. The *Richmond Enquirer* vigorously denounced his economic ideas as promoting federal despotic power and linked his economic writings with the Adams administration and Clay. The *Enquirer* also gleefully reported Raymond's poor electoral showing.[42]

The national politics of slavery continued to thwart colonizationists' plans, but local supporters persisted in their hopes that Baltimore and Philadelphia would become fertile grounds for African colonization. In 1826, Baltimore's Charles C. Harper ran for a seat in the Maryland Assembly, declaring that he "would devote all the means" at his command to the support of African colonization. Despite his efforts to distance himself from abolitionism, Harper fared only slightly better than did Raymond, falling far short of winning the seat. Privately, ACS agents admitted that free black Baltimoreans' support for colonization had been disappointing.[43]

In Philadelphia, however, the ACS seemed to make some progress among white opponents of slavery. Gurley visited the city in 1826 and reported that "the sentiments of the Quakers have, I believe, changed much in our favor." Shortly thereafter, Philadelphians formed an auxiliary to the ACS. But the group's agents continued to be disappointed by the lack of public support for colonization, especially among free blacks.[44]

As the year closed, Baltimore supporters of African colonization hoped that they had achieved a breakthrough. Harper and John H. B. Latrobe, white agents for the Maryland Colonization Society, organized two meetings of free black Baltimoreans. The first, held at Bethel Church, was only moderately attended, but the second, at the Sharp Street African Church, attracted a much larger crowd. Harper and Latrobe introduced a resolution representing the sentiments of "respectable free people of color," and according to Harper, an "immense majority" supported this proposal, though a minority led by Jacob Greener opposed it.[45]

These sorts of meetings had often been a forum for denunciations of African colonization, but ACS agents now sought to repudiate the 1817 Philadelphia protest by turning the Baltimore resolution into a public relations coup, proving that free blacks desired to leave the United States for Africa. Within the month, the Sharp Street memorial was reprinted in the *African Repository*. The document's language does not denigrate free blacks as much as the discourse of colonization often did, probably because free black leaders had suggested some changes to the resolution presented by the white ACS agents. Nevertheless, the language contributes to the idea that free blacks recognized and consented to their exclusion from American citizenship: "We reside among you, and yet are strangers; natives, and yet not citizens.... Our difference of colour, the servitude of many and most of our brethren, and the prejudices which those circumstances have naturally occasioned, will not allow us to hope, even if we could desire, to mingle with you someday, in the benefits of citizenship." The memorial used natural metaphors for African colonization, likening it to the removal of an "extraneous mass" to promote the "health and moral sense of the body politic." Overall the presence of free blacks in the United States is depicted as unnatural and unhealthy for all.[46]

At the same time, ACS allies in Congress pushed for active government support for colonization. Ezekiel Chambers, a senator from Maryland, introduced a memorial to that end, prompting Hayne immediately to rise and protest the ACS as "wild, impractical [and] mischievous." The proposal ultimately went nowhere. In March 1827, the Maryland legislature passed a bill to appropriate one thousand dollars per year for the ACS, far less than would be necessary but perhaps, the organization hoped, a step in the right direction. The Pennsylvania legislature soon took up a similar bill.[47]

Seeing that the colonizationists were making political progress, free blacks worked hard to counter the impression that they had embraced the ACS's language, particularly the idea that they had no interest in becoming full citizens of their native country. Writing in the *Genius of Universal Emancipation*, "Africanus" insisted,

> Born in the United States it would be very unnatural for me to have no love for my country. My taste, manners, habits, customs and opinions prove my attachment to the American Republic; and it is impossible for me to resist the desire of remaining peaceable under the protection of its laws, perfectly contented to share the blessings that flow from the institutions resulting from its free principles.[48]

The writer also disputed the idea that the memorial embodied the true sentiments of Baltimore's free blacks, taking issue with the language used. The author was less concerned about whether some individuals wished to emigrate and more focused on what free blacks' actions and the words that colonizationists tried to associate with those actions say about African Americans' place in American society.

Writing as "a colored Baltimorean," William Watkins reiterated these points as he dissected the memorial's wording to counter the lines that were most objectionable. Watkins, too, rejected the idea that free blacks had no hope to "mingle with you one day in the benefits of citizenship." He also argued that even those who supported the memorial did so not as a general statement of the sentiment of the free black community (as the ACS had presented it) but rather as a narrow statement of those who did wish to leave. Since, as Watkins pointed out, only ten Baltimoreans had sailed on a recent ship to Africa, any attempt to apply their sentiments to the larger black community was a misrepresentation. He also hoped to reassure his free black brethren in New York and Philadelphia that most of Baltimore's free blacks shared their animosity toward African colonization.[49]

Black Philadelphians expressed their support for their colleagues to the south. Writing to the recently established *Freedom's Journal*, James Forten echoed the two Baltimore writers, declaring that the memorial was the work of Harper and Latrobe and did not reflect the true feelings of the free blacks of Baltimore. He also noted that not a single attendee at a recent meeting in Philadelphia had supported "colonization in any foreign country whatever." *Freedom's Journal* buttressed Forten's claims by reprinting a piece in which Russell Parrott declared unequivocally, "With all her imperfections, still she is my country, the home of my affections, in which is centered my most ardent hopes."[50]

Few African Americans in the mid-Atlantic accepted the premise that black people could not be American, yet many continued to see themselves through a broadly international lens. For some, like Daniel Coker, a mission to West Africa under the aegis of the ACS satisfied this broad, African identity. For many others, Haiti offered an opportunity to embrace an expansive, international black identity while maintaining claims on American citizenship and continuing the struggle against American slavery. The growing attention paid to Haiti, in turn, complicated the politics of colonization, paradoxically alienating both free blacks and white slaveholders from the ACS.

PART II

Black Politics on the Border

CHAPTER 3

Interstate Diplomacy and Fugitive Slaves

Traversing the streets of Philadelphia in October 1822, James Forten recognized Congressman Samuel Breck and offered his hand. Though Breck apparently was unaccustomed to being approached on the street by black men, he recognized Forten's "respectability" and accepted the offered greeting. Forten announced proudly that in the recent election, he had taken all of his white employees to the polls and that they had voted for Breck. Forten was eager to demonstrate his political influence but had almost certainly not cast a vote himself.[1]

Pennsylvania had stood at the forefront as states dramatically reduced property restrictions in the wake of the American Revolution. The state's 1776 constitution had allowed nearly universal manhood suffrage, but custom—and intimidation—generally excluded black men from the polls.[2] In addition, Philadelphia's electoral politics might have deterred Forten and other free black men from engaging in risky attempts at voting. While the Federalist Party suffered dramatic national losses after the end of the War of 1812, Philadelphia consistently returned its Federalist congressmen to Washington. Pennsylvania political parties were particularly muddled in these years, engaging in what one historian has described as "a game without rules." Newspapers printing the 1820 election returns did not label candidates by party, in keeping with the usual practice, since it was impossible to label each candidate with the name of a single party. Federalist congressmen such as John Sergeant staunchly criticized slavery extension, but it was less clear where state and local politicians stood on issues related to free blacks. White abolitionist William Rawle believed that the political coalitions he observed in Philadelphia were absurd, and he remarked in his journals on "the strange involutions of parties." In such an environment voting or attempting to do so might not have seemed worth the risk.[3]

Although black Philadelphians did not necessarily believe that denying them the right to vote was just, in this particular context, they did not see that citizenship right as most pressing. While Americans later came to see the right to vote as the essence of citizenship and the Supreme Court and amendments to the U.S. Constitution eventually helped to establish the idea of a national citizenship, in the early nineteenth century, citizenship was more diffuse and complicated. As historian William J. Novak has written, "Membership in and exclusion from a range of differentiated associations determined one's bundle of privileges, obligations and immunities much more than the abstract and underdeveloped constitutional category of national citizenship." Citizenship flowed from the bottom up, and although the right to vote was certainly an important marker of citizenship, it was hardly the only one.[4]

In this light, the independent institutions of free black life that flourished in this period must be seen not as a means of withdrawal from public life but rather as assertions of black citizenship—as a part of black engagement with a broader, public world. Chief among these institutions were black churches, but they also included benevolent societies, schools, masonic lodges, and cultural institutions. Novak notes that early American associations were "distinctly public rather than private" in character. As such, they were often chartered and regulated by state authorities. For example, in 1815, Robert Green had brought suit against Richard Allen's Bethel African Methodist Episcopal Church on the grounds that the church had unlawfully expelled him as a trustee without a fair hearing. The Pennsylvania Supreme Court ruled against Bethel, yet as Allen's biographer, Richard S. Newman, points out, the court's decision essentially recognized Allen's church and held it to the same standards as any other body incorporated in Pennsylvania.[5] The recognition of this public dimension of black institutions implied that in certain respects, African Americans were citizens.

The political and legal status of free African Americans became especially important in early American struggles over fugitive slaves, which meant that the stakes were particularly high in the border cities of Baltimore and Philadelphia. Not only were free blacks actively engaged in aiding fugitives, but black citizenship came to be seen as a threat to recovery of fugitive slaves. Recognition of black citizenship in Pennsylvania, as limited as that recognition might be, therefore became a threat to slavery in Maryland. In this way, debates over black citizenship came to play a critical role in state and national politics, and free blacks themselves came to be important political actors without casting a single vote.

Fugitive Slaves, Kidnappers, and Black Citizenship

Free black Philadelphians, living as they did on the borderlands of slavery, recognized that their liberty was precarious. Maryland slaveholders' desire to recover fugitives and the lucrative possibilities of slave catching led to what historian Julie Winch has termed "the other underground railroad."[6] While some fugitives from slavery found their way north, many African Americans, legally enslaved or not, were captured and sold south. Kidnapping, often carried out by organized rings, posed a constant threat to black Philadelphians. Violent stories of the capture of free blacks by sinister "mansteaters" were a fairly common feature of Philadelphia newspapers. The young and the poor were particularly vulnerable, but even the wealthy and respected were not immune.[7]

Dramatic stories may have brought tales of kidnapping to the attention of the public, but free blacks and their white allies fought to capitalize on that attention and to provide legal defense against kidnappers. A large portion of the business of the Pennsylvania Abolition Society (PAS) and its acting committee was devoted to efforts to return those who had been illegally seized and sold into slavery. Though the PAS restricted its official membership to whites, it seems to have worked closely with black abolitionists regarding kidnapping.[8] In addition to its work on individual cases, the PAS drafted resolutions for Congress defending the rights of free blacks and hired an agent to work to get the state legislature to pass measures to prevent kidnapping.[9]

As early as 1799, black Philadelphians had petitioned Congress to deal with the kidnapping problem. In December 1816 and January 1817, at the same time that the American Colonization Society was founded, Pennsylvania and Maryland congressman introduced a series of resolutions intended to defend the rights of "persons of color, free, or entitled to freedom at a given time," who were being "carried into perpetual slavery."[10]

In December 1817, Congress responded to this agitation with a bill "to amend the act respecting the recovery of fugitives from justice, and persons escaping from the service of their masters." It was reported by John Pindall, a representative from Virginia. Antislavery forces initially supported the bill, hoping that they would be able to attach measures to protect the rights of free blacks. When it became clear that the bill would in fact strengthen masters' efforts to recover fugitives and do nothing to defend against kidnapping, they turned against it. The bill was defeated handily.[11]

The enemies of slavery in Pennsylvania then turned their eyes to the state legislature. In January 1819, the PAS resolved to send a bill to Harrisburg to correct "the outrage committed on the people of colour under the Fugitive Slave Law of the United States." Proponents of the bill were particularly concerned with preventing aldermen and justices of the peace from conspiring with kidnappers. The law passed on March 27, 1820, made kidnapping a felony punishable by a fine of between five hundred and one thousand dollars and between seven and twenty-one years of hard labor. It also fined justices of the peace who cooperated with kidnappers. Some legislators had worried that the bill would deter legitimate attempts to recapture fugitives, and by the gubernatorial elections of that year, the kidnapping bill had become a political issue. Philadelphia Democrats charged Federalist candidate Joseph Hiester with indifference to the crime of "manstealing." The politics of race and slavery were hardly clear, however, as the same Democratic partisans insisted that Hiester had won the election with the aid of illegal votes, including some cast by "negroes who were runaway slaves."[12]

The Pennsylvania law quickly provoked response from states to the south. Members of Congress from Virginia and South Carolina sought to challenge the provisions of the law that they argued undermined the operation of the federal Fugitive Slave Law, though their efforts garnered no results. In Maryland, the response was particularly pointed. One 1821 celebration of the Fourth of July included a toast to "Our Sister States, north of us, whose *philanthropy* it is to deprive us of our fugitive slaves—the receiver is as culpable as the thief." Maryland legislators soon began to receive petitions calling for them to counteract their northern neighbors' efforts to hobble the Fugitive Slave Law.[13]

The tension between the two states was exacerbated in 1821 when fugitive slave John Read, who had escaped from his Baltimore master, Samuel Griffith, and settled just west of Philadelphia, killed Griffith and an overseer who were attempting to reenslave Read. Maryland slaveholders were particularly disturbed when the judge at Read's trial told the jury that if Griffith had not intended to take Read before a judge, then Griffith was in violation of the 1820 law and that Read therefore had been acting to prevent the commission of a felony. As a result, the jury acquitted him of Griffith's murder (but convicted him for killing the overseer). In response, the Maryland legislature called on the state's governor to confer with his Pennsylvania counterpart to resolve tensions between citizens of the two states. In his annual message, Pennsylvania's Hiester acknowledged these tensions, expressing sympathy for the owners of runaway slaves but also declaring the need to protect free blacks from the threat of kidnapping.[14]

The PAS countered Maryland slaveholders' attempts to pressure Pennsylvania's elected officials with a petition declaring that the Marylanders were fortunate that their Pennsylvanian neighbors did not do more to undermine an institution they profoundly loathed. The petitioners remained hopeful that harmony between the two states could be preserved but insisted their state bore responsibility for defending the rights of all of its citizens: "In our constitution no distinction of colour is to be found."[15] The idea that black Pennsylvanians were citizens of Pennsylvania (whatever the specific meanings of citizenship) was a central part of efforts to defend free blacks from kidnapping and not coincidentally to undermine efforts to recover fugitive slaves.

This idea profoundly troubled Maryland's slaveholders. They could assert a certain amount of control over free blacks within Maryland's borders, but the movement of black bodies across state lines or the threat of such movement meant that the laws of Pennsylvania had implications for neighboring states. This movement and efforts to control it made the borderland between Baltimore and Philadelphia a place of fierce conflict.

At the same time, events far to the south raised tensions to a fever pitch. In May 1822, white South Carolinians began to uncover what seemed to be a massive conspiracy led by Denmark Vesey, a free black carpenter. Investigators later pieced together evidence of a plan for free and enslaved blacks in and around Charleston to seize the city's arsenal and slaughter whites in an effort to strike a blow against slavery. The local African Methodist Episcopal (AME) church, of which Vesey was a leader, seemed to be at the center of the plot. News soon began to filter north, with ominous reports appearing in Baltimore and Philadelphia papers. Some warned that some conspirators had settled in Philadelphia, and the city's *Democratic Press* lamented that Philadelphia was becoming a penal colony "to receive the convicts of the southern states."[16]

These claims contained some truth. Richard Allen and his Philadelphia church welcomed hundreds of refugees from the Charleston AME church. In particular, Allen took in pastor Morris Brown, who soon became Allen's close friend, confidant, and spiritual ally, serving on Bethel's board of trustees. Brown and Allen later traveled together, preaching and organizing the AME Church.[17]

Close ties between black Methodists up and down the Atlantic coast reinforced the feeling of solidarity between free blacks in Philadelphia and African Americans in the South, but many southern whites found these ties profoundly disturbing. Equally troubling was the role that free blacks had played in the conspiracy. In December 1822, South Carolina passed the Negro Seaman Act, whose goal was "the better regulation of free negroes and persons of color." It sought to prevent contact between slaves and free black sailors by requiring black seamen to be jailed upon entering any South Carolina port and released only when their ship departed. Doing so, legislators hoped, would prevent black sailors from spreading "the moral contagion of their pernicious principles and morals."[18]

The Negro Seaman Act represented more than a response to paranoia: it constituted an attempt to undermine the very real influence that free blacks, especially sailors, had on slavery. Throughout the Atlantic, sailors served as "vectors of revolution," a multiethnic, multiracial class of workers who for decades had played a crucial role in fomenting conflict. More narrowly, black sailors had been a source of at least some of the antislavery literature that had found its way into the hands of enslaved South Carolinians, and Vesey himself had spent time at sea. Perhaps more disturbing to whites, the conspirators of 1822 had hoped to receive assistance from Haiti and had attempted to enlist the aid of the island nation's president, Jean-Pierre Boyer.[19]

The South Carolina legislature showed that in much of the Deep South, fear of slave rebellion trumped the legal rights of free blacks, but these actions raised serious questions elsewhere. Could the fear of slave revolt justify the denial of equal protection under the law to citizens, even if those citizens were free blacks? For that matter, could free blacks be citizens?[20]

The actions of southern legislatures once again forced northerners to address the question of black citizenship, a question that many preferred to avoid. African Americans' acquiescence to the customary denial of the full rights of citizenship allowed Philadelphia's whites to sidestep the thorny problem of the exact status of free blacks. The veneer of consent helped to conceal the forces that confined African Americans to a distinctly second-class citizenship.

Southerners highlighted the hypocrisy of northern antislavery, yet at least in the 1820s, many northerners balked at denying free blacks all claims to citizenship. A memorial from "Masters of American vessels, lying in the Port of Charleston" protested the Negro Seaman Act not only because of the economic costs it imposed but also because it resulted in the unlawful imprisonment of "free coloured persons, native citizens of the United States." Even in Maryland, where whites had gone to great lengths to establish legal controls over free blacks, some observers expressed concerns about the complete denial of free blacks' legal rights. A Baltimore newspaper noted that the law violated "the first clause in our declaration of independence."[21]

The Negro Seaman Act also produced problems for U.S. diplomacy, since non-American ships also sailed into Charleston Harbor. The imprisonment of free black sailors who were British subjects violated the Commercial Convention of 1815, which had guaranteed American and British seamen free access to ports. When ship captains brought their complaints to the attention of U.S. Supreme Court justice William Johnson, he declared the law unconstitutional, though the South Carolina court upheld the law. The British minister to the United states, Stratford Canning, protested the act to Secretary of State John Quincy Adams, finally moving the U.S. government to act: within weeks, black sailors were once again free to sail into Charleston Harbor without fear of immediate imprisonment. Yet prominent South Carolinians almost immediately banded together in "An Association" to enforce through private means what had been untenable as public policy.[22]

While these matters might have seemed distant to some free blacks in Baltimore and Philadelphia, others surely saw profound implications for their own citizenship claims. The local press's reporting on the controversy and the presence of so many refugees from South Carolina would have made residents of the two cities aware of the situation. At the heart of this conflict lay the question of the legal status of free blacks, not only in South Carolina but also in the United States and internationally. In addition, the South Carolina legislature had explicitly declared that the rights of free blacks threatened the stability of slavery.

As important as these issues of black citizenship were in the abstract, they became concrete in the borderland between Philadelphia and Baltimore when masters attempted to recover fugitive slaves. In 1823, a Maryland master advertised in the *Baltimore Patriot* for the return of fugitive Frank Reed. "As he has relations in the neighborhood of Philadelphia," noted the owner, "it is supposed he may have gone there." Though the number of slaves who escaped to Pennsylvania may have been exaggerated, the threat posed by the proximity of free black communities across the border profoundly disturbed Maryland slaveholders. This perceived threat provided an incentive for Baltimore slaveholders to offer their slaves an opportunity to purchase their freedom. Owners assumed that slaves who saw some possibility of a negotiated freedom rather than an assured lifetime of bondage would be less likely to flee, and used that possibility as a means of control.[23]

Self-purchase provided Baltimore slaves' most common route to freedom. For at least a time, these concessions by owners slowed the flight of fugitives, but the creation of a large free black community in Baltimore had unintended consequences for the institution of slavery. Fugitives could "melt into anonymity" among the free blacks of Baltimore, either as a permanent escape from slavery, or as a way to prepare for a flight to the north.[24]

The growth of this free black community and the threat that it posed to slavery provoked Maryland into imposing an abundance of legal restrictions on the economic, social, and political rights of its free blacks. "Vagrants" could be seized and sold into forced labor, while the children of those who had been seized were bound as apprentices. Free blacks had to obtain licenses to purchase firearms or liquor and were prohibited from selling a variety of goods without the written permission of either a justice of the peace or of three "respectable persons" who could vouch for the sellers. Free blacks were not allowed to operate boats without white supervision, and African American religious services had to be supervised by white pastors. Actions deemed to promote the escape of slaves could lead free blacks to be punished as slaves. In practice, many of these restrictions were unevenly enforced, though over time white Marylanders became increasingly willing to take extreme measures to control this growing free black population.[25]

Such laws also had consequences for free blacks living to the north. Enforced or not, these Black Codes were well known to black Pennsylvanians and served as a potent warning about what sort of restrictions some white Pennsylvanians desired. When black Philadelphians called on white allies to defend their black neighbors' citizenship rights, they often envisioned the sorts of rights denied to free blacks in Maryland.

Fugitive Slaves and State Politics

Disagreements over what citizenship rights were to be accorded to free blacks caused particular controversy when African Americans crossed state lines. Many Marylanders thought that Pennsylvania was far too generous in its treatment of African Americans. Black citizens in Pennsylvania threatened slavery in Maryland, and Maryland slaveholders were not content to leave these matters to their northern neighbors.

In 1826, after years of inaction by the governments of neighboring states, the Maryland legislature empowered a delegation to confer directly with legislatures in adjoining states. After securing the passage of a Delaware law to facilitate the return of fugitives, the delegates traveled to Harrisburg to push for similar legislation in Pennsylvania. Benjamin Lundy mocked the "accommodating disposition" shown by the Delaware legislature and hoped that Pennsylvanians would provide more resistance. Democratic newspapers also noted the delegation's impending arrival, pointing out the "respectability" and intelligence of the Marylanders. Two of the commissioners, Ezekiel Chambers and Robert Goldsborough, were active supporters of African colonization.[26]

The arrival of the commissioners stirred up considerable debate in the Philadelphia press. The editors of the *Democratic Press* called on the legislature to work closely with the Maryland delegation, insisting that it was their "constitutional" responsibility to do so. The *Aurora* similarly defended the commissioners, insisting that "every friend of good order and of the poor negroes themselves must desire to see it passed." Both papers denied that their support of the bill indicated a love of slavery but instead pointed to the need to promote the union and reminded readers that slavery had not been entirely extinguished from Pennsylvania. They hoped that interstate compromise rather than antislavery activism would lead to the gradual end of slavery in both states.[27]

Others in Philadelphia did not look so kindly on the Maryland delegation. Readers of *Poulson's American Daily Advertiser* flooded the paper with letters on the subject, most of them opposing the bill. Some emphasized the extravagance and pomp with which the commissioners were greeted by Harrisburg, depicting them as southern aristocrats seeking to dominate their northern neighbors. Others simply saw the whole controversy as a distraction from the real business at hand. One supporter of the bill, however, admitted the evils of slavery but insisted that the bill would improve the lives of slaves since it would deter them from running away and thus ultimately lead to better treatment.[28]

Many opponents of the proposed measure argued that Pennsylvania must defend the liberties of its free black citizens. In fact, opposition to the Maryland delegation led white Pennsylvanians to assert the citizenship of the commonwealth's free blacks more explicitly than ever before. One writer warned, "Let us beware, lest by allowing a door for kidnappers to seize on one class of our free and equal citizens we barter the principles of our liberties for the good opinion of the state of Maryland." The PAS also invoked the need to defend "the rights of our own citizens" in its formal protest to the state legislature.[29]

The vital place occupied by claims of black citizenship in the opposition to the fugitive bill reinforced for black Philadelphians the importance of maintaining those claims despite free blacks' ambiguous place in Pennsylvania. While many blacks were willing to forgo their right of suffrage in the face of custom (and the threat of violence), the crisis provoked by the Maryland commissioners demonstrated that free blacks could not afford to do without some of the rights accorded to citizens of Pennsylvania. It also illustrated how black citizenship in one state could be a powerful tool to undermine slavery in another. The fugitive bill also provoked the most direct political action by free blacks that Pennsylvanians had yet witnessed, including the stagecoach journey to Harrisburg on which Richard Allen met Jonathan Roberts.[30]

The legislature remained deadlocked over the measure until a young representative from Philadelphia, William Morris Meredith, offered a compromise. Meredith had been in frequent contact with Philadelphia abolitionists, including Allen, and Meredith's father kept him apprised of the increasingly intense opposition in his home district to any accommodation to what one correspondent termed the "Maryland invasion." Meredith's compromise strengthened the protections against kidnapping while making it easier for slaveholders to capture those whom they could legally claim. While opponents of the bill were genuinely concerned about the kidnapping of free blacks, Meredith was at least partly correct that the bill's detractors were really interested in preventing the recovery of fugitive slaves.[31]

Meredith's leadership in the passage of this bill illustrates the entanglement of the politics of fugitive slaves and other political questions. It is perhaps surprising that Meredith would take such a prominent role in a controversial bill of this sort. Though opinion in his home district was mixed, the opposition to compromise was fierce (Meredith's father termed it "the hurricane that is blowing"), while support seems to have been lukewarm. Meredith might have left this matter to others but instead took the lead, arguing that Pennsylvania had a constitutional imperative to support efforts to recover slaves. To ensure that he was not perceived as simply a tool of Maryland slaveholders, Meredith's compromise included a strengthened defense of the rights of free blacks, and he pressed for emancipation of Pennsylvania's few remaining slaves.[32]

Meredith's public and private defense of his actions illuminates the complex politics of this issue. Elected in January 1826 to replace a recently deceased representative, Meredith came into office eager to promote a vigorous program of internal improvements. Support for elements of the American System was more or less a requirement for Philadelphia politicians, as the young lawyer discovered. According to one letter writer, Meredith had been left off of the ballot in the previous election because he had been deemed insufficiently supportive of such projects. By the time he won the special election, he was considered a "zealous" supporter of the internal improvements. In particular, Meredith was eager to demonstrate to his constituents that he was a capable advocate of government support for canal building.[33]

The canal Philadelphians were most eager to promote was the Chesapeake and Delaware Canal. For some time, Philadelphia merchants had been warily eyeing Baltimore, which grew dramatically in the decades after the revolution. Its location on the Chesapeake gave it access to the farmers of the Susquehanna Valley, a market that many Philadelphians felt was rightfully theirs. Since the eighteenth century, some Philadelphians had explored the possibility of a canal that would link the Delaware and Chesapeake Bays and thus provide Philadelphia with access to the Susquehanna, but the project proved troublesome. In 1825, Congress had passed a bill supporting the canal, but as was always the case in such projects, this support depended on the conviction that it would be in the national interest, not simply in the interest of some state or section. The parties that did not stand to profit from the proposed projects tended to call into question the proposition that the general interest was being served.[34]

In this case, the state through which most of the canal would pass, Delaware, stood to benefit relatively little. The main beneficiary would be Philadelphia; the big loser would be Baltimore, though the Eastern Shore of Maryland would presumably benefit. Support for the canal, therefore, depended on cordial relations between Pennsylvanians and Marylanders. Both the Pennsylvania and Maryland legislatures had purchased stock in the canal company (as had the federal government), and in his defense of the fugitive bill, Philadelphia congressman Joseph Hemphill noted that the Maryland legislature had been the first to incorporate a company to construct such a canal. Nevertheless, Baltimoreans remained concerned about the effects of the new waterway.[35]

"Zealous" advocates of the Chesapeake and Delaware Canal, therefore, had an incentive to promote harmony between the Maryland and Pennsylvania governments. Meredith defended his support for the fugitive bill by emphasizing the need for regional harmony, though he did not explicitly state that such harmony was essential for canal building. He emphasized the common ground between Pennsylvanians and Marylanders despite their differences of "feelings" concerning slavery, and he denounced those who would label "our fellow citizens of the Southern States" as "man-stealers." He called for moderation and understanding of "our *Southern* brethren." Though ostensibly the bill was intended to protect the rights of both free blacks and slaveholders, Meredith focused on the need for cooperation between the white citizens of Pennsylvania and Maryland.[36]

Other suggestions linked the fugitive slave issue with the need to cooperate on internal improvements. When the Maryland legislature had resolved to send its delegation to Pennsylvania, Baltimore legislator Benjamin Howard (who had defeated Daniel Raymond and who was a prosperous lawyer) had suggested empowering the delegation to confer with Pennsylvania's legislature both on the fugitive slave question and "on the subject of Canals," though the legislature ultimately left the two questions separate. Perhaps not coincidentally, Howard's father, John E. Howard, had been an early and vigorous advocate of the American Colonization Society.[37]

The "problems" created by free blacks thus had the potential to disrupt the delicate harmony on which the support for federal internal improvements depended, not just on a national level but on a regional one as well. A broadly conceived American System needed to address these problems if it hoped to have any success. African colonization sought to promote sectional harmony and ultimately economic development by removing free blacks from the United States altogether. Other supporters of internal improvements sought to promote interstate harmony by attempting to prevent fugitive slaves from seeking a safe haven across state lines.

These discussions concerning specific and limited notions of black citizenship and fugitive slaves were accompanied by broader debates of slavery. Many partisan leaders worked hard to keep the issue of slavery out of political discourse, but it kept reemerging in Philadelphia politics. In 1826, Hemphill, a Federalist who had migrated into Andrew Jackson's camp, resigned his seat due to poor health. His resignation came not long after his much-publicized speech on the Panama mission.[38]

Many observers ultimately saw the race to replace Hemphill as a referendum on the politics of slavery. The October 1826 election pitted former Federalist John Sergeant, the Adams candidate, against Jacksonian Henry Horn and Federalist Thomas Kittera. Sergeant and Horn finished in a tie, and the seat remained open until the following October, when Sergeant won the second special election. Partisans explicitly framed the 1827 contest as a battle between the

1824 presidential candidates, Jackson and Adams, and over the issue of slavery. On the eve of the election, Jacksonian editor Duff Green warned that Sergeant's allies, "the Aristocracy, the Bank, the Abolition Society and the bar of Philadelphia," sought to reopen the slavery question. Sergeant's defenders pronounced his victory a triumph for political antislavery. "Pennsylvanians no slavites," trumpeted Benjamin Lundy in the *Genius of Universal Emancipation*, proclaiming Sergeant the "celebrated advocate of the anti-slavery cause." Philadelphian William Rawle recorded in his journal that he had voted for Sergeant despite his dislike for Adams: "I think the best interests of the country require that the Southern Policy should not obtain too much ascendancy."[39]

As the 1828 presidential election approached, supporters of the Adams administration and enemies of Andrew Jackson hoped to use the issue of slavery to woo Pennsylvania voters. James Buchanan wrote to Jackson in late 1826 that the general's opponents had attempted to link him with some of his more radical southern allies but that the strategy had not worked. In 1828 however, anti-Jacksonians in Philadelphia, especially the editor of the *Democratic Press*, John Binns, tried a new approach, depicting Jackson not simply as a slaveholder but also as a slave trader. Binns printed broadsides with a famous iconic image of a chained slave and the words, "Am I not a man and Brother? General Jackson has been a slave dealer—a trafficker in human flesh, a Buyer and Seller of Men, women and Children for filthy lucre." Jackson personally denied these allegations, while his Philadelphia supporters attempted to refute them in print.[40]

Adams partisans chose to focus on the more sensational slave-trading charge rather than on the more concrete, sectional contrast of a pair of northerners (Adams and Richard Rush) opposed to a ticket of southern slaveholders (Jackson and John C. Calhoun). While Pennsylvanians generally opposed slavery, they tended to be most disturbed by slavery when it touched them in some way. The kidnapping of free blacks and the possibility that their state and local governments might be forced to defend slavery profoundly concerned Pennsylvanians and may have led Binns and others to believe that allegations of slave trading would resonate with Pennsylvania voters. As the landslide victory of the Jackson-Calhoun ticket showed, however, the implications of the presidential election for the issue of slavery had failed to dissuade nominally antislavery Pennsylvanians from supporting the Hero of New Orleans. In fact, some Philadelphia supporters of the general felt comfortable enough with their candidate's connections with the institution of slavery to turn it into a kind of badge of honor. According to one report, joyous Jackson partisans had celebrated their victory by parading around Philadelphia with "what appears to be a vile print of a negro driver, with a hickory whip in one hand, and pointing scornfully at a negro but with the other, as an emblem of their victory."[41]

The extent to which slavery became an issue in this election certainly had implications for the citizenship rights of free blacks. *Freedom's Journal*, which provided fairly extensive coverage of the actions of black Philadelphians, made only passing reference to the claim that Jackson had been a slave trader, but anyone who would celebrate Jackson's election by parading through the streets and mocking opponents as whipped slaves would obviously have little sympathy for African Americans' citizenship rights.[42]

The political implications of black citizenship and of the political engagement of black Philadelphians are evident in a satirical print from the series "Life in Philadelphia" by Edward Williams Clay. A political supporter of Henry Clay (whom Edward claimed was a distant relation, though he lacked any evidence to support that claim) and bitter critic of Jackson, Edward Clay drew a series of images mocking the pretensions of black Philadelphians (especially the wealthy).[43]

One print depicts an older, respectably dressed black man who grabs a shabbily attired black youth and shouts, "What de debil you hurrah for General Jackson for?" The older man has a copy of the anti-Jackson *Democratic Press*, while the younger one wears a hat made of the pro-Jackson *Mercury*. In one sense, this image mocks black Philadelphians' attempts to act in "racially inappropriate" ways and provides evidence that white Philadelphians of all po-

Edward Williams Clay, "What de debil you hurrah for General Jackson for?," 1828. Courtesy of the Library Company of Philadelphia.

litical persuasions found the prospect of black political engagement worthy of ridicule. However, it also mocks the young boy, who does not seem to know enough to avoid supporting the slaveholder. The print also features a throng of white celebrants in the background, and the boy may also serve as a stand-in for all Philadelphians too foolish to recognize that they had been deceived by the Jackson movement; in essence, a black Philadelphian who supports Jackson is only slightly less ridiculous than any Philadelphian doing so.

The image also hints, perhaps unintentionally, at black political engagement. Though it is unlikely that any black Philadelphians voted in the election, they may have closely watched electoral politics. The image implies that the two black Philadelphians have been following the election in the partisan press and that the man feels that it is important to set the boy straight, to guide his political allegiances. The older figure echoes Samuel Breck's depiction of the "respectable" Forten, the exceptional black leader among a generally degraded mass of black Philadelphians.

Despite Clay's derisive depiction of such political advocacy, some free blacks clearly saw themselves as political actors, and African Americans continued to assert their citizenship rights in a variety of ways. Recognizing that full legal equality was not a realistic goal at the time, free blacks and their allies framed their struggle for essential legal protections as a struggle for black citizenship. Many whites, however, perceived even limited notions of black citizenship as a threat to slavery and interstate cooperation and objected to suggestions that African Americans be considered citizens in any respect. This was true across the United States, but the nature of the Philadelphia-Baltimore borderland, the concentration of free blacks, the seeming ease with which they crossed the legal boundary between freedom and slavery, meant that the questions surrounding black citizenship had particular resonance in this mid-Atlantic region.

CHAPTER 4

Black Citizenship in the Age of Nat Turner

Writing to the *Liberator* in early 1831, James Forten celebrated "the change in the British Ministry" and the resulting "determination to do away with the curse of slavery in the colonies." Forten predicted similar changes in his own country and looked at the progress of British emancipation as an omen that the coming year would witness "great events": "the tyrants of this country, must tremble." He had no way of knowing that in an obscure corner of Virginia, Nat Turner was making plans to bring about "great events" in his own way.[1]

Turner's rebellion would have consequences far beyond southeastern Virginia. White fears of slave uprising that had previously focused on Haiti now had a new domestic face. These fears spurred a renewed debate on the institution of slavery and its future. Some Americans saw slavery itself—the inherent instability of the institution of human bondage—as the cause of slave rebellion. For many others, though, the country's free black population bore the brunt of the blame for provoking the violence of Southampton, Virginia.

Fears about free blacks and the threat they posed to slavery had particular resonance in Philadelphia and Baltimore. Turner's rebellion led to a resurgence in efforts by whites in both cities to deal with what they perceived to be the dangers posed by the free blacks in their midst. This backlash included a more openly coercive form of African colonization as well as other means of controlling free African Americans. Free blacks in Philadelphia and Baltimore were compelled to defend their claims on American citizenship, both in terms of their right to remain in the United States and in regard to the limited rights they had enjoyed as free persons of color. At the same time, efforts to use colonization as a means of resolving the sectional tensions produced by slavery helped to push the issue of black citizenship into the very heart of the politics of union.

Nat Turner and Reactions on the Border

The reaction to Turner's rebellion played out in distinctive ways in the border region between Baltimore and Philadelphia. Existing anxieties about the movement of African Americans were heightened by renewed worries about slave rebellion and sectional conflict. These anxieties provoked both local and state responses that threatened free blacks' already tenuous citizenship rights.

In late August 1831, dark rumors of a slave revolt began to filter north from southeastern Virginia. While initial newspaper reports in Baltimore and Philadelphia and throughout the nation were vague, the outlines of the events unfolding in Southampton County soon became clear. The initial stories, drawing heavily on the written accounts of eyewitnesses, at times estimated the number of insurgents in the hundreds and at other times reassured readers that the cause was only "plunder, and not with a view to a more important object." Lists of the white victims were also reproduced. Before long, newspapers informed readers that the insurrection had been put down, though they continued to follow the story as Turner himself eluded authorities.[2]

The reports of the successful suppression of Nat Turner's rebellion seem to have done little to assuage white Baltimoreans' fears that Turner, like so many black fugitives before him, had found his way to their city. According to one report, a black man who had recently been committed to the Baltimore jail on a charge of horse stealing was in fact "General Turner" himself. Though the press quickly refuted the story, the claim spread to papers in other cities, including Philadelphia.[3]

In addition, white Marylanders heard reports that rebellion had spread south into North Carolina and, more disturbingly north, up the Eastern Shore of Maryland and even into Delaware. Within months of the Turner insurrection, the mayor of Baltimore had received reports of alleged conspiracies in and around Baltimore. Many Baltimore slave owners looked to remove the threat by selling their enslaved property—over the two years following the rebellion, slave sales doubled in Baltimore. Yet many white Marylanders saw the city's large free black population as the obvious source of instability.[4]

To solve the problem, white citizens called on the state government to act. "The good people of South River," on the Western Shore of Maryland, "have no hesitation in expressing their belief that the diabolical spirit which induced the misguided wretches of our sister state to the perpetration of such abominable and hellish crimes has been infused into a certain portion of our population throughout the state." Participants at this and other meetings in the southern portion of the state called not for some form of emancipation but rather for the more careful control of free blacks and for their deportation if possible. Another meeting declared emancipation "repugnant to the rest of the state" and called for its prohibition. However, whites did not speak with one voice on the subject. Citizens in Queen Anne's County, on the Eastern Shore, denounced the proposed restriction on manumission as "cruel, impolitic, unjust, dangerous, and unauthorized by the constitution." Instead, they advocated the removal of free blacks from the state as part of the gradual emancipation of all Maryland slaves.[5]

Petitions representing these diverse positions were directed to a joint committee of the Maryland legislature, chaired by Henry Brawner, who owned more than fifty slaves and represented a district dominated by slaveholders. Six of the seven committee members represented districts in the southern portion of the state, and the seventh owned six slaves himself. Yet in March 1832, when Brawner's committee issued its report on the state's black population, the document declared slavery an "admitted and awful evil." The Brawner Report called for the removal of all blacks, both free and enslaved, from Maryland. The committee assumed that the state's free blacks would go first and called for a strengthened force to police any remaining free blacks.[6]

While the report looked to the "recent events" to the South as confirmation of the threat posed by slavery, it was also clearly shaped by Maryland's northern border with Pennsylvania. According to the report, Maryland's "situation, along the border of a free state," had made obvious the virtues of free labor over enslaved. The removal of blacks would encourage white immigration from other states, promote economic development, and allow the state to invest in northern-style free schools. Intellectual and scientific achievements would follow.[7]

The Brawner Report envisioned African colonization as an integral part of the plan to free Maryland of its black residents but differed in one crucial way from the colonization societies. Brawner and his associates acknowledged slaveholders' right to their property and therefore admitted that "without their owners consent, none of them can be touched." In this way, they shared the attitude of the leaders of the American Colonization Society (ACS). Yet for Maryland's free blacks as well as those who would become free, consent was no longer necessary. Brawner recognized, perhaps as a consequence of more than a decade of free black opposition to African colonization, that consensual emigration would not remove all of Maryland's free black population. Force would be necessary to spur such a migration.[8]

In response to Brawner's report, the Maryland legislature passed two bills, "an act relating to the people of colour of this state" and "an act relating to free negroes and slaves." Together, these bills sought to promote the gradual end of slavery in the state and to remove the state's black population. The first bill required that newly freed blacks leave the state, preferably for Liberia, and appropriated money to pay for transportation to the colony. The second bill required that all free blacks entering the state leave within ten days. Those who failed to do so would receive fines of fifty dollars per week; people unable to pay this fine would be arrested and their labor auctioned off to cover the fine. The importation of enslaved blacks was also prohibited, and any remaining free blacks were subject to more stringent controls, with a particular eye on preventing the cooperation between the free and the enslaved. The measures severely restricted African Americans' ownership of firearms and right to gather (whether for religious or "tumultuous" purposes). In certain cases, free blacks could be punished in the same way as slaves.[9]

While the new legislation allowed the coercive power of the government to promote the removal of black Marylanders, it proved largely unsuccessful. Over the next decade, Maryland's free black population continued to grow both in raw numbers and as a percentage of the state's total population. Slave owners in northern Maryland frequently continued to manumit slaves without securing their removal from the state, taking advantage of a loophole that allowed judges to grant manumitted slaves who exhibited "extraordinary good conduct and character" a one-year permit to remain in the state. If the framers of the two bills sought to create an all-white Maryland, many white Marylanders seemed content to take advantage of the labor of free blacks while depending on the law to control them.[10]

Securing state cooperation represented a victory for the Maryland State Colonization Society. By 1831, the society had been languishing. Convinced that the parent ACS was limiting Maryland's ability to promote its own colonization plans, leading state colonizationists founded a new society that "explicitly disclaim[ed] all intention to interfere in the smallest degree with the slave population. It would teach the slave obedience, rather than create in his breast one feeling of disaffection." The new society targeted free blacks, though it also suggested that colonization might ultimately lead to voluntary emancipation.[11]

If the legislation spurred by the Brawner Report helped address the colonization movement's chronic shortage of funds, it was less successful in addressing the resistance of free blacks. Writing as "A Colored Baltimorean" in the *Genius of Universal Emancipation*, William Watkins continued to dispute those who called for free blacks to embrace colonization. Black Baltimoreans also continued to use mass meetings as a way of demonstrating popular opposition to colonization. A March 1831 "respectable meeting of persons of color" of Baltimore expressed its distrust of the ACS and lamented the group's success in seducing "many of our warm and sincere friends." For black opponents of colonization and the whites who listened to them, the actions of the Maryland legislature laid bare the fiction that colonization rested on the consent of free blacks. Commenting on this meeting in the *Liberator*, William Lloyd Garrison compared the colonizationists to the people of Georgia who sought to justify the removal of the Cherokees as consensual.[12]

Watkins also sought to turn the ACS's appropriation of the Fourth of July on its head, claiming for African Americans the rights announced in the Declaration of Independence. He denounced the efforts of colonizationists to link the national day of celebration with the idea that free blacks could never enjoy the "rights of freemen" in the United States. Colonizationists' success in doing so, he lamented, led him, "pensive and solitary, to contemplate the past and the present as connected with our history in the land of our nativity." As in previous African American discourse, perhaps most famously in David Walker's *Appeal to the Colored Citizens of the World*, Watkins coupled claims of abstract, natural rights with an expression of a physical attachment to the land of African Americans' birth. Like Walker, Watkins denounced the blindness of whites that prevented them from seeing that slaves and their descendants had done more to earn citizenship than nearly all white Americans. Watkins closed with the hope that black connection to the United States and to its republican institutions would soon lead white Americans to recognize the claims of "300,000 homeborn citizens of the United States."[13]

Opponents of colonization recognized that the willingness of significant numbers of black Baltimoreans to emigrate to West Africa served as an implicit rebuke to their public claims that the vast majority of free blacks opposed colonization, so while the public sphere remained a crucial ground on which free blacks resisted the work of colonization, it was not the only ground. Black Baltimoreans used direct tactics to undermine colonization. In 1831, the Maryland Colonization Society chartered a ship, the *Orion*, with the intention of sending more than sixty emigrants to Liberia. As the date of departure grew near, black opponents of colonization worked to dissuade people from leaving, going so far as to follow people on board the ship as it prepared to depart. The vessel ultimately set sail with only thirty-one emigrants.[14]

In the face of such organized opposition, the Maryland Colonization Society stepped up its public appeals to prospective emigrants. Many of the organization's leaders believed that the opposition stemmed from the willful misrepresentations of "some of the leading coloured people" of Baltimore and hoped that "true" representations of the conditions in Liberia, especially from black settlers, would set the record straight. Maryland colonizationists issued at least two separate pamphlets quoting Francis Devany, high sheriff of Liberia, a former slave who had gone on to work for Forten in Philadelphia as a sail maker. Devany's testimony not only depicted Liberia as possessing effortlessly prosperous farms but also noted, "We serve as jurymen, and are tried by jurymen of our own colour.... Schools are provided for all the children in the Colony."[15] Despite the threats of coercion evident in the Brawner Report and the legislation it spawned, Maryland colonizationists continued to hope that black Baltimoreans would emigrate willingly since restrictive laws and laws mandating deportation could be difficult to enforce.

Philadelphians were geographically further removed from Southampton, Virginia, but did not by any means feel themselves immune from the events of Turner's rebellion. *Poulson's American Daily Advertiser* predicted that the United States would experience riots that would rival the Haitian Revolution and warned that these conflicts would not stop at Pennsylvania's southern border. The *Inquirer* printed the panicked letter of a man who claimed that "five hundred!!!" free blacks had arrived at the port of Philadelphia in the past few months, and another claimed to have witnessed "eight or ten other colored men [who] had just arrived here *from Southampton*, Virginia." White Philadelphians already uneasy about the free blacks in their midst now felt that they had new justification for their suspicions.[16]

Philadelphians had been debating African colonization for more than a decade, but Turner's rebellion added urgency to the topic. A number of concerned citizens met on the evening of November 23, 1831, to promote African colonization. The meeting appointed officers and a committee of four to draft resolutions, which were approved unanimously. Participants claimed to have "ample demonstration that the free colored people of the northern and eastern states were the original and ostensible, if not real cause of the creation of the present disaffection existing among the slaves." The group warned that the "recent massacres in the southern states" were a harbinger of "an approaching crisis" in the American republic. Despite their stated abhorrence of slavery, the colonizationists insisted that they recognized the rights of slaveholders and sought to reassure their "friends and countrymen of the south" that they did not wish to provoke insurrection among slaves. The removal of northern free blacks might represent the first step on the road to gradual emancipation, but the primary reason for colonization was to help prevent future slave rebellions. Colonization would save the republic itself.[17]

This meeting constituted a significant change from previous efforts to promote African colonization. First, its resolutions emphasized the national threat posed by black Philadelphians rather than their "degraded status"; only those opposed to colonization were "idle and profligate." Second, these colonizationists came close to dropping the veneer of consent, at least as far as free blacks were concerned: "The time [is] rapidly approaching when it will be found indispensably requisite . . . that all negroes within the boundaries of the United States be removed to Liberia or some other place as easily accessible." Third, this meeting sought to speak for the "working class," which participants singled out as particularly supportive of colonization. They warned of the threat posed by black emigration to the nearby "foreign power" of Canada and denounced southern states' efforts to push emancipated slaves into the free states. The leaders of this meeting also seem to have been distinct from those of previous and subsequent colonization groups, and their methods seem to much more closely mirror those of partisan politics. The gathering resolved to organize on a ward-by-ward basis to promote colonization.[18] If earlier efforts had been the province of respectable members of the city's elite, this new form of colonization was aggressive and populist.

Black Philadelphians seem to have recognized these changes in the rhetoric of colonization, and their criticism changed accordingly. While earlier criticism of local colonizationists had been gentle and respectful, black Philadelphians dropped the gloves to take on these colonizationists. One black correspondent to the *Liberator* expressed hope that the legislature would ignore the words of "a set of tippling shopkeepers and their customers." A resolution drafted by a meeting of black Philadelphians, including William Whipper and Robert Purvis, commented ironically on "these *gentry*" who were calling for colonization.[19] Biting and sarcastic, these comments attacked not just the colonizationist project but the character of its advocates. In so doing, Whipper and Purvis implicitly compared their respectability with the character of these disreputable whites.

Whipper and Purvis also explicitly invoked black Philadelphians' citizenship rights in criticizing this new form of colonization. They termed the colonization meeting a "caucus" in which "a few *officious* young men in a Republican country, presume[ed] to legislate for a respectable body of their fellow citizens, possessing rights as sacred and dear as theirs, *without making them a part in their legislation*."[20] The authors framed themselves and by extension all black Philadelphians as respectable, patriotic citizens and contended that the colonizationists were attempting to use antirepublican means to deny black Philadelphians that citizenship.

This sort of rhetoric became characteristic of Purvis and Whipper, who emerged as two of the most prominent black leaders of the next generation. Robert Purvis was born in 1810 in South Carolina to a white cotton merchant, William Purvis, and his mixed-race wife, Harriet Judah. The elder Purvis moved his family to Philadelphia in 1819, intending eventually to move on to Britain, though he died before doing so and left his children a substantial estate. Robert grew up among the city's black elite, attended school in Massachusetts, but

Robert Purvis, ca. 1840s.
Courtesy of Boston Public Library.

returned to Philadelphia and married Forten's daughter. Purvis distinguished himself as a community leader and one of the most prominent black abolitionists in the United States.[21]

William Whipper was born in somewhat humbler circumstances in Lancaster County, Pennsylvania, in 1804. By the late 1820s he had moved to Philadelphia, where he worked steam cleaning clothes. Whipper had already distinguished himself with his rhetorical and literary skills, and he went on to have a successful business career. He arose to a position of leadership not through economic status but through his intellectual abilities and his commitment to the causes of abolition and black rights.[22]

As the latest wave of support for African colonization seemed to confirm black suspicions that the threat of force lay behind the consensual rhetoric of colonization, developments in the state legislature led Purvis and Whipper to fear that their state's southern boundary hardly constituted a firm defense against the political power of slavery. In December 1831, Franklin Vansant, a Democrat from Philadelphia Country, submitted a resolution calling for measures to prevent the emigration of free blacks into Pennsylvania unless they posted a five-hundred-dollar bond to ensure "good behavior." Similar laws had long been on the books in Ohio and Illinois. Other legislators introduced measures to control the movements of free blacks already residing in Pennsylvania, including requiring a registry of free blacks and forcing blacks to prove their legal residence in the state before they could move to a different county. The legislature also considered ways to strengthen the state's efforts to assist in returning fugitive slaves.[23]

Black Philadelphians' responses to these proposed measures demonstrate the importance of the concept of black citizenship, however contested, to their efforts to secure their liberties in the face of the legal protections afforded slavery. In a memorial to the legislature protesting the proposed legislation, free blacks openly claimed the rights of citizens. Whatever the status of other questions, they had assumed that they were "citizens for protection"—that is, they expected equal protection under the law. They denied asking for any new privileges or pushing for disputed rights like suffrage (though they insisted in an aside that they deserved this right as well). Free blacks thus cautiously positioned themselves as the defenders of existing rights and cast their opponents as seeking radical change. The fact that white Pennsylvanians rejected such laws suggests that the argument for black citizenship resonated more with white Pennsylvanians than with white residents of other border states in the North, especially those of the Old Northwest.[24]

The reactions to Nat Turner's rebellion in Maryland and Pennsylvania reveal a volatile borderland in the slavery debates. For many whites in both of these states, the ability of blacks, whether free or enslaved, to move across this border was disturbing and needed to be controlled. For the men who drafted Maryland's Brawner Report, the proximity of free territory destabilized slavery even as it held out the promise of a more prosperous and harmonious Maryland devoid of black people. The border also made problematic a paternalistic defense of slavery. Even if free blacks were the cause of discontent among the slaves and white Marylanders removed that troublesome population from their state, they could do little about those who lived just to the north.

Many white Pennsylvanians, conversely, believed that their state needed to enact laws to defuse the threat posed by fugitives taking advantage of the protection offered by Pennsylvania's free soil. The danger that Maryland would simply push its unwanted black population across the border and upset Pennsylvania's delicate racial balance seemed horrifying, and free blacks' claims to citizenship and to the protection of the law seemed to take on an added menace.

Yet these events also demonstrated the existence of potential white allies on both sides of the state line. The Pennsylvania legislature defeated the proposed law to restrict black emigration, and some white Philadelphians objected to the idea of forced deportations. The editors of the *United States Gazette* reprinted the resolutions of the November 1831 pro-colonization meeting but expressed their disagreement with many of its principles. They doubted that northern free blacks had been in any way responsible for Turner's rebellion and suggested that black Philadelphians were less likely to suffer in the area of "moral deportment" than similarly situated whites. The editors claimed to support colonization but echoed free blacks' insistence that anyone born in the United States had no natural connection to Africa: whites had no more right to send free blacks across the Atlantic than they did to expel whites. For the editors of the *Gazette*, colonization seemed one of many ways that free blacks might improve themselves.[25]

Although coerced removal from Maryland had become the law, Baltimore's free black population continued to grow. Enslaved men and women exploited the economic and social conditions of Baltimore to secure manumission and to remain in the state thereafter. Even with state funding, most free blacks refused the ACS's offers of resettlement and encouraged their friends and neighbors to do the same. This black resistance disheartened even the most ardent of Maryland colonizationists, who had assumed that free blacks would jump at the chance to "return" to Africa: wrote Moses Sheppard in October 1833, "I shall hereafter, if I live, do less; if I apply my time, I will not give money, if I give money I will not occupy my time, the blacks are not sensible of the favor offered them, and the whites are not conscious of the importance of the measure."[26]

Free blacks living in Baltimore and Philadelphia could not afford to ignore politics or public policy. The response to Nat Turner had shown that many whites were eager to use the coercive power of the government to deprive blacks of many of the legal protections that they enjoyed, including their right to remain in the land of their birth. However, developments in the aftermath of Turner's rebellion also demonstrated other whites' latent opposition to the use of such coercive force as well as the need for free blacks to marshal this sentiment for their own defense. In particular, free blacks in both cities sought to show that African colonization was necessarily coercive. They hoped that even whites who remained broadly opposed to arguments for black equality would nevertheless recognize that blacks had a right to legal protection and at least some measure of citizenship rights.

African Colonization and the Power of the State

The politics of black citizenship were often contested locally or in the halls of statehouses, but the implications of those contests had regional and national consequences. As colonizationists sought to promote their movement as a part of a long-term plan to assuage sectional tensions over slavery, the local and state maneuverings of colonizationists in Philadelphia, Baltimore, and elsewhere became enmeshed in the national politics of sectionalism and state power.

At the same time that residents of those cities were struggling with the aftermath of Nat Turner's rebellion, African colonization reemerged as a contentious issue in national politics and a crisis arose over South Carolina's nullification of the "Tariff of Abominations." Though many slaveholding politicians, especially those from the Lower South, feared colonization as the first step on the way to federally mandated emancipation, Border South politicians continued to promote colonization as an integral part of sectional reconciliation. In this way, colonizationists' efforts to answer criticisms lodged by Lower South defenders of slavery while responding to skeptical free blacks helped to draw the issue of black citizenship into the politics of union.

The Nullification Crisis ostensibly involved the unequal consequences of the 1824 tariff, but as historian William Freehling has convincingly demonstrated, the fears that the federal government would assume the power to abolish slavery lurked behind protests over unfair taxation. South Carolinians had suffered from the economic hard times of the 1820s and saw the tariff, which was meant to protect northern manufacturers from cheap English goods, as the chief cause of their economic troubles. By 1828, the state legislature asked John C. Calhoun to lay out the case for state nullification of the tariff. South Carolina had first nullified federal law when it refused to recognize the legitimacy of the Supreme Court decision declaring the post-Vesey Negro Seaman Act unconstitutional. At that time, the State Senate had declared that South Carolina's need to suppress slave rebellion surpassed "all *laws*, all *treaties*, all *constitutions*," and South Carolina had continued to imprison black seamen in violation of federal law. Now, Carolinians again sought to nullify federal law to defend slavery. Calhoun's anonymously published treatise asserted the right of states to nullify federal law but framed this claim as a defense of rather than a threat to the federal union. Only by defending minority rights through nullification could disunion be averted.[27]

At the same time, Henry Clay was pushing a different legislative program intended to promote union. Clay had taken the lead in backing federal support of African colonization. Perhaps the clearest attempt to integrate colonization into Clay's broader American System, however, came with the 1832 Public Lands Bill. On April 16, Clay reported to the Senate a bill providing that the bulk of the proceeds of the sale of public land would be distributed by the federal government back to the states, which would be empowered to use these monies to fund internal improvements, education, or African colonization.[28]

The debates over the bill proved contentious, especially with regard to the federal government's role in promoting African colonization. Opponents might have been particularly sensitive to even this sort of indirect interference in the institution of slavery as a consequence of the fact that abolitionists had increasingly been arguing for the federal government's right to regulate the interstate trade in slaves as a way of dealing a blow to slavery itself. Clay sought to head off concerns over excessive federal power by reaffirming his belief that the federal government had no authority over slavery. Clay countered arguments that the whole nation should not be forced to financially support colonization because it benefited only a select few eastern states by saying that "the evil of a free black population is not restricted to a particular state, but extends to and is felt by all." This question, he insisted, remained distinct from slavery. He noted that a number of slave states had in fact supported colonization with state funds. The bill finally passed the Senate, but the House postponed the measure until the next legislative session as a consequence of opposition by southern and western congressmen.[29]

At the same time, the Nullification Crisis was reaching its climax. Despite Calhoun's insistence that nullification offered a means of saving the union, not destroying it, many leading proponents of the idea were less cautious in denouncing the threat of federal power and warned that disunion would surely follow if the government persisted in its course. In response to this stance, President Andrew Jackson denounced the nullifiers on December 10, 1832. While he acknowledged that their arguments against the tariff may have been legitimate, he denied that states had the legal right to nullify federal law and declared, "Disunion by armed force is *treason*." Jackson hoped to appeal to the patriotism of the people of South Carolina, who he claimed had been deceived by their leaders.[30]

Clay stepped into this crisis, hoping to once again avert a potential sectional showdown. At least one of Clay's Philadelphia correspondents insisted that the Upper South slaveholder was the only national politician who had the "power to heal the dissensions between the North & the South." Clay pushed through Congress a legislative compromise that included a tariff reduction as well as a "force" bill that granted the president authority to use the armed forces to enforce the law.[31]

Yet Clay continued to push his public lands bill, along with its provision for support of African colonization, as a part of his larger effort to undermine sectionalism. Many slaveholders still opposed this bill, in part because, in the words of Alexander Buckner, a Jacksonian senator from Missouri, it was "well calculated to disturb the quiet and peaceable enjoyment of a certain description of property in the slaveholding states." Nevertheless, the bill again passed the

Senate as well as the House on March 1, the same day that both the compromise tariff and force bills were enacted. "Yesterday was perhaps the most important Congressional day that ever occurred," wrote a jubilant Clay, "the Compromise bill, the Land bill and the Enforcing bill having all passed during it." Jackson signed both the compromise tariff and the force bill the next day, though he pocket vetoed the public land bill.[32] Jackson clearly accepted the more narrowly conceived measures designed to address nullification but rejected Clay's broader vision for wielding the power of the state to promote the union, in part through African colonization.

The connections between the Nullification Crisis and slavery were recognized outside the halls of Congress as well. "It will not be denied that modest Pennsylvania has equal rights with her proud sister Carolina, and if Carolina can nullify a law then Pennsylvania can do the same," noted a letter to *Poulson's American Daily Advertiser*. The author suggested that Pennsylvanians might nullify the Fugitive Slave Law, which his state opposed as fully as Carolinians opposed the tariff: "Now this law Pennsylvania does not like, and suppose she should follow the example of Carolina and nullify this obnoxious law? What would be the consequence?"[33] In this formulation, the Pennsylvanian becomes the defender of the union through his willingness to support a law he deems odious. But it also illustrates that federal power was presently marshaled in defense of slavery, especially in the border states.

The Nullification Crisis also presented an opportunity for northern protectionists to depict themselves as virtuous defenders of the Constitution. Pennsylvania supporters of the tariff argued that "blighting, blasting, withering" slavery, not protectionism, was the source of South Carolina's economic distress. The peculiar institution, they argued, constituted both a drag on the economy and a threat to the federal union. One Philadelphia broadside predicted that this dissolution of the Constitution would come as soon as January 1834.[34]

Colonizationists saw their cause as the only solution to the political threat that slavery posed to the union, but just as Clay needed to navigate the thickets of American federalism to secure congressional funding for colonization, colonization societies themselves had to negotiate sectional tensions. They did so with a federal structure that in certain ways paralleled that of the government. The ACS had initially attempted to assuage sectional differences with vague language, but now, as a consequence of challenges from the white defenders of slavery and from white and black abolitionists, this task had become more difficult. These challenges had illuminated the inherent tensions in colonization's national coalition.

This tension was particularly acute in Maryland. While that state's slaveholders might have been more favorable to depictions of slavery as a "necessary evil" than their Virginia counterparts, they still feared any implication that government power might be used to force emancipation on them. Maryland colonizationists therefore consistently asserted their devotion to the principle "that any action upon the subject of slavery belongs exclusively to the States respectively, in which the Institution exists."[35] While this position to some extent reflected the opinion of many of the state's supporters of colonization, it also constituted a reassurance to slaveholders in Maryland and elsewhere, an effort to stave off the criticism that such slaveholders had leveled at colonization.

Yet unlike many colonizationists further south, Marylanders generally portrayed their organization as a means of ultimately emancipating their state's slaves. "The State Society looks forward to the time, and by all proper means would hasten it, when Maryland shall cease to be a slave holding State." Privately, Maryland colonizationists feared that connections to colleagues in the Lower South were undermining their ability to promote colonization in their own state and to appeal to northerners for financial support.[36] Free blacks in Baltimore and elsewhere had played a key role in shaping colonization in Maryland, so proponents of the idea could not go too far in their efforts to appease slaveholders that they alienated even more free blacks.

Maryland colonizationists sought to operate a state society independent of the ACS as a means of resolving these sectional tensions within the movement. Some of the organization's supporters argued that Maryland was uniquely situated to serve as the model of African colonization. The Maryland Colonization Society's 1834 annual report declared, "If Maryland, thus situated, cannot succeed in the experiment, other states may well despair, and the friends of the cause throughout the land may well be disheartened." Maryland-based colonizationists privately urged the national organization to focus its efforts on their state. "Tell the rational friends of freedom and Emancipation," wrote Moses Sheppard, "their efforts are weakened by being diffused over the vast Southern and Western Country, let them concentrate their force on Maryland." These men sought to make Maryland into a bulwark against the radical abolitionism of the North while reassuring moderately antislavery northerners of the society's commitment to the ultimate end of slavery.[37]

Baltimore's free blacks found themselves caught in a catch-22. On one hand, white supporters of colonization argued that it was impossible for free blacks to live peacefully in Maryland. On the other hand, foes of abolition contrasted the "peaceful" behavior of Baltimore's free blacks with the degraded and volatile free blacks in other parts of the country. In response to one anonymous inquiry by "A White Citizen" as to whether they would turn their backs on their "peaceable and orderly" past, three black pastors chose to emphasize their respectability and stake in society as a guarantee of their continued good behavior.

The *Niles Register* published a letter in which John Fortie, Nathaniel Peck, and William Levington reassured white readers they and other black Baltimoreans "have always been a docile people." William Watkins wrote to Garrison of his displeasure at the subservient tone of these pastors yet also requested that Garrison not publish the letter. If Watkins found the pastors' strategy upsetting, he certainly recognized that in the context of mid-1830s Baltimore, it made a certain sense. Maryland colonizationists pointed to the riots in cities to the North as evidence for the need to remove free blacks to Africa and as a demonstration that the life of the enslaved black was preferable to that of the free. The three pastors used the "docility" of black Baltimoreans and the stability of their community as an implicit argument against the need for colonization. Riots along the lines of those in Philadelphia and New York would only have strengthened the arguments in favor of removing all free blacks from Maryland. Whereas colonizationists insisted that free blacks had sparked Turner's rebellion, the pastors pointed to colonizationists as the real threat to the city's order.[38]

As Maryland colonizationists sought to use their state society to avoid the contradictions within colonization, black opponents hoped to undermine the idea by highlighting these contradictions. Privately, Sheppard acknowledged that some slaveholders supported colonization as a means of rendering their slave property more secure. He hoped that such men could be forced unintentionally to do the work of emancipation. Sheppard also argued that an African colony initially had to be peopled by free blacks: only after free persons had established the colony could it incorporate the newly emancipated.[39]

Baltimore free blacks had little confidence in more philanthropic colonizationists' ability to win out over their more pro-slavery colleagues. In a series of letters to the *Liberator*, Watkins used the contradictions of Maryland colonization to thwart efforts to take advantage of the society's federal structure. Writing for an audience of abolitionists, both black and white, Watkins challenged the idea that Maryland's colonizationists were truly devoted to emancipation and insisted that they, like their counterparts in the Lower South, were really interested in strengthening the grip of slaveholders on their property. He noted that Maryland colonizationists praised the intelligence of free black colonists and required them to make a pledge of temperance before departing for Liberia yet considered those who remained behind incapable of self-control or self-government. Watkins labeled this inconsistency "the legitimate fruit of colonization," mocking attempts to appeal both to slavery's northern foes and to its southern defenders.[40]

Black Baltimoreans' responses to colonization illustrate that they understood the complexity of the colonization debate and recognized the need to appeal to a variety of audiences. Watkins wrote in a style that differed dramatically from that used by Fortie, Peck, and Levington, but the two approaches had a great deal in common as well. Like Watkins, the three pastors sought to exploit inconsistencies in white rhetoric. Watkins makes a forceful argument that free blacks have a right to remain in the land of their birth, while the pastors also argue for their right to continue to live as free men in their native land, to enjoy the limited legal rights granted by the state of Maryland and the city of Baltimore. Perhaps the most important difference arises from the audience for these two documents. Watkins wrote for a northern, abolitionist audience, while Fortie, Peck, and Levington addressed a local public, but both letters made the case for black citizenship.

Free blacks in Philadelphia and Baltimore also understood colonizationists' willingness to use the force of government to stifle dissent. While visiting Baltimore in the summer of 1832, Philadelphia Methodist pastor Charles Gardner received a warning that he was in violation of the Maryland state law dictating that free blacks visiting the state could not stay longer than ten days. Though the law had been intended to prevent free blacks from instigating slave rebellions, colonizationists used it to prevent northern free blacks from "poison[ing] the minds of the colored people" against colonization. Gardner sought passage back to Philadelphia but was arrested onboard a ship before he could depart and informed that "the Colonization Society has obtained a warrant against you for staying over your time." Gardner ultimately escaped conviction on the grounds that illness had prevented his departure, but colonizationists clearly sought to use the power of the government to prevent black Philadelphians from spreading their influence in Baltimore.[41]

On both sides of the Maryland-Pennsylvania border, free blacks had no choice but to address the political realities of the backlash against Turner's rebellion: black citizenship rights were under assault. African Americans in the mid-Atlantic saw opportunities as well.

Born into slavery on Maryland's Eastern Shore in 1817, Frederick Bailey developed a great desire to see Baltimore. In his view, "Even the Great House itself, with all its pictures, was far inferior to many buildings in Baltimore." By the late 1820s, Bailey was living there. He initially found the city bewildering, and boys tormented him as "Eastern Shore Man," but he soon acclimated himself to life in the city.[42]

Baltimore presented opportunities not available in his former home, most significantly the chance to become literate. Despite his master's disapproval, young Frederick taught himself to read, taking advantage of occasional help from white playmates. Literacy opened Bailey's eyes to the world beyond his immediate surroundings. He had heard others whisper the word *abolitionist* as the cause for a slave's disobedience, but it did not make sense until he obtained a copy of the *Baltimore American* that detailed northerners' efforts to end slavery in the District of Columbia. From that day forward, he recalled, whenever abolition was mentioned, he drew closer to listen.[43]

Although the young man's progress resulted in part from his own initiative, he also benefited from struggles of free blacks in Baltimore. Bailey later commented that "a city slave is almost a freeman, compared to a slave on a plantation," but still he looked north, paying "particular attention to the direction which the steamboats took to go to Philadelphia." While waiting for an opportunity to escape, Bailey immersed himself in the political institutions of black Baltimore. He participated in the debates hosted by the East Baltimore Mental Improvement Society (an organization made up primarily of free blacks). He joined the Bethel African Methodist Church but left after five of the trustees published a letter condemning northern abolitionists. He later joined the Sharp Street Church, whose pastor, John Fortie, had signed the letter defending the peacefulness of Baltimore's black community.[44]

In September 1838, Frederick Bailey, who soon changed his name to Frederick Douglass, escaped to the North, perhaps the most significant political act that a slave could undertake.[45] His escape had been made possible by a network of black institutions that must also be seen as political. Black churches were centers of the black community and negotiated with white legal and ecclesiastical authorities for power and autonomy. In many cases, they tied their parishioners to coreligionists in the northern states. Churches and a host of other black institutions fought to shape the public perception of Baltimore's black population and sought to empower their congregations in the face of white supremacy. Perhaps most important, black institutions helped make the borders of slavery less stable, providing opportunities for the enslaved to escape from bondage. Baltimore, with its rich if constrained black public life, proved a crucial political school for Frederick Douglass.[46]

Douglass's escape took him through Philadelphia, but at the urging of a black porter, he caught the first train he could for New York City.[47] Many other fugitives, however, settled in Philadelphia and in other areas along Pennsylvania's southern border. Many whites feared that if nothing were done, even more would do so, threatening the institution of slavery in Maryland.[48] At the same time, Philadelphia's free blacks fought for some legal recognition of their right to be considered citizens, and other whites became tentative allies, in this struggle.

PART III

*The Politics of
Black Moral Reform*

CHAPTER 5

Black Citizenship and Reform

In 1838, after accepting the position as editor of the *Pennsylvania Freeman*, abolitionist poet John Greenleaf Whittier noted his impressions of his new home in Philadelphia: "Politics has much more to do with our cause here than in New England," he wrote, "reforms are carried out at the ballot-box instead of the Church." Pennsylvania has not often been seen as a main front in the political struggle against slavery, providing only tepid support for the Liberty Party in the 1840s, for example.[1] Yet the struggle for black citizenship and against slavery in the 1830s demonstrated that free blacks in Pennsylvania were engaged in a different sort of antislavery politics that often eschewed ideological purity in favor of practical necessity and sought to build coalitions. It helped to develop a rhetoric that emphasized the defense of northern rights against the encroachment of slaveholders' power. In short, it prefigured much of what would characterize antislavery politics in later years.

Particularly in the border city of Philadelphia, African Americans had by the early 1830s come to recognize that their struggles for citizenship rights were intertwined with broader political struggles, and they stood at the center of these political developments. National black conventions, the process of rewriting the Pennsylvania Constitution, and reform organizations became forums for black politics and presented opportunities to defend black citizenship rights. It was not enough to simply advance abstract notions of equality or to challenge white racism; the fight for black citizenship pushed African Americans to engage with a political system from which they were increasingly formally excluded. If they hoped to have any success in this fight, African Americans needed to appeal to whites who feared the prospect of racial equality but who were also uncomfortable denying all citizenship rights to their black neighbors.

"A Christian Party in Politics":
Reform, Temperance, and Antislavery in Philadelphia

African Americans in Philadelphia and Baltimore recognized that the threats they faced were to some extent faced by free blacks throughout the United States. Therefore, as African Americans in those cities considered how to address local concerns, they expanded their connections with free blacks from other parts of the nation and sought to build political coalitions that would expand the appeal of their claims on citizenship rights and broaden the struggle against slavery.

In the fall of 1830, "the Coloured Citizens of Philadelphia" called for a meeting of "their brethren throughout the U States." The group suggested the creation of a nationwide network of free blacks, working together to "devise and pursue all legal means for the speedy elevation of ourselves and brethren to the scale and standing of men." One of those means was the promotion of black settlements in Canada, but they stressed that this effort did not indicate that they had abandoned their claims to American citizenship grounded in the Declaration of Independence.[2]

This national convention movement and other types of free black activism in the early 1830s provide ample evidence of black political engagement. The conventions sought not simply to mimic the form of white politics but also to influence it, in part through connections to broader white-led reform politics. These black activists stressed the connections between black citizenship and the fight against slavery as well as the idea that slavery and related attempts to deny the citizenship rights of free blacks constituted an assault on the liberties of all Americans.[3]

The first black convention met in Philadelphia in September 1830 and took up the cause of Cincinnati's free blacks. Alarmed at the rapid growth of Ohio's free black population, city authorities had declared in 1829 that they would begin enforcing Black Codes that had been on the books for decades. Municipal authorities gave free blacks thirty days to comply with the laws, which required every African American to post a five-hundred-dollar bond to ensure good behavior. White mobs refused to wait for the laws to take effect, terrorizing Cincinnati's black neighborhoods and causing between one thousand and two thousand free blacks to flee the city, most for Canada.[4]

With these events in mind, delegates from seven states met at Richard Allen's Mother Bethel AME Church on September 20–24. The convention had initially been championed by Hezekiah Grice of Baltimore, but Pennsylvanians dominated, with Allen elected president. The men from these borderland cities took the lead, in large part because the events of the past few years had made them acutely sensitive to the kinds of threats faced by free blacks in Cincinnati, another border city. Twelve of the twenty-six convention delegates were from Pennsylvania, while among other states only Maryland sent as many as four. The meeting established the "American Society of Free People of Color for improving their condition in the United States; for purchasing lands; and for the establishment of a settlement in the Province of Upper Canada" and drafted a constitution detailing the new institution's goals and form. Officers would be elected at an annual meeting, and the society itself would meet quarterly. Auxiliaries would be established throughout the nation.[5]

The organization's name hints at a tension that existed from the start: the contradictory goals of supporting a new settlement outside the United States and retaining claims on their native land. The organization agreed to assist in the founding of a Canadian settlement but coupled that support with opposition to African colonization. In fact, the conditions of the "afflicted country" of Africa were contrasted with "the language, climate, soil and productions" of Canada, which bore a remarkable resemblance to those of the United States. The delegates stressed that the decision to emigrate to Canada was not made freely but was coerced by unjust laws. To reiterate their contention that most free blacks would remain in the United States, the society also made a commitment to improving conditions for African Americans south of the Canadian border.[6]

At the group's first annual meeting, held the following year, delegates continued to seek a balance between cosmopolitanism and nationalism. While the group reasserted its intention to support the colony in Upper Canada, participants repeatedly returned to arguments that African Americans had a right to remain in the land of their birth and that they deserved to be American citizens. The benevolent work of emancipation being carried out in Britain and Denmark and the opportunity presented by the British territory of Upper Canada were contrasted with the cruel laws of "our own native land ... the birthplace of our *fathers* ... the land for whose prosperity their blood and our sweat have been shed and cruelly extorted." The same language was used to denounce the efforts of the American Colonization Society. The convention also reiterated its position that "the spirit of persecution" rather than any consensual relinquishment of American citizenship underlay free blacks' willingness to consider emigration to Canada.[7]

In addition, the meeting introduced a twinned embrace of the Declaration of Independence and the U.S. Constitution as sources of black citizenship, balancing philosophical and legal justifications for participants' claims. The convention resolved to read both documents at every subsequent meeting, noting that the principle of equality enshrined in the Declaration was "incontrovertible." Furthermore, the Fourth of July should be set aside as a day of "humiliation, fasting and prayer," at which collections should be made in support of the national convention movement. This idea mirrored the efforts of colonizationists, who had for several years employed the day for their own purposes, and contrasted free blacks' orderly and pious observation of the day with the often-raucous public displays from which African Americans were excluded. With this goal in mind, the convention also counseled against black public processions on any day.[8]

The convention, particularly the Conventional Address drafted by Philadelphians Belfast Burton, Junius Morel, and William Whipper, also took up a language of constitutionalism that had not been prevalent in previous black discourse. The Constitution, these men declared, "guarantees in letter and spirit to every freeman born in this country, all the rights and immunities of citizenship." Framing rights in terms of national law rather than transcendent morals, the convention termed efforts to deny blacks these rights "unconstitutional" rather than simply un-Christian or unjust.[9]

Looking to the Constitution as source of black citizenship suggests a level of pragmatism and a political orientation that not all abolitionists shared. By 1832, William Lloyd Garrison was already describing the Constitution as "the most bloody and heaven-daring arrangement ever made by men."[10] Some African Americans sympathized with Garrison's rhetorical assaults on the Constitution, but for the men of the black conventions, committed to asserting their own claims on American citizenship in the face of efforts to insist that they were somehow aliens in the land of their birth, the Constitution remained an ally.

Garrison and those who shared his views stepped up their assaults on the Constitution over the course of the decade, leading ultimately to a split in the American Anti-Slavery Society in 1840. The issue of politics encompassed more than simply the morality of voting. Many Garrisonian abolitionists believed in voting. But the larger issue was the possibility of fighting slavery within a political system that was so profoundly shaped by slavery.[11]

Garrison's attitude toward politics and voting was much less clear in the early 1830s, though even then carefully delineated what sorts of political action were appropriate. In an 1834 letter to the "Colored Inhabitants of Boston" printed in the *Liberator*, Garrison lamented Black Bostonians' apparent support for Whig candidates. In Garrison's view, "If there be a party which you should dread and oppose more than any other, it is THE WHIG PARTY," which was in league with slavery and which bore most of the responsibility for the recent riots in New York and Philadelphia. In addition, he noted, at the head of the party stood Henry Clay, a slaveholder and colonizationist. But Garrison did not denounce African Americans' willingness to vote or political parties as a whole; rather, he called for a particular kind of politics and a particular kind of party.

> We do indeed need a *christian* party in politics—and not made up of this or that sect or denomination, but of all who fear God and keep his commandments, and who sincerely desire to seek judgment and relieve the oppressed. I know it is the belief of many professedly good men, that they ought not to "meddle" with politics; but they are cherishing a delusion, which, if it do not prove fatal to their own souls, may prove the destruction of their country.

His call for a "Christian party in politics" is a political analogue to his call to purify the Christian church of the taint of slavery. Garrison noted that though he was specifically addressing the black voters of Boston, he hoped that his words would be heeded by all blacks who possessed the right to vote.[12]

By the early 1830s, Garrison had embraced antimasonry, and powerful ideological and organizational bonds tied together the abolition and antimasonic movements. In the 1834 election, Garrison endorsed the Anti-Masonic congressional candidates.[13] When he spoke of a "*christian* party in politics," then, if he was not specifically calling for support of the Anti-Masons, their particular brand of partisan politics was on his mind.

Moreover, Garrison's phrasing referenced an 1827 Fourth of July sermon in which the Reverend Ezra Stiles Ely, pastor of Philadelphia's Third Presbyterian Church, called for the creation of "a *Christian Party in politics*, which I am desirous all good men in our country should join." Ely argued that a union of all the members of "any one of the denominations of true Christians" would drive from politics the enemies of Christianity, among which he included deists, Socinians, and others of unorthodox belief. Ely had initially supported fellow Presbyterian Andrew Jackson rather than the Unitarian John Quincy Adams but took up the antimasonic cause by 1830. Antimasons quickly seized on Ely's conception of a Christian party, and many saw their movement as fulfilling that idea.[14]

In Pennsylvania and elsewhere, antimasonry held out some promise for those who hoped to advance the antislavery cause. From the late 1820s to the early 1830s, Pennsylvania's antimasonic movement gradually built its political organization and electoral strength. The party's 1829 gubernatorial candidate, Joseph Ritner, a former state legislator and Speaker of the Pennsylvania House, had backed Jackson in 1828 even though the two men disagreed on many policy positions. Ritner supported the tariff, public education, temperance, and ultimately the antislavery movement. Ritner lost the election despite polling a respectable 40 percent of the vote. Desire to check the political influence of Freemasonry was, of course, the party's raison d'être, but the party quickly broadened into a political coalition. Historian Ronald P. Formisano notes the existence of a certain sympathy between abolitionists and Anti-Masons, both of whom "refused to compromise with institutions they believed were corrupting the American republic." Always a largely regional political movement, antimasonry proved far more amenable to antislavery policies than did more consciously national political parties.[15]

Many National Republicans recognized the need to cultivate alliances with this new movement as the number of Anti-Masonic members in the state legislature grew from fifteen in 1829 to thirty-three in 1832. Others, however, were less optimistic about the possibility of such a coalition: "We cannot by any course we may pursue conciliate the Antimasons," wrote Philadelphian John Sergeant to Henry Clay, "or gain from them a single vote. They go on doggedly for antimasonry, and, I believe, are more opposed to us than they are to Jacksonism." Some of Clay's other correspondents from Philadelphia recognized the necessity of conciliating the antimasons as well as of conducting such political maneuvering delicately. In 1829, resentment against Philadelphia had been a focus of antimasonic rhetoric, placing the city and county among Ritner's weakest counties; by 1832, however, many National Republicans, especially in Philadelphia, had made their peace with antimasonry. Ritner's vote in the city of Philadelphia jumped from 7 to 58 percent, and although he once again lost to George Wolf, this time he did so by the slimmest of margins. Statewide he won more than 49 percent of the vote.[16] Ritner's positions on the questions of slavery and black rights were not yet clear, though he soon proved himself an ally of abolitionists and even something of a friend to Pennsylvania's black citizens.

Despite the promise of antimasonry, black Philadelphians struggled to develop their own vision of antislavery politics. In the early 1830s, the clearest model for an antislavery politics was not to be found in any American legislative body but in the British Parliament. Perhaps the most prominent figure in the British antislavery movement was William Wilberforce, and when he died in July 1833, black abolitionists determined publicly to honor his memory. Black Philadelphians appointed a committee of seven to arrange for the celebration of Wilberforce's life, and the committee voted unanimously to ask William Whipper to deliver the eulogy. The printed account of this eulogy included these organizational details, perhaps as a means of arguing for the legitimacy of Whipper's view as an expression of the black community but also as a performance of black politics, a demonstration that black men employed the same forms of civic engagement that were a customary part of white politics. Whipper addressed his eulogy to "my fellow citizens."[17]

Whipper's eulogy emphasized Wilberforce's combination of evangelical charisma and political savvy, holding him up as a model of Christian virtue and defender of true religion: "To celebrate his acts and to reverence his memory is to render homage to the cause of religion, morality, and public as well as private virtue." Yet Whipper also devoted a substantial portion of his address to Wilberforce's political efforts—to his decades of work within Parliament and the skill with which he advanced a series of antislavery measures. Wilberforce became a skillful political tactician, and "though so often defeated, had sufficiently learned the encampments and bulwarks of the enemy, to understand what materials were necessary to be obtained to carry the citadel." His work, in Whipper's eyes, embodied a Christian republican politics, uniting moral suasion and practical politics. Many other Americans agreed, viewing Wilberforce as an ideal of Christian statesmanship and perhaps as the model for the kind of leader that Ezra Stiles Ely had hoped would head a "Christian Party in politics."[18]

In celebrating Wilberforce and explicitly contrasting British antislavery politics with U.S. politics, Whipper reasserted black claims on American citizenship, reminding his audience that he and all native-born African Americans had the right to criticize the United States not as an outsider but as a citizen. "When we speak of America," he declared, "we do it with those feelings of respect that are due to it as our country—not as the land of our adoption, nor with the alienated breath of foreigners; but with the instinctive love of native born citizens."[19] Wilberforce exemplified the potential effectiveness of a politics of Christian reform, but Whipper recognized that if African Americans were to play a role in that politics, they would have to do so not simply as men or even as Christians but as Americans.

The black conventions of the early 1830s also became a forum in which free blacks, among them Whipper, envisioned a purified form of American politics in which they would play a crucial role. In this, black conventions echoed the antipartisan themes that abounded in early nineteenth-century politics. Subsequent conventions reiterated the resolution of the first meeting that discouraged black processions, especially those which were held on July 4 or 5. Instead, free blacks were encouraged to meet on those days to pray and discuss subjects relevant to their "moral and political improvement." In fact, the members of the conventions turned the denial of certain political rights into a kind of public virtue: declared the 1834 convention, "Let us refuse to be allured by the glittering endowments of official stations, or enchanted with the robe of American citizenship."[20] Black conventioneers not only claimed the rights of citizenship but positioned themselves as ideal, uncorrupted republican citizens. Recognition of black citizenship, they argued, would serve as a means of purifying American politics.

Similarly, a call to support temperance served a dual political purpose within the black convention movement and in black politics in general. From the first, the conventions depicted moral reform as central to their mission, and temperance was the quintessential moral reform. In fact, both black and white temperance reformers argued that their efforts were important not simply on their own merits, but because temperance provided the foundation for all moral reform.[21] Black temperance primarily constituted an effort to make blacks more worthy of citizenship in white eyes but also constituted a performance of political action. Participation in temperance societies rendered free blacks fit for politics as well as demonstrated black self-governance and citizenship.

Crucial to this political performance was the insistence that black temperance did not equate to an admission that blacks were more intemperate than whites. The report of the committee on temperance at the third annual convention argued that the opposite was true but also noted that whites held free blacks to a higher standard.[22] Black temperance, then, sought not to bring free blacks up to the level of whites but rather to push for a level of virtue and self-control among free blacks that even whites would have to recognize.

The push for temperance, like the fights against slavery and for black citizenship, combined moral suasion with direct political action. The earliest temperance reformers had emphasized the need for better enforcement of legal measures—for example, restrictions on the licensing of liquor sellers—that were designed to curb drunkenness but were largely unenforced. In the 1820s, in the face of unprecedented drunkenness, temperance began to take on a new character, in certain ways foreshadowing abolition's turn toward "immediatism." The new temperance reformers insisted that respectable men must totally renounce the use of alcohol: any moderation in this course would ultimately undermine efforts to combat drunkenness. Self-reform would lead to a transformation in public opinion, which would in turn lead to the prohibition of alcohol. This reform was to be produced by a loose confederation of local and state organizations under the umbrella of the American Society for the Promotion of Temperance and later the American Temperance Union, organized in Philadelphia in 1833.[23]

Antimasons often proved useful allies for promoters of temperance. In Pennsylvania, for example, antimasonry helped inject temperance into the political struggles of the early 1830s. In the 1832 gubernatorial election, Democrat George Wolf sought to appeal to temperance voters even though his opponent, Anti-Mason Joseph Ritner, was known as a temperance man. Wolf's efforts were undone, however, when his support for licensing oyster cellars in Philadelphia became known. Anti-Masons insisted that Wolf was not a genuine friend of temperance but rather would favor "any scheme that promises him popularity, as is proved by his professing himself the friend of temperance, and licensing a thousand grogshops, that he may gain the votes of Philadelphia."[24] As this line of criticism suggests, Anti-Masons not only saw drunkenness as a social ill which needed to be rooted out (in part by legislation), they also depicted drink as a fundamental part of the corrupt party politics they hoped to destroy.

Many Americans also linked temperance to antislavery.[25] Southern representatives to the 1833 convention that organized the American Temperance Union called for a resolution stating explicitly that the subject of slavery was "entirely disconnected" from that of temperance. Another southerner called for a rule banning any representative of the group from speaking on any subject other than temperance on the grounds that perceived connections between temperance and antislavery undermined temperance efforts in the slaveholding states. These resolutions were defeated by those who argued both that such a disclaimer was unnecessary and that it would give tacit approval to slavery.[26]

In fact, temperance reformers had done much to forge rhetorical links between slavery and drunkenness. Perhaps the most famous analogy came from Lyman Beecher, who argued that the horrors of drunkenness were just as great as those of the Atlantic slave trade: "Yes in this nation there is a middle passage of slavery, and darkness, and chains, and disease, and death. But it is a middle passage not from Africa to America, but from time to eternity, and not of slaves whom death will release from suffering, but of those whose sufferings at death do but begin."[27] Although Beecher compared drinking to the slave trade rather than to slavery itself, his words helped connect and popularize connections between slavery and drunkenness.

Free blacks who sought to unite the fight against slavery with the fight against alcohol were not, then, the first to do so, yet their efforts differed in some important ways from those of their white predecessors. In 1832, at the second black convention, Whipper proposed the creation of black temperance societies to support "total abstinence from the use of ardent spirits." He was elected president of the Colored Temperance Society of Philadelphia two years later and delivered his thoughts on the two related reforms in his address to the society's annual meeting.[28]

Unlike Beecher, Whipper compared intemperance not to the slave trade but to slavery itself. Beecher had used the middle passage as a point of comparison because all of his listeners could recognize the enormity of that evil. The members of Whipper's audience felt the same unanimity on the question of slavery, but Whipper went further, using slavery as an extended metaphor for intemperance. While Beecher had merely compared the numbers involved and the level of suffering, Whipper examined the related tyrannies of drink and slavery, using one to illuminate the other. Most damning was alcohol's ability to induce the willing surrender of self-control: "The slave hates his situation, and only remains in it because his bonds are forcible. The other loves it, because having slain his reason and self-respect, it promotes his animal luxury." Whipper's words demonstrate his understanding, as one historian has argued, "how intemperance, racism, and slavery worked systematically to prevent black advancement and limit black freedom." His analogy places black resistance at the heart of his call for temperance and implicitly argues against a paternalistic view of slavery. Slavery is the lesser evil only because the enslaved resist it.[29]

Whipper called for his audience to support temperance not only because drunkenness was akin to slavery but also because temperance constituted a form of antislavery. If his listeners embraced the principles of temperance, "the moral force and influence would disperse slavery from our land."[30] More than simply a means of promoting and demonstrating black respectability, temperance offered a way of purifying American politics and clearing the path for abolition. This proposition would be naive if Whipper's call were not part of a larger reform vision. Whipper sought to merge the specific concerns of black Philadelphians with the broader reform politics around him, arguing that temperance reformers "are exercising the highest order of legislation." After insisting that the "political elevation of our whole people" needed to be a part of temperance reform, he made the case that such reform was necessary because of the political influence of alcohol, which wielded a power that was "strongly felt in our legislative assemblies" and "more than partially rule[d] our government." As with slavery, this political power could be overcome only by a change in grassroots public opinion, at which point "government power" could be used to legislate against the evils of "uncontrolled liberty."[31]

Whipper closed with an even more direct claim about the connections between antislavery and temperance: "Wherever we see what we term a true abolitionist, he is invariably a friend of the temperance cause."[32] Whipper recognized that antislavery and the fight for black citizenship rights needed to be a part of a broader reform politics.

Efforts to promote black citizenship and to develop a coherent black reform politics were accompanied by a disturbing escalation of interracial violence on the streets of Philadelphia. White assaults on black citizens were not new, of course, but the mobs of the 1830s achieved a level of brutality and destruction that had rarely been previously seen.[33]

This new breed of violence appeared on a Sunday afternoon, November 22, 1829, and some observers linked it to white resentment of black worship services. In the eyes of the editors of the *Philadelphia Chronicle*, however, the riot resulted from the actions of the mass of free blacks whose conduct was not deserving of respect, and the mayor needed to act to keep them in order: "On Sundays, especially, they seem to think themselves above all restraint, and their insolence is intolerable." In other words, some white Philadelphians criticized their black neighbors for disorder and "insolence" on a day when they should be in church; other whites criticized black churches themselves as insolent. In choosing to cultivate one set of white allies, black Philadelphians antagonized another group of whites, with sometimes violent consequences.[34]

In July 1834, black Philadelphians received ominous warnings of violence. Benjamin Lundy warned in the *Genius of Universal Emancipation* that "the professed lovers of 'Union and Equal Rights'" were planning "to get up a mob," similar to the one that had recently tormented black and white abolitionists in New York. On August 9, after a small skirmish between blacks and a white fire company raised tensions, a gang of fifty or sixty attacked one of James Forten's sons while he was out running an errand. Three nights later, whites attacked a series of black establishments, including a church and residences, before being dispersed by the mayor and constables.[35]

The next night, the white mob returned in force. Rioters targeted black residences and churches in an area astride the city's southern border. The black Methodist church on Wharton Street was completely destroyed, and the African Presbyterian Church was severely damaged. Three more days of rioting resulted in the looting and destruction of thousands of dollars in property. The mayor and sheriff ultimately swore in three hundred special constables, who joined with the militia to quell the violence.[36]

Antiblack mob violence surely had a multitude of causes, but looming large among them was white resentment of the politics of black reform. A commission investigating the riot declared that white rioters were motivated by concerns that they were losing jobs to their black neighbors, yet historian Emma Jones Lapsansky has found that white resentment, especially among Irish immigrants, of black social "progress" was equally important. Rioters bypassed scores of black homes in favor of targets that symbolized black success. The mob's actions thus constituted a backlash against the black strategy of self-improvement and its public performance.[37]

Partisan newspapers quickly fit the rioters' motives into a larger political and cultural conflict. Whig publications attributed the violence to "ruffian foreigners" and claimed that it was intended to advance the Democratic Party. The *Pennsylvanian* disputed this claim, insisting that the riots had been instigated by supporters of the Second Bank of the United States in its struggle against Andrew Jackson and by incendiary abolitionist publications that also stoked Irish-born Philadelphians' resentment of the Whig Party. In the partisan press, the riots were not simply a response to the fight for black citizenship or to the struggle for abolition; those already contentious questions were intimately connected with other politically volatile issues.[38]

For their part, black Philadelphians turned the riots into a demonstration of the superiority of the black victims over their white adversaries. At the following year's black convention, Whipper introduced a resolution (seconded by Robert Purvis) regarding the riots:

> Resolved, That the Christian forbearance practiced by our people during their persecution by those mob riots of 1834, merits the praise and respect of the whole Christian world; and is a most successful refutation of the pro-slavery arguments advanced in this country, by men who are marked by inveterate and warlike dispositions.
>
> Resolved, That their peace, quietude and humility, during that period of excitement, have, in point of civilization and Christian kindness, placed them far above the agitators, abettors, or actors of that humiliating and degrading persecution.[39]

Whipper challenged the argument against abolition that former slaves would inevitably seek revenge against whites. He also painted the rioters as part of a larger, pro-slavery movement and not motivated simply by hatred of their black neighbors. The members of the mob, along with their "agitators" and "abettors," were pushing a national, pro-slavery argument. Whipper did not explicitly raise the issue of black citizenship, but the contrast between white disorder and black restraint made that case implicitly.

Jury Trials, Black Citizenship, and Pennsylvania's Constitution

Among the citizenship rights claimed by black Philadelphians, none was more essential than the right to the protection of the laws of Pennsylvania. This protection was especially critical in kidnapping and fugitive slave cases. For black Pennsylvanians, the ability to claim citizenship enabled them to demand the protection of the law rather than simply ask for the benevolent protection of whites. It also enabled African Americans to cast kidnapping and the reclamation of fugitive slaves as southern assaults on the free state of Pennsylvania.[40]

The questions of black citizenship and its implications for slaveholders had occasionally surfaced in the Pennsylvania legislature. In 1831, the issue of whether the Pennsylvania House could grant a black man a divorce induced significant anxiety about inadvertently asserting a black citizenship right.[41] In late 1836, however, free blacks and their white allies began a coordinated effort to push for a bill granting a jury trial to those accused as fugitive slaves. This campaign bore many of the hallmarks of what would later be identified as political antislavery.

In the fall of 1836, the Young Men's Anti-Slavery Society of the City and County of Philadelphia, an organization in which Philadelphia's black elite played an active role, began circulating a memorial intended for the state legislature. A bill granting the right of trial by jury to a claimed fugitive had been introduced during the preceding session, and the signers asked that the legislature take up this measure as a "safeguard of justice." Abolitionists in Pittsburgh had drafted a similar document, noting that this right was enshrined in the Declaration of Independence.[42]

Over the next few months, the campaign for the bill broadened. Under the headline "The United States Constitution Will Destroy Slavery," the *Pennsylvania Freeman* argued that by granting a jury trial to fugitives, Pennsylvania not only would be defending "the rights of citizens" but also would be striking a critical blow against slavery, asking, "How few fugitives from slavery will be reclaimed when the claimants shall find themselves compelled to establish their claim before an open court?" According to the editors, although slavery's defenders invoked the Constitution as their defense, the document was in fact a weapon against slavery. The *Freeman* also reprinted a memorial from Pittsburgh citing the prevalence of light-skinned slaves in the South as evidence that all citizens of Pennsylvania were at risk, not merely those easily identified as black. The "moderate" Pennsylvania Abolition Society also drafted a resolution calling for the trial by jury for accused fugitives, as did the state antislavery convention that met in Harrisburg in January 1837.[43]

In the midst of this campaign, Pennsylvanians received the most encouraging sign yet regarding the progress of political antislavery. In his annual address to the state legislature, Governor Ritner denounced the national government's efforts to undermine "all the principles of Pennsylvania policy." He listed numerous state interests that had been thwarted by the presidential administration, including national funding for internal improvements, Clay's land distribution bill, the protective tariff, the U.S. Bank, "and last, but worst of all, ... the base bowing of the knee to the dark spirit of Slavery." He laid out a political antislavery platform: "opposition to slavery at home," opposition to the admission of new slaveholding states, and opposition to slavery in the District of Columbia. Ritner admitted that the constitutional rights of other states had to be respected but warned that allowing southern states to dictate concessions on this issue, especially any ban on the free discussion of it, risked turning a consensual union into "subjection."[44]

Pennsylvania's opponents of slavery responded with overwhelming support for their Anti-Masonic governor. The Young Men's Anti-Slavery Society passed a resolution praising Ritner's "bold determination and honest rectitude of purpose in fearlessly asserting and nobly defending our right to think and act for ourselves, independent of the will of southern dictators." The society contrasted this manly stance with the "servile and fawning policy of other northern rulers." The Pennsylvania Abolition Society also expressed its support for the governor, and the *Pennsylvania Inquirer*, though hardly an advocate for abolitionism, noted with approval Ritner's denunciation of slavery's political power. The national abolitionist press also took note, with the *Liberator* approvingly quoting Ritner's address.[45]

Whittier, in Harrisburg for the state antislavery convention, also praised the governor. The poet and newspaper editor believed that latent support for antislavery existed, and Ritner, "the sturdy farmer," was helping to awaken it by flying "the banner of Free Discussion" in the "mountain breezes of Pennsylvania." After the two men met, Whittier came away impressed and Ritner expressed support for the convention, in which one of his sons served as a Washington County delegate.[46]

Supporters of political antislavery in Pennsylvania recognized that even though Whigs and Anti-Masons had entered into a political coalition, not all members of that partnership were equally friendly to the rights of free blacks. Support for legislation that would buttress black citizenship rights provoked a fierce and highly partisan legislative debate. "The Senate have done no other thing all this week than debate the Negro Bill," complained state senator George Baker, a Philadelphia Democrat, in March 1837.[47] Despite the lengthy debate and the antislavery sentiments of the state's chief executive, the legislature rejected the bill. The legislative fight nevertheless provided political antislavery supporters with some hope. Although the Senate defeated the jury bill, every Anti-Masonic senator supported it. "The defeat of the Bill," wrote Whittier, "is to be ascribed entirely to party feeling. Every Whig and Van Buren member of the Senate voted against it: the anti-masonic members only sustaining it."[48]

The state constitution developed into the chief battleground in the fight over black citizenship. Pennsylvanians had expressed their dissatisfaction with the 1790 constitution at various times over the ensuing four decades, but reform efforts failed to gain traction until the mid-1830s. Opposition to constitutional reform had often cut across party lines, but in 1834 some Democrats took up the cause. They formed a statewide association that advocated a constitutional convention, and the legislature passed a bill putting the issue to a referendum in October 1835. The referendum was approved, and a constitutional convention assembled in Harrisburg on May 2, 1837, with a Whig–Anti-Mason coalition enjoying a one-vote majority over its Democratic opponents and electing John Sergeant as convention president.[49]

The issue of black citizenship had not been a particular concern of those who had called for the convention, but black Philadelphians worried that opponents of black legal and political rights might seize the opportunity. These free African Americans decided to reach out to allies who would oppose such efforts before the issue was raised. Black leaders convened a meeting at Mother Bethel on June 5. After the meeting opened with hymns and prayer, Frederick Hinton, a prosperous barber and leader of the city's black community, addressed the group, sharing information he had received from the convention. Attendees drafted a memorial denouncing any attempt to deprive black Pennsylvanians of their right to vote and dispatched Hinton and Charles Gardner, a black Presbyterian minister, to take the memorial to the convention in hopes that they would "be heard on their own behalf, before the bar of the Convention."[50]

Black Philadelphians' fears were well founded. During the discussion of the suffrage article of the new convention, John Sterigere, a Democratic delegate from just west of Philadelphia, moved to restrict voting eligibility to "whites." On June 19, the convention took up the issue, with Sterigere's supporters, among them Benjamin Martin of Philadelphia County, emphasizing the public prejudice against blacks and suggesting that advocates of black voting sought "to degrade the poor laboring white man." Opponents pointed to the indeterminacy of the word *white*, leading Sterigere to withdraw his proposal.[51]

On June 22, Martin made another attempt to add language to restrict the franchise to whites, citing both the increase in the free black population, especially in Philadelphia, and what he claimed was blacks' inability to be elevated to the level of whites. According to Martin, "Much has been done for these people, schools have been kept up—they have been instructed in all the sciences, and in the rudiments of religion, and I have known but one solitary instance of a good result." That exception was James Forten. After a brief debate, Martin's language went down in a vote that crossed party lines. Many delegates apparently saw the vote not as a final resolution of the issue but as a means of putting it off for the moment. At least one delegate suggested that the decision would be made for the convention by a pending court case in Luzerne County, in northeastern Pennsylvania.[52]

As important as the issue of black suffrage was at a state level, it had national political implications as well. The issue was again raised indirectly by the convention's debate over Pittsburgh blacks' petition for the defense of their right to vote. Foreshadowing later events, Charles Jared Ingersoll of Philadelphia argued that he opposed allowing African Americans to vote, at least in part because doing so constituted an affront to "those who were born in the southern portion of the Union." Thaddeus Stevens, an antislavery lawyer and politician, wryly responded that he "never had heard of a nabob or despot who lacked defenders" and turned Ingersoll's argument on its head: "Are we to be told, sir, that we are not to print this memorial because it will be offensive to the South?" Such a decision, insisted Stevens, constituted "a servile and unworthy motive of action." This discussion paralleled the fight in the U.S. Congress over how to handle abolitionist petitions, though it is not clear whether the national debate determined local attitudes. In any case, the convention voted to print the memorial.[53]

Though the convention adjourned without restricting suffrage to whites, black advocates for political equality could hardly declare victory. By the time the convention reconvened in January 1838 in Philadelphia, the issue of black voting had become both more prominent and more contentious. Democrats running for election in Bucks County, just north of Philadelphia, claimed that they had lost as a consequence of illegal black votes and challenged the election in county court. In addition, the issue of black voting became increasingly tied to the national struggle over abolition and the political power of slavery, especially the fight over the congressional Gag Rule, which sought to prevent the discussion of abolitionist petitions.[54] Black voters were far more likely to cast their ballots for Whigs/Anti-Masons, but those potential beneficiaries had to worry about the larger danger that those votes posed to sectional peace and the union.

Supporters of black voting therefore sought to frame black suffrage not as a radical change but as a long recognized if rarely exercised right of black citizenship. On January 6, 1838, Hinton and Gardner presented Philadelphia delegate James C. Biddle with the memorial from the Bethel meeting. One of the document's ten resolutions focused on black progress as an argument against disfranchisement, and one made a universal appeal to the divinely ordained equality of men. The rest of the resolutions, however, constituted a pragmatic attempt to address the political realities of the debate over black voting, emphasizing the idea that restricting suffrage to whites constituted the removal of rights that Pennsylvania had long recognized belonged to free blacks.[55] Whereas opponents of black suffrage argued that blacks had never been granted this right and depicted attempts to promote black voting as a "modern" innovation, defenders of black suffrage sought to portray themselves as advocates of the status quo and their opponents as advocates of change.

One recent study of the Pennsylvania convention and the attempt to restrict the franchise to whites has characterized it as the culmination of a shift from racial paternalism to racial ascriptivism. While white Pennsylvanians had previously hoped that blacks could be raised to the level of whites and thus granted citizenship, by 1838, whites believed that African Americans were incapable of citizenship in a white republic. In this telling, free blacks trying to demonstrate their worthiness were fighting a hopeless, rearguard battle against forces that increasingly held that no amount of self-improvement could make a black worthy of political rights.[56] The debate over the measure to restrict suffrage, however, indicates that this narrative oversimplifies the racial attitudes of the delegates to the convention.

Democrats who supported restricting the vote to whites had various reasons for taking this position. In many cases, support for restriction was based on a belief in the inherent inferiority of blacks. Nevertheless, proponents of this view felt the need to expand their argument, perhaps in hopes of swaying those who were uncomfortable with a position that rested on inherent and immutable racial difference. John McCahen of Philadelphia County, for example, contended that lack of military service rendered blacks undeserving of the right to vote. George Woodward pointed to the difference between white and black emigration as a basis for racial restriction. Europeans had consented to become Americans, whereas "the negroes never assented, and their presence here, since it was procured by fraud and force, could not be construed into an adoption of the country, or an acquiescence in its forms of government." Despite the problems with and inconsistencies of these arguments—African Americans had, of course, served in both the American Revolution and the War of 1812—they point to the fact that the arguments for racial restriction encompassed more than simple racial inferiority. Even Sterigere, the convention delegate who had introduced the idea of restricting suffrage, felt the need to distinguish the "political rights" under discussion from the "natural rights" of the Declaration of Independence which he conceded had included blacks.[57]

Supporters of racial restriction, whether Democrats or members of other parties, also pointed to the implications of black voting for the national politics of slavery. William Meredith, a Philadelphia Whig, straddled the fence, admitting the intelligence and virtue of some blacks while supporting distinctions within citizenship. He also warned that black voters would be interested primarily in undermining slavery and that the convention was under an obligation "not to interfere in the domestic affairs of the people of the south." Democrat Robert Fleming noted that granting citizenship to blacks might produce constitutional problems if blacks from Pennsylvania sought to have a southern state respect those rights. Woodward, another Democrat, stressed the national stakes of the debate: "If this point could be gained," he insisted, "if the negro could be elevated to political equality with the white voters of Pennsylvania, this excitement would acquire a new impulse, and the war of the abolitionists against our southern brethren would be waged with redoubled ferocity." He admitted that blacks were capable of self-government but insisted that white prejudice meant that they could be permitted to govern themselves only in Africa. Even some delegates who voted against racial restriction expressed wariness about other states' concerns.[58]

Many delegates—not merely Democrats but also Whigs—had narrowly partisan reasons to avoid antagonizing slaveholders. While Pennsylvania Whigs might be more critical of slavery than their Democratic opponents, Whigs in many parts of the South sought to prove themselves slavery's true defenders.[59] Any hopes that their party would succeed on a national level would be threatened if Pennsylvania Whigs embraced the controversial issue of black suffrage.

Supporters of black voting also noted the national implications of the issue but saw those implications as a reason to support black suffrage. "My principal objection," contended Anti-Masonic delegate Emanuel Reigart, "is that it will be viewed in the south as a triumph of southern principles in a northern state." Walter Forward insisted that notions about blacks' inability to govern themselves were part of an old aristocratic doctrine that had somehow found its way from South Carolina to Pennsylvania.[60] Backers of the black franchise combined abstract defenses of the constitutional rights of free blacks with moral appeals, but the most pointed denunciations of racial restriction took the form of warnings that it constituted an attempt by southern slaveholders to impose their power on the state of Pennsylvania.

More delegates seem to have believed that black political activity was a threat that needed to be eliminated. As the debate drew to a close and the vote neared, the presence of black spectators in the gallery became controversial. A group of black Philadelphians, including James Forten Jr., was forcibly expelled from the convention. Soon after, the convention voted seventy-seven to forty-five to limit suffrage to whites, with many Whigs, including Philadelphia's William Meredith and Joseph Hopkinson, supporting the change.[61] Both men had national political connections, and Meredith harbored larger political ambitions. Neither supported, at least publicly, the notion that blacks were inherently inferior, and Hopkinson had argued that the 1790 constitution had permitted free blacks to vote, yet both men voted for racial restriction.[62] The issue was not the abstract question of racial difference but rather the practical political problems posed by black suffrage. The Whigs who opposed racial restriction portrayed themselves as moderates seeking to diffuse a potentially explosive issue.

Although the Philadelphia petition did not have the results envisioned by its drafters, the document reflected the sorts of political arguments that were ultimately crucial to the success of the amendment to disfranchise blacks. Hinton and Gardner had argued that black disfranchisement would promote rather than soothe political conflict, creating dissension in society by creating artificial distinctions.[63]

When the convention later rejected a proposal to provide jury trials to accused fugitive slaves on the grounds that such a measure constituted a threat to the union, it also demonstrated that at issue was a larger conception of black citizenship, not just a narrowly conceived voting privilege. As Thomas Earle pointed out, many defenders of restricting the right to vote had argued that doing so simply denied free blacks "political rights" while they retained "civil rights." The rejection of the right to trial by jury, however, proved that such distinctions were far from clear and that the protection of the union and the defense of southern rights demanded ever larger concessions. William Yates, a Philadelphia correspondent for the *Colored American*, echoed Ritner's assessment that the convention had engaged in "a base bowing of the knee to the spirit of slavery."[64]

Black Philadelphians found themselves on the defensive. They were discouraged by the convention's actions but quickly mobilized to oppose the ratification of the new constitution. They also needed to respond to two recent legal decisions declaring that free blacks had never held the legal right to vote in Pennsylvania.[65] A committee headed by Purvis drafted the "Appeal of Forty Thousand Citizens, Threatened with Disfranchisement, to the People of Pennsylvania," which was read before a public meeting in the First Presbyterian Church, and demonstrated a complicated engagement with the arguments that had been made at the convention.

The Appeal is conservative in that it points not to black progress but to the precedent of black citizenship and to African Americans' contributions to the United States. Black Pennsylvanians did not need to earn equal citizenship because they and their ancestors had already done so: "We honor Pennsylvania and her noble institutions too much to part with our birthright, as her free citizens, without a struggle."[66] Like other opponents of suffrage restrictions, Purvis was calling for black suffrage not as a radical change but as the preservation of an existing right and depicted the convention's proposed change as a radical departure from previous practices.

Even worse, Purvis argued, this radical change resulted from Pennsylvania politicians' subservience to the interests of slaveholders. "We do not believe our disfranchisement would have been proposed," argued Purvis, "but for the desire which is felt by political aspirants to gain the favor of the slaveholding States. This is not the first time that northern statesmen have 'bowed the knee to the dark spirit of slavery,' but it is the first time that they have bowed so low!" He characterized this change and the refusal to provide jury trials for accused fugitives as part of a southern plot to extend slavery to the North. But since Pennsylvania had relatively few blacks, the "Appeal" warned, the slaveholders "may demand that a portion of the white tax-payers should be unmanned and turned into chattels." The new constitution thus represented nothing less than an attempt to enslave free Pennsylvanians.[67]

Purvis and others continued to place the American Colonization Society at the center of this conspiracy to deprive black Pennsylvanians of their citizenship. Advocates of disfranchisement had hoped that it would encourage free blacks "to look to Africa for a home" (though Walter Forward and other opponents had also argued in favor of colonization).[68] Yet free blacks, especially in Philadelphia, had always imbued opposition to colonization with a broader significance. Colonization stood as a symbol for how good men who considered themselves friends of slaves could fall under the sway of slaveholders. Black political rhetoric focused on these men, since African American leaders had little reason to appeal to people who considered blacks unalterably inferior to whites or those who consciously sought alliances with slaveholders. However, men who had more conflicted views on the issue might be convinced that they were inadvertently doing the work of slavery.

Fierce public discussion of the issue of black citizenship only heightened Philadelphia's existing tensions over abolition. Because abolitionists often had difficulty finding halls open to their meetings, they built Pennsylvania Hall to serve as a place where "liberty, equality and civil rights could be freely discussed," an explicit reference to the congressional Gag Rule. At the hall's May 14, 1838, opening, Philadelphia abolitionist David Paul Brown addressed a large crowd on the subject of "Liberty," followed by a lecture on "The Duty of Temperance Men at the Ballot-Box." Over the next several days, the Pennsylvania Hall hosted a number of abolitionist speakers, including some from the Anti-Slavery Convention of American Women.[69]

Philadelphians opposed to abolition immediately made known their displeasure, and rumors spread that "amalgamation" was taking place in the hall. On the night of May 17, a large mob gathered outside, threatening Pennsylvania Hall and those inside. Mayor John Swift convinced the abolitionists to adjourn for the evening, assuring them that if they did, he would disperse the mob. But soon after the mayor departed, the crowd set fire to the hall, burning it to the ground. Over the next two days, the mob turned its sights on black Philadelphians, torching the Shelter for Colored Orphans and attacking a black church.[70]

Contemporaries saw Pennsylvania Hall's destruction as a fiery fulfillment of the political struggle over black citizenship rights. The building's stockholders denounced its destruction as a blow against free discussion and as the work of the South. The Democratic *Philadelphia Pennsylvanian* lamented the mob's violence but insisted that the abolitionists themselves were mostly to blame: the editors "utterly condemn every effort to admit the negro race to the right of suf-

"Destruction by fire of Pennsylvania Hall, the new building of the Abolition Society, on the night of the 17th May," 1838. Courtesy of the Library of Congress Prints and Photographs Division.

frage, as contended for by our opponents in the reform convention, as we do the attempts now making to effect a first step toward the amalgamation of the races, giving them an equality in social intercourse."[71]

The grand jury's report on Pennsylvania Hall's destruction no doubt strengthened black abolitionists' impression that colonization lay behind the assault on the building. Led by foreman Elliott Cresson, a prominent colonizationist, the jury expressed lukewarm criticism of the rioters and placed the blame for the riot largely on the shoulders of abolitionists. In particular, the jury criticized the abolitionists' offense to "the nicer feelings of the public" when "individuals were brought into close and familiar intercourse, whom long habits and a well ascertained and established sense of propriety had invariably kept asunder."[72]

Slavery and black citizenship rights again rose to the fore in Pennsylvania's October elections. Not only did the ratification of the constitution appear on the ballot, but slavery and sectionalism emerged as important issues in other races as well. Governor Ritner was up for reelection, and the *Pennsylvanian* mocked the sitting governor both for declaring himself an abolitionist and for allowing his allies to deny this claim. In the Third Congressional District, which included northern Philadelphia County, Ingersoll, a Democrat, ran against incumbent Whig Charles Naylor. Ingersoll had been one of the convention's most prominent defenders of racial restriction and an eloquent champion of southern rights. His Whig opponents depicted him as a southern aristocrat, disdainful of the "laborers of the North" and an advocate of "Lynch Law." Naylor and Ritner, conversely, were celebrated for "lifting the key-stone above the reach of national dictation and oppression."[73]

If black voting had not begun as a primary concern of the debate over constitutional reform, it had emerged as one of the most visible and contentious elements of the proposed constitution. Whigs/Anti-Masons sought to strike a balance befitting their mixed position on black suffrage. For the most part, the antiratification rhetoric focused on the "staunch heart-of-oak roof" that had been the old constitution, contrasted it with the new partisan patchwork. Opponents of the new constitution did not, however, ignore the issue of black voting. In one of a series of essays, "Young Hickory" denounced the suffrage clause, though he admitted that he did not personally support black voting. Democrats were not nearly as circumspect in their campaign on behalf of ratification. On Election Day, the front page of the *Pennsylvanian* declared in large print,

> All who are opposed to NEGROES voting—
> All who are opposed to LIFE OFFICES—
> All who desire an extension of the Right of Suffrage—
> WILL VOTE FOR THE AMENDMENTS[74]

The ratification of the constitution involved much more than the question of black suffrage, yet both supporters and opponents depicted that issue as a central feature of the proposed constitution. Thus, the election must be seen at least in part as a repudiation of black suffrage and of Ritner's perceived abolitionism. Yet black Pennsylvanians also had reason to hope. Democrat David Porter defeated Ritner by a mere 2 percent, and Ritner received more votes than he had in his victorious 1835 effort. The constitution was approved by an even slimmer margin, with just 50.3 percent support. The partisan composition of the State House remained unchanged, while the Whig/Anti-Masonic coalition increased its majority in the Senate.[75] The politicians who made up the convention might have voted overwhelmingly for disfranchisement, but the voters of Pennsylvania expressed less avid support. And Ritner's narrow loss and the continuing strength of the Whig/Anti-Mason coalition offered hope that the state government might eventually prove to be an ally in the struggle against slavery and for black citizenship.

The convention debates and the campaign against ratification illustrated that Pennsylvanians had not reached a consensus around hard racism. White Pennsylvanians may not have considered blacks equals, but some residents of the state sought to afford their African American neighbors some citizenship rights, and even more were profoundly uncomfortable with the idea that southern slaveholders could influence these questions on Pennsylvania's soil. Free blacks continued to exploit these two lines of argument to shape a formal politics that now legally excluded them. African American leaders also recognized that the battle within the state's Whig/Anti-Mason coalition was crucial. As in the fight against colonization, free blacks needed to convince potential allies that denying American citizenship rights to free blacks was tantamount to defending slavery.

Reform, the Church, and Tactical Disagreements in Black Abolition

Black Pennsylvanians found themselves on the defensive on the issue of voting, but African Americans asserted their right to be considered citizens in other ways. Like free blacks elsewhere, black Philadelphians had long advocated a strategy of black uplift, but in the 1830s organizations promoting moral reform among free blacks wrestled with the implications of their work for citizenship claims. Black Philadelphians fiercely disagreed over the ways to balance moral reform and the fight for black citizenship. They also found themselves a part of other contentious questions that divided abolitionists in these years and had profound implications for black citizenship rights.

Visiting the August 1837 meeting of the American Moral Reform Society (AMRS) in Philadelphia, the editor of the *Colored American*, Samuel Cornish, had high hopes. The AMRS, had emerged from the black convention movement and was led by members of Philadelphia's black elite, balancing a commitment to the promotion of the principles of moral reform "among the colored race" with denunciations of "national or complexional distinctions." In Cornish's view, the group held a critical position in the struggle against slavery. Yet the editor did not like what he saw. "The colored citizens of Philadelphia, many of them wealthy and intellectual, are visionary in the extreme," he explained to his readers. But the AMRS's leaders, most notably Purvis and Whipper, were "vague, wild, indefinite and confused in their views. They created shadows, fought the wind, and bayed the moon, for more than three days." Cornish was especially troubled by the leaders' insistence the organization should avoid all "complexional" designations. Philadelphian Frederick Hinton concurred with Cornish's assessment of the "blind and furious objections" which were urged against the admission of the designation "free people of color" and added criticism of the leaders' declaration that the society would seek to aid all men, not simply "the colored community."[76]

The black press engaged in a robust contest over the merits of the AMRS and its aims and tactics. The issue of the group's name was particularly contentious, in part because critics saw it as emblematic of the organization's entire approach.[77] Cornish in particular exhorted Philadelphians to channel their efforts into practical efforts to promote black moral reform. Whipper became the AMRS's de facto spokesman and defended the group in the pages of the *Colored American*.

Though critics claimed that AMRS leaders sought to avoid use of racially specific language because they were ashamed of their color, defenders saw the linguistic disagreement as reflecting tactical differences over how best to eliminate caste in American society and how best to promote African American citizenship rights. AMRS leaders contended that any embrace of exclusively black institutions would undermine their larger efforts to eliminate complexional differences. According to Whipper, "All unnecessary distinctions among men, ought at once and forever, to cease.... [T]hey should only be distinguished by their virtues and vices." He refused to apologize for this admittedly "visionary" notion. In addition to refusing to use racial language, Whipper and his allies insisted that their organization should seek moral reform of all people and in so doing undermine America's racial order.[78]

In practical terms, however, the AMRS remained a black organization. Though sympathetic whites were invited to participate, free blacks maintained the leadership positions. Moreover, while the AMRS was rhetorically dedicated to color-blind moral reform, the practical meaning of this ideology remained unclear. The organization's moral reform efforts seem generally to have targeted free blacks.[79] The critique of the AMRS's position on color seems to have resonated because it buttressed the claim that the society was impractical, and critics seems to have valued practicality above all else.

In 1838, while the AMRS maintained its opposition to the use of the term *colored*, the *Colored American* added a Philadelphia edition under the proprietorship of the Reverend Stephen Gloucester to its original New York edition. Gloucester had been active within the AMRS, and he initially wore both hats, though differences soon emerged. An August 28, 1838, meeting in support of the *Colored American* demonstrated that many black Philadelphians saw support for the newspaper as criticism of the AMRS's "visionary" position on complexional institutions. The meeting denounced the society's principles as "frivolous ... founded on the most incorrect principles, and calculated (if adhered to by our people) to reflect disgrace upon them, and retard the advancement of their best interest." Going further, participants declared that they would not support the newspaper under any other name. Some of the men who attended this meeting were also active in the rival Philadelphia Association for the Moral and Mental Improvement of the People of Color," which specifically devoted itself to the promotion of moral reform among "people of color."[80]

Baltimore's William Watkins also emerged as a prominent though somewhat more moderate critic of the AMRS. In a letter to John Burr, a supporter of the group, Watkins used a parable to justify the existence of institutions that exclusively aided blacks: While journeying to Philadelphia, he wrote, he had witnessed two men, one white and one black, fall overboard. The white men who remained on board immediately set about helping the white man but ignored the drowning black man because of their "deep-rooted hatred against a sable hue." Watkins, however, devoted his energies to rescuing the black man, a course of action he saw as neither selfish nor inconsistent with the principle of racial equality but simply as a practical response to the reality of white racism.

Some AMRS backers insisted that critics were exaggerating the distance between the group's supporters and its detractors. The *Colored American* published Watkins's letter as evidence of the AMRS's flaws, and Whipper subsequently published the letter in the *National Reformer* (the AMRS's official organ). Whipper denied that his position on the color issue was as fanatical as his opponents claimed and contended that no real differences existed between his and Watkins's positions. Watkins admitted that he opposed the "prodigal use, or unnecessary parade" of the word *colored* despite his insistence on its practical necessity. Watkins also admired the principle of moral reform for all, regardless of color, though he doubted that it could be put into practice. Above all, Watkins called for the parties to find common ground. If Whipper could plausibly claim that his position did not differ substantially from Watkins's, he had more difficulty countering Watkins's assertion that the emphasis on these questions had undermined the AMRS's ability to provide concrete benefits for Philadelphia's free black population. AMRS leaders seem to have recognized as much, though they attributed their failure to the vastness of the task before them rather than to their own tactical missteps.[81]

If disputes over whether to focus solely on African Americans were most prominent, they were not the only sources of disagreement surrounding the AMRS's approach. At the society's 1838 meeting, Gloucester objected to a resolution penned by Whipper that attributed the "disabilities under which we labor" to the "spirit of the Church and the government under which we live." Gloucester, pastor of the Second African Presbyterian Church, which hosted the meeting, sought to change the second part of the resolution to read, "the worldly spirit of a great portion of professed Christians." Gloucester, like many black pastors, believed that the church needed to play a central role in any moral reform project. The AMRS, however, became increasingly vehement in denouncing the church, including black churches, and took a position close to William Lloyd Garrison's on the issue. The convention voted nineteen to eleven in favor of Whipper's original resolution, and Gloucester and many of his Presbyterian allies withdrew from the AMRS after the convention.[82]

This was not Gloucester's first attempt to promote the role of the black church in the antislavery movement. In 1837, New York–based abolitionist publisher Joshua Leavitt had lectured at Gloucester's church on the Christian duty to promote emancipation. The congregation was moved by the address and resolved to create an antislavery society, which they named for the speaker who had inspired them. After the burning of Pennsylvania Hall, the organization appointed Gloucester and two other men to a committee charged with finding a location for antislavery speakers. In addition to his involvement with the Leavitt Anti-Slavery Society, Gloucester was one of the founders of the American and Foreign Anti-Slavery Society after the American Anti-Slavery Society split.[83] Gloucester was only the most prominent of the many black pastors who disagreed with the blanket rejection of churches as pro-slavery and who sought to work within the Protestant denominations to promote moral reform and to fight slavery.

Disagreements in abolitionists' approach to politics also played an important role in the 1840 split in national antislavery. By the late 1830s, many abolitionists had grown dissatisfied with Garrison's leadership and contended that the Garrisonians' increasingly critical stance toward the church, support of women's rights, and resistance to coordinated political action had become an obstacle to an effective antislavery movement. Not all of Garrison's critics opposed him on all of these grounds, but the disagreements on these issues combined to shatter the American Anti-Slavery Society. Many of the men who formed the church-oriented American and Foreign Anti-Slavery Society also criticized Garrison's position on voting, though many Christian abolitionists continued to hope to work through the existing parties.[84]

The AMRS took a thoroughly Garrisonian attitude toward the church, but its position on voting was less orthodox and reflected members' focus on black citizenship rights. On July 31, 1839, abolitionists converged on Albany, New York, to discuss the antislavery movement's direction, especially regarding voting and political action. Despite Garrisonian objections, the meeting strongly endorsed political antislavery tactics, calling on all abolitionists to use their vote to fight slavery. Whipper and the *National Reformer* took a middle-of-the-road approach, insisting that both moral and political action were needed weapons in the war against slavery. When the Anti-Slavery Society for Eastern Pennsylvania met in May 1840, it passed a resolution disapproving of the Albany Convention and advising abolitionists to "scatter their votes, or absent themselves from the polls." Though the resolution passed overwhelmingly—ninety-three to twenty-seven—members of the AMRS (including Gardner, Daniel Payne, and Purvis) were conspicuous among the nays.[85] Whatever their position on the church and its place in the fight against slavery, black Philadelphians seem to have taken a practical attitude toward morality.

Leaders of the AMRS challenged the allegation that they were impractical visionaries in other ways, perhaps none more important than by supporting the work of the Vigilant Committee of Philadelphia. Indeed, their proximity to the border helped to produce a distinctive form of "practical abolition" among Philadelphia's free blacks.[86] Black Philadelphians had long been crucial supporters of fugitives from slavery, but the increasing numbers of those fleeing north into Pennsylvania convinced many residents that a formal organization was needed to support this work. In August 1837, Purvis and other men established the Vigilant Committee of Philadelphia, electing black dentist James McCrummell as its first president. The group met openly and raised money through advertisements in the *Pennsylvania Freeman* and through public celebrations. By 1839 the group had grown substantially and was reorganized with Purvis as its president. The standing committee and officers of the newly organized Vigilant Committee included both supporters of the AMRS and those who had been highly critical of it. The *National Reformer* printed accounts of the committee's meetings, and Whipper used the pages of his journal to raise funds for the group. For Whipper, the AMRS's struggle to eliminate the racial caste system and to promote black citizenship were a part of the fight to defend fugitive slaves from being taken back into bondage.[87]

Many African Americans continued to see churches as crucial battlegrounds in the fight for black citizenship. Though many black churches were part of specifically African American denominations, others operated within white-dominated ecclesiastical bodies, and black citizenship posed just as much of a threat to denominational unity as to more formally political institutions. These national organizations generally sought to assuage sectional differences over slavery, often by disfranchising black parishioners within the denomination. Black Christians refused to accept this disfranchisement. Though some white and black abolitionists called for a withdrawal from corrupt, compromising churches, many free blacks on the border saw their work within their churches as an essential form of practical antislavery. To an extent, this effort formed part of free blacks' larger strategy to depict themselves as sober, virtuous citizens.

Many denominations recognized that the status of black church members was intimately related to larger political debates about black citizenship. In the spring of 1840, the General Conference of the Methodist Episcopal Church met in Baltimore. Tensions over slavery had been growing within the church, and members had divided into three factions: southerners, abolitionists (including the church's seventy thousand African American members), and northern conservatives. The conflict between southerners and abolitionists dominated the conference, while conservatives did their best to hold the church together. The conference voted seventy-five to fifty-six in favor of a resolution submitted by a prominent Georgia pastor, Ignatius Few:

> *Resolved*, That it is inexpedient and unjustifiable in any of our ministers *to admit the testimony of colored persons against white persons*, in church trials, in those states and territories where the testimony of such persons is rejected in the courts of law.[88]

The members of Baltimore's Sharp Street and Asbury Churches met in May to draft a resolution objecting to the General Conference's actions: "We feel called upon most solemnly to PROTEST against this act of the General Conference, whereby every colored member of the church is unjustifiably and unnecessarily disfranchised and degraded." The Baltimoreans contended that the resolution both undermined the work of the church and strengthened "that unholy pride of caste." They reasserted their determination to remain within their church while insisting on their right to be heard. Though representatives of the Baltimore churchmen presented their resolution to the bishops, it was not read before the conference as a whole. However, according to Watkins, the protest had an effect on those who read it, and it was reprinted in the abolitionist press. Some white Methodists also took up the cause of their black brethren, and references to the Few resolution featured prominently in calls for a meeting of antislavery Methodists in the fall of 1840.[89]

Conservatives within the church had sought to preserve the unity of Methodism for ecclesiastical and political reasons. Methodists not only were concerned that the splintering of the church would undermine its ability to carry out its religious commitment to save souls but also believed that their church played an important role in promoting morality in American politics, and this role would be compromised if unity could not be preserved. The question of church discipline and its connection to the law formed an essential part of Methodism's understanding of its relationship to American civic life. Conservatives had previously seen abolitionists as the most dangerous threat to church unity (though southern defenses of slavery were also somewhat disturbing). After the 1840 conference, however, northern conservatives increasingly saw subservience of ecclesiastical law to civil law in these matters as an affront to Methodism itself. Abolitionists, especially the most radical among them, increasingly left the Methodist Episcopal Church, but many conservatives who remained saw Few's resolution as a great embarrassment and as evidence that Methodism could not continue to appease slaveholders while hoping to accept blacks into their church as spiritual equals. This conservative antislavery, with its resistance to southern domination, split the church in 1844.[90]

Free blacks found their citizenship rights under attack in many places: in print, in statehouses, on the streets, and in churches. Their defense of the rights of citizenship, therefore, took a number of forms. Black Pennsylvanians and their allies denounced what they saw as the new constitution's radical transformation of suffrage into a racially delimited citizenship right. Many African Americans, especially in Philadelphia, embraced moral reform as a means of demonstrating and promoting the respectability of free blacks, yet they also wrestled with the implications of "complexional" organizations, concerned that they might unwittingly reinforce white beliefs regarding African Americans' unworthiness of citizenship rights. Other African Americans struggled for citizenship rights within white-dominated churches. To advance the cause of black citizenship or at a minimum to combat efforts to restrict existing citizenship rights, African Americans needed to navigate the churning waters of partisan politics, building coalitions and cultivating white allies wherever they could be found.

CHAPTER 6

White Immigrants, Black Natives

Black activists had engaged in a number of contentious debates about tactical issues, but almost all free blacks were united by a commitment to aiding fugitive slaves. This commitment, in turn, raised serious questions about what rights free blacks should enjoy. Pennsylvania's African Americans continued to push for jury trials, which would have protected against kidnapping but which also would have complicated matters for masters seeking to recover fugitive slaves. The Maryland state legislature considered further restrictions on free blacks' legal rights. In both states, political struggles pitted slavery's defenders, who called for dramatic restrictions on black citizenship rights, against white moderates' sometimes tepid support for limited black citizenship. Recognizing the importance of even small victories in this struggle, African Americans found themselves engaged in a world of partisan politics.

Free blacks also faced a more ideological argument against their right to be seen as citizens: the denial of their Americanness. Free African Americans had long used their birth on American soil as a part of a broader argument for their rights as U.S. citizens. But this somewhat abstract notion increasingly came to be seen through the prism of European immigration to the United States. As white immigrants embraced their whiteness as a means of securing American citizenship rights, free blacks pointed to the rights afforded to new Americans as providing support for African Americans' claims. The fight over black citizenship rights remained a part of the borderland struggle over the security of slavery, but it also became entangled with emerging political conflicts surrounding white immigrants and the question of who was truly American.

Black Citizenship and Border Politics

Free African Americans had learned that the struggle for black citizenship needed to be fought at all levels of government. The issue crossed geographic boundaries, with national politics attuned to developments at the state level and the politics of one state influenced by those of others. To advance the fight for black citizenship rights, whether that right was suffrage, trial by jury, or the protection of state laws, African Americans along the mid-Atlantic border embraced practicality over ideological purity.

Protection by local officials could be just as important as the protection of state and national governments. In this regard, the 1838 election was not a complete disappointment for Pennsylvania abolitionists. As usual, Whigs maintained their hold over Philadelphia, but when the city's common and select councils met to choose the mayor, they voted eighteen to twelve for Isaac Roach rather than incumbent John Swift. Many abolitionists were profoundly disappointed by Swift's inability to defend Pennsylvania Hall from the rioters who set fire to it. Swift's supporters announced their opposition to the councils' decision and attributed Roach's victory to the "the abolition party, and secret enemies in the Whig ranks."[1] Abolitionists had considerable influence in Philadelphia politics, and as had been the case during the reform convention, the crucial battle was often within the Whig Party.

Efforts on behalf of the right to vote had also helped make black abolitionists in general more amenable to political action than their white colleagues. African American abolitionists might criticize political corruption or the parties' subservience to the Slave Power, but few, even among William Lloyd Garrison's most ardent devotees, spurned voting in principle. Even those who might theoretically have been sympathetic to nonvoting saw the tremendous symbolism of the franchise. It was one thing for a white man to refuse to vote on principle; for a black man to denounce voting as immoral would have called into question efforts to secure the right to vote. Free blacks had long seen the right to vote as a part of the larger fight for citizenship rights, and whatever their disagreements on other questions, by 1840, African Americans largely agreed on the importance of black citizenship to their efforts to fight against slavery.

Even subtle qualifications of this assertion fell away. William Whipper had long argued that moral reform needed to play an essential role in making African Americans good citizens, though he had always stressed that he was not implying that whites were superior. In 1839, Whipper declared that his earlier assertion that free blacks needed to be elevated prior to becoming citizens had been a mistake: "We now utterly discard it and ask pardon for our former errors. We do now henceforth and forever deny that in the republican sense of the term, the colored population need to be elevated," he wrote in the *National Reformer*. "If we are asked, what evidences we bring to sustain our qualifications for citizenship, we will offer them certificates of our BIRTH and NATIVITY."[2]

Many whites disputed this assertion. On March 21, 1840, the Maryland Senate and House passed a measure intended to strengthen the 1831 laws in regard to free people of color. The new legislation declared that no free black could enter Maryland, whether that person "intends settling in this state or not," and imposed a twenty-dollar penalty for the first offense and five-hundred-dollar fine for a second offense. The sheriff was empowered to sell any offender who could not or would not pay the fine to the highest bidder. Proceeds from fines and sales would go to the state colonization society.[3] This measure offered free blacks the clearest evidence yet not only that colonization was a proslavery conspiracy but also that it sought to enslave any free blacks who did not leave "by their own consent." It also demonstrated Maryland slaveholders' fear that their state's position on the border—in particular, its proximity to Philadelphia's vibrant and activist free black community—threatened slavery.

Black Philadelphians used the Maryland law to call into question the motives of the city's colonizationists. In a published letter to the general agent of the Pennsylvania Colonization Society, Charles Gardner recalled his experiences in Maryland in 1832, when he was arrested at the request of the Maryland Colonization Society. That society had now become the direct beneficiary of "kidnapping and selling of free men," yet no branch of the American Colonization Society (including Pennsylvania's) had denounced this arrangement. The Pennsylvania Society had, in fact, petitioned for a related law that would have taxed free blacks to support colonization. While Pennsylvania colonizationists might have hoped to distance themselves from their southern colleagues, Gardner reminded his readers that "the enlightened colored man has not been deceived as yet."[4]

That summer, David Ruggles, a black New York abolitionist, called for a "National Reform Convention of the Colored Inhabitants of the United States of America" in New Haven, Connecticut. The convention was intended to organize more effective opposition to slavery and colonization, but the Maryland law gave urgency to that effort. According to the call for the convention, "The existence of the late Maryland *Black Law* should arouse every colored inhabitant of this Nation to a proper sense of his endangered condition, and inspire every bosom with a righteous and indignant zeal against oppression." The call was cosigned by an impressive array of black activists from across the North, including a substantial number of Pennsylvanians. Both Whipper and Robert Purvis signed on, though they eventually withdrew their support, explaining to Ruggles that they could not attend a convention organized on "complexional lines."[5]

If Purvis at times seemed to privilege ideological purity over practical concerns, he also recognized that practical needs could overwhelm ideological differences. Only a few months after the disagreement with Ruggles, Purvis served as the secretary for a meeting at the Methodist Episcopal Wesley Church on Lombard Street to support the *Colored American*. Purvis spoke at length, reiterating his opposition to racially exclusive institutions but noting that "the Colored American should be sustained." The importance of maintaining the black press trumped Purvis's continuing belief that "complexional" organizations or designations were counterproductive. Though he did not mention it, the need to support the *Colored American* had become even clearer in light of the closing of Whipper and Purvis's *National Reformer* the previous winter.[6] Practical necessity trumped ideological purity.

Practical-minded abolitionists also recognized that elections remained tremendously important to the antislavery struggle. Even as abolitionists, white and black, struggled over the question of political action, they found themselves embroiled in the coming presidential election. Henry Clay had provoked the ire of many abolitionists, even those who had previously supported him, with his February 1839 speech criticizing abolition. Clay had known that the address would cost him some support in the North, but he hoped that those losses would be counterbalanced by stronger support among southern Whigs. Antimasons and abolitionists within the Whig Party rallied to William Henry Harrison, who ultimately emerged as the party's candidate. The executive committee of the Pennsylvania Anti-Slavery Society later pointed to Clay's defeat as "another indication of the increased deference paid by politicians to the wishes of abolitionists" and applauded "the substitution of one at least less prominent on the pro-slavery list." Though the abolitionists took credit for Clay's defeat, they were hardly warm friends of the Hero of Tippecanoe, and they recognized the value of such incremental changes in the politics of slavery.[7]

Though Harrison was no abolitionist, many abolitionists remained devoted to the Whig Party. John Greenleaf Whittier claimed that many Pennsylvania abolitionists opposed the Liberty Party and its candidate, James G. Birney, because they saw it as "a Van Buren trick to defeat the Whigs." For their part, Pennsylvania Democrats sought to reinforce this connection between Whigs and abolition. James Buchanan publicly termed Harrison "the candidate of the united Whig, Antimasonic and Abolition party!" and privately expressed doubts that "any of the Southern States, after the recent developments on the subject of abolition, [would] give its vote to Harrison."[8] Voters may not have been motivated primarily by their concerns about slavery, but it remained a potent element in the complicated presidential politics of 1840.

Though black Philadelphians lacked the franchise, they generally supported political action and seem not to have taken a strong position on the Liberty Party, perhaps as a consequence of its general weakness in Pennsylvania. Despite this silence, at least some white Philadelphians saw a connection between African Americans and the presidential election. On the evening of the vote, a mob attacked Mother Bethel African Methodist Episcopal Church, breaking most of its front windows.[9] Black churches symbolized the political influence of their congregations, and some white Philadelphians disturbed by the interjection of antislavery into partisan politics blamed black churches for this development. An assault on an African American church served as a denunciation of black citizenship.

The connection between the black church and electoral politics was reinforced by a meeting at the African Episcopal Church of St. Thomas on January 13, 1841. With Robert C. Gordon Jr. in the chair, participants discussed how blacks could regain the right of suffrage in Pennsylvania. The group decided to petition the state legislature to restore black suffrage and to grant jury trials to accused fugitives. Accounts of the meeting indicate some disagreement over the propriety of using the word *colored* in the petition, but a large majority supported it.[10]

Apparently by coincidence, a group of free blacks had convened in Pittsburgh for the same purpose a day earlier. The Pittsburgh meeting settled on a statewide convention as the best means to secure black suffrage, while Philadelphians emphasized the importance of petitioning the legislature. On one hand, too much should not be made of this difference. An April meeting of the "disfranchised citizens of the city and county of Philadelphia" expressed its support for the statewide convention while reaffirming the importance of petitioning the legislature. While the AMRS condemned the proposed convention on the grounds that it had been called on "complexional grounds," another group of Philadelphians met in August and repudiated this argument, appointing fifteen delegates to the convention. These men ultimately did not attend, though they were placed on the convention roll, but instead sent a letter of support that was entered into the minutes of the convention.[11]

On the other hand, the differences between the political strategies in eastern and western Pennsylvania speak to underlying philosophical differences. Philadelphians seem to have been more inclined to work within the existing political system, petitioning the state legislature rather than calling for a state convention. This tendency went hand in hand with the link black Philadelphians made between the right to vote and the right to trial by jury for fugitives. Black Philadelphians saw suffrage as part of a larger set of citizenship rights that would use Pennsylvania law to protect African Americans from slavery. By necessity, this approach involved a willingness to work within the existing political system. Tendencies should not be mistaken for hard differences, however. The Pittsburgh convention also noted the importance of using Pennsylvania law to protect free blacks: "We pay our taxes, then, not the less for our vote, but the more for the protection of the laws." Defenders of the convention recognized that it, like the petition, ultimately depended on the support of white Pennsylvanians; supporters of the statewide convention simply felt that it was the most effective means of convincing whites.[12]

Free blacks in Maryland had reason to fear a decline in white support for even minimal legal rights. Maryland colonizationists had increasingly hinted at a willingness to support coerced black removal. While the 1841 convention declared its hope that free blacks would voluntarily remove themselves from the state, it warned that such might not always be the case.

> If regardless of what has been done to provide them with an asylum, they continue to persist in remaining in Maryland, in the hope of enjoying here an equality of social and political rights—they ought to be solemnly warned, that in the opinion of this Convention, the day must arrive when circumstances that cannot be controlled, and which are now maturing—will deprive them of the freedom of choice, and leave them no alternative but removal.[13]

This passage provoked an impassioned denunciation from a meeting of free blacks as far away as New Bedford, Massachusetts, chaired by former Baltimore resident Frederick Douglass, who had not yet emerged as a national figure.[14] Douglass surely knew that the implications that coercion ultimately lay behind the colonization societies' mask of consent were not new, but the threat of forced removal soon became all too real for Maryland's free blacks.

While colonizationists showed that "moderate" whites were increasingly willing to disregard the customary legal rights of free blacks, more radical critics of black citizenship rights were also ascendant. In January 1842, a meeting of Maryland slaveholders convened in the House of Delegates to discuss the growing free black population and the danger it posed to the institution of slavery. According to one speaker, slaveholders needed to further regulate the enslaved "so as to make them more valuable and to lessen the influence of the free negroes with them." From the beginning, the delegates recognized the delicacy of the issues they debated and sought to control the portrayal of their meeting. No reporter would be admitted unless "his veracity could be vouched for by any gentleman a member of this convention." The delegates wanted to make sure that their actions did not provoke abolitionists.[15]

But as the delegates feared, Charles Torrey, a Boston abolitionist operating in Washington, gained admittance to the convention as a reporter. He aroused delegates' suspicions and was asked to leave; when he resisted, he was arrested and jailed for several days before a judge released him.[16]

Torrey's imprisonment was reported on in the North, where it increased the perception that slaveholders sought to infringe on the liberties of white men as well as black. The abolitionist press was outraged, with the *Liberator* denouncing "southern cowardice and ruffianism." The mainstream press also reported the story: the *Philadelphia Public Ledger* declared that "taking notes" should not constitute a criminal offense "even in a slaveholding state, jealous as it is of its institutions."[17] Rather than preventing knowledge of the slaveholders' meeting from becoming public, Torrey's arrest brought wider northern public attention to the Annapolis gathering.

The Annapolis group's recommendations included new restrictions on private manumissions and more stringent controls on the behavior of free blacks. Several measures also sought to cut down on slaves' ability to flee the state. The publication of these suggestions promptly provoked opposition by many Marylanders and by the state's white Methodist churches. The Light Street Methodist Church hosted a large interdenominational protest against the proposed legislation. Participants declared that the new laws would violate the civil rights of both blacks and whites and denounced the Annapolis meeting as a betrayal of Maryland's "medium position between the two great sections of our country." Thanks in part to this opposition, the bill containing the slaveholders' recommendations failed to pass the State Senate.[18] Whereas a year earlier, the Methodist Church's annual conference had refused to recognize a petition from black congregations, white Methodists now defended the rights of free blacks.

In late 1840, as William Johnson traveled through Pennsylvania to secure support for the *Colored American*, he submitted his observations for publication in the paper. While in Philadelphia, he was pleased with the backing he found for his efforts and noted,

> There is one fact touching Bethel Church, which you will be proud to have decorate the columns of our paper, viz: at the monthly concert of prayer, on the last Monday evening in each month, for the emancipation of the enslaved millions in our country, a collection is taken up for the Philadelphia Committee of Vigilance.

When he returned to Philadelphia after visiting the rest of the state, he found himself attending yet another meeting in support of the Vigilant Committee of Philadelphia, this one held at the African Episcopal Church of St. Thomas. Both white and black abolitionists addressed the crowd, which consisted of both men and women. The Reverend Daniel Payne closed the meeting with an exhortation to take the money that would have been spent on unnecessary food, clothing, and entertainment and instead lay it "upon the altar of the bleeding fugitive." In this way, Johnson noted, enough was raised to "colonize $5,500 worth of cattle in Canada, with their own consent."[19]

Whatever their disagreements on other issues, black Philadelphians came together to support efforts to aid fugitives from slavery. Under Purvis's leadership, the Vigilant Committee provided crucial support to hundreds of fugitives. Those fleeing slavery were given shelter, medical care, and legal assistance and were ultimately shuttled north. The committee worked with its counterpart in New York, bridging differences between activists in the two cities. Black pastors and black churches played crucial roles in the functioning of the Vigilant Committee, both publicly and in its more clandestine work.[20]

Efforts to aid fugitives took both legal and extralegal forms. The protectors of fugitive slaves faced hostility from a significant portion of the white population but made no real secret of their existence or of their purpose, demonstrating that they also depended on white public opinion. Public fund-raising efforts exposed activists to violence from opponents. Even when the Vigilant Committee operated extralegally, it depended on state laws and sympathetic officials to undermine slave catchers' attempts to recover runaways.

The laws on which the Vigilant Committee depended were called into question by a legal case, *Prigg vs. Pennsylvania*. In 1832, Margaret Morgan, who had been living as a free woman in Maryland though her owner had not formally emancipated her, moved to Pennsylvania with her husband, who had freedom papers. In 1837, after the death of Morgan's owner, Margaret Ashmore claimed to have inherited title to Morgan and sent an agent, Edward Prigg to recover her. Prigg received warrants to recover runaways from the justice of the peace in York County, Pennsylvania, and seized Morgan and her children and returned with them to Maryland. A Pennsylvania grand jury subsequently indicted him for kidnapping under the 1826 law.[21]

The incident escalated into a conflict between Maryland and Pennsylvania laws about accused fugitives crossing the border. The governor of Pennsylvania requested that the governor of Maryland extradite the accused kidnappers. Maryland's governor refused, handing the issue over to the legislature, which passed resolutions declaring that the Pennsylvania kidnapping law was in conflict with the U.S. Constitution and sent representatives to the Pennsylvania legislature to address these concerns. Pennsylvania legislators refused to amend their law, but both sides agreed to present the case to the judiciary for resolution. In May 1840, the case reached the U.S. Supreme Court.[22]

On March 1, 1842, Justice Joseph Story delivered the Court's opinion declaring the Pennsylvania law unconstitutional because it interfered with the slaveholder's right to reclaim his property. Prigg could not, therefore, be prosecuted as a kidnapper. But Story's decision also opened up other legal avenues for the protection of fugitives. The right to reclaim a fugitive slave, Story reasoned, was a legal relationship between the slave owner and the federal government, but states could not be compelled to act. They could choose to pass laws to facilitate the return of fugitives, unless doing so was "prohibited by State legislation." Numerous northern states subsequently seized this loophole as a way to prevent masters from recovering fugitives.[23]

"No state magistrate, officer, or citizen in the Free States can be compelled to aid the recaption of a fugitive," noted the *Emancipator*. Though the decision had nationalized slavery, the paper pointed out, Chief Justice Roger B. Taney had dissented from the opinion because it did not compel the states to aid in the recovery of fugitive slaves. The *National Anti-Slavery Standard* also picked up on the decision's potential: "Already the Marylanders have had reason to chasten their exultation at the decision. . . . The Marylanders will find that the law is against them, let it decide as it will."[24]

Black Philadelphians remained intent on taking advantage of what they saw as the latent sympathy for limited black citizenship rights. When the Vigilant Committee reorganized itself in December 1843, it did so publicly, and the Pennsylvania Anti-Slavery Society continued to praise the committee, attributing to its work "a continuous procession of fugitives from southern injustice to the land of freedom."[25] The *Prigg* decision showed that black citizenship rights were often contested far from where those rights would be enjoyed, but Philadelphia's free blacks were determined to show that the fight for black citizenship would be decided on the ground as well.

Who Is an American?

For African Americans to secure citizenship rights, they increasingly needed to establish themselves as truly American even though most had been born in the United States and had never lived anywhere else. At the same time, white immigrants arriving in the United States faced challenges but quickly received citizenship rights that American-born free blacks were denied. Many of these white immigrants emphasized their supposed superiority to black people as a means of laying claim to American citizenship. African Americans and their allies saw the ease with which white immigrants were granted the rights of citizenship as the clearest illustration of the injustice of American racism, and white immigration became an important lens through which the struggle for black citizenship was understood.

By the late 1830s, the abolitionist critique of colonization, financial mismanagement, and the economic hardship that followed the Panic of 1837 had dealt a substantial blow to the American Colonization Society, but the colonization movement proved resilient. Increasingly, local and state societies in the North sought to operate independent of the national society, along the lines of the Maryland model. The American Colonization Society reorganized itself in 1838, dramatically stripping down the national organization and becoming a federation of state societies. Northern societies subsequently had more latitude to claim to be the real advocates of emancipation while continuing to cast abolitionists as fanatics and visionaries.[26]

In October 1838, Joseph Ingersoll, president of the Pennsylvania Colonization Society, addressed the group's annual meeting and positioned colonization as the middle ground between the defenders of slavery and radical abolitionists. Ingersoll was active in Whig politics, winning election to the U.S. House of Representatives in 1834. "American colonization neither proposes nor effects by any of its measures the continuance, or the immediate abolition of slavery," he insisted. "Of its ultimate consequences every one may judge, for it has no concealment or disguise in its movements or aims." Ingersoll denied that blacks were inherently inferior to whites but believed that race was a product of environmental conditions. However, according to Ingersoll, these conditions were nearly impossible to overcome: "How powerful must be the causes that give to identity the seeming and the effect of irreconcilable difference." To make sense of this difference, Ingersoll returned to a metaphor that colonizationists had used before, though with a new twist. White prejudice had made blacks "pilgrims and strangers here," and "the African population is colonized already; colonized in the heart of the land of their birth, in the centre of their earliest and only recollections."[27] By declaring that American prejudice already made African Americans aliens, Ingersoll countered black claims that birth on American soil entitled them to citizenship.

Ingersoll hammered home his point by pointing to white immigration: "We welcome to our shores yearly as many emigrants as would rapidly melt away a mass equal to the whole of our coloured population, and they too not aided, encouraged, urged." During this period, the United States (and especially the midAtlantic cities of Philadelphia and Baltimore) saw an unprecedented level of immigration, so it is not surprising that immigration came to shape Ingersoll's and others' understanding of attempts to spur emigration.[28] Seeing colonization as immigration in reverse performed substantial ideological work. On one hand, it was a crucial part of convincing the public that African colonization was feasible. Backers of the idea did not intend to pay for or coordinate the transportation of all of America's free blacks but merely sought to set in motion a process whereby blacks would ultimately remove themselves from the United States.

By comparing colonization to immigration, supporters also assured free blacks that leaving the United States was the same thing that white immigrants were doing of their own free will. Despite occasional threats of force, colonizationists generally still maintained the veneer that colonization was to be consensual. Colonizationists also hoped to quell black concerns about cultural differences between Africa and the United States. White European immigrants, Ingersoll suggested, rapidly integrated into American society. Similarly, in Africa, former chattels would easily transform "into makers and administrators of law."[29] Colonization could transform both Africa and the United States if the dynamics that pushed immigrants out of Europe and pulled them to the United States could be reversed.

Colonists used the immigration parallel to portray African colonization as natural and inevitable. This approach also helped to reframe race as the primary marker of American citizenship even as it ostensibly claimed that race was merely a product of environment. In a report presented at the 1838 annual meeting of the Maryland Colonization Society, the organization's president, John Latrobe, echoed Ingersoll in pointing to European immigration as a crucial model. The report took the position that free blacks would never be willing to emigrate to Africa until they saw that doing so was in their interests. The Colonization Society, therefore, needed to create a colony prosperous enough to draw Maryland's free blacks. Annual immigration from Europe, the report noted, was triple the annual growth of the free black population, and "these emigrants come here with their own means. . . . [T]hey come because it is more attractive to come to America than to stay at home. They come because they think it is in their interest to come." The report emphasized the society's promotion of the pull from the African end but also noted the significant push from the United States: in light of the powerful "inducements for the colored man to remove from America," "the tide of emigration from this country will set in that direction, even more strongly than the tide now sets from Europe to the United States."[30]

Despite such arguments, colonizationists in Baltimore and Philadelphia seem to have recognized that black opposition remained a serious obstacle. Stephen Gloucester had tried to gain access to the Philadelphia colonization meeting but was denied entrance. "They had an officer at the door," he informed the editor of the *Colored American*, "and said that the Society or Managers had said, no blacks could come in." This exclusion gave credence to black suspicions regarding the movement's underlying motivations.[31] Even if they hoped to win over free blacks, colonizationists were under no illusions regarding current opinion.

Opposition to African colonization remained an important part of black political discourse. Soon after the July 1838 publication of the Common Council of Philadelphia's report on the burning of Pennsylvania Hall, a Philadelphia correspondent wrote to the *Colored American* with a scathing account of the report, damning it as an affront to the U.S. Constitution and claiming that it was built on the lies of the colonization movement. The writer, "Censor," denounced the report as inconsistent with the rights of speech and assembly that the Constitution guaranteed to all citizens. The report even hinted that the invitation of "citizens from distant States" to speak at the hall had contributed to its destruction, though "Censor" noted that the Constitution also stated that "citizens of each State, shall be entitled to all the privileges and immunities of citizens in the several States."[32]

The correspondent cast colonizationists and the mob as innovators and abolitionists as the defenders of traditional constitutional liberties. The report's tacit defense of the rioters rested on the claim that abolitionists had promoted racial amalgamation, presenting a scene of interracial social intercourse not seen "since the days of William Penn." The mob was, according to the report, defending the traditional racial order. "Censor," in contrast, insisted that white fears about racial amalgamation were a product of colonization propaganda. "Black and white walking arm in arm," he maintained, "was *very common* in the city of Penn, until the colonization 'mad dog' cry of 'amalgamation,' admonished a peaceable people to discontinue the 'social intercourse.'"[33] Once again, the denial of black citizenship rights was depicted as a radical departure.

Black Philadelphians had often defended themselves by contrasting their sober, orderly actions with the drunken riots of their oppressors, but "Censor" took this rhetoric a step further. He denounced claims that the managers of Pennsylvania Hall had allowed "unpatriotic speeches" as "Jesuitical." Whereas abolitionists often were denounced for religious infidelity, this writer consciously chose to claim the banner of religious orthodoxy. He later made the religious contrast into a political one:

> The managers of "Pennsylvania Hall," as citizens, had as undoubted a right to erect a building and dedicate it to "free discussion," as Deists and free thinkers have, who are protected in their orgies in "Tammany Hall," and to expect *that* protection from the civil authorities that the laws of the land have guaranteed to them.[34]

This account contrasted the actions of the abolitionists, virtuous and patriotic, with the quintessential symbol of Democratic partisanship.

Some historians have depicted the mid-nineteenth century as the pinnacle of American party politics, yet amid this partisanship, many Americans continued to express devotion to an antipartisan (though not nonpartisan) ideal . While many reform movements of this era claimed the antipartisan mantle, political parties (often though not always third parties) also proclaimed themselves opponents of partisanship. The Whig Party in particular appealed to voters on antipartisan grounds. This phenomenon had deep roots in American political history. As David Waldstreicher notes, nationalism allowed partisans to portray themselves as antipartisan "if one identified one's own party, not as a party, but as the real nation."³⁵

Such partisan antipartisanship could serve as a potent argument for black citizenship rights. "Censor" linked the rioters and their defenders both to Deists and to Jesuits, religious outsiders who nevertheless were protected by the American Constitution. Tying them together under the partisan banner of the Democratic Party allows "Censor" to depict himself and black abolitionists in general as antipartisan and therefore as the true representatives of the nation—as ideal citizens.

Whipper offered his take on antipartisan partisanship in his account of the 1838 Pennsylvania election. Writing in the *National Reformer*, he lamented that the parties were trying to outdo each other in depicting their candidates as the defenders of slavery and asserted that had blacks been allowed to vote, "the disfranchised voters could have re-elected our patriotic governor," Ritner. In Whipper's view, although both parties were corrupted by a desire to appeal to the Slave Power, a politician—even one nominated by one of those parties—could stand above partisanship. Partisanship and subservience to slavery went hand in hand, but patriotism enabled even a party politician to resist "southern thralldom."³⁶

While African Americans struggled to depict themselves as virtuous American citizens, some abolitionists hoped that another group of American citizens, Irish immigrants, might be enlisted in the fight against slavery and in support of black citizenship. In 1840, American abolitionists had recruited Irish political leader Daniel O'Connell to appeal to his countrymen in the United States to support the abolition movement. O'Connell and more than sixty thousand other residents of Ireland signed "An Address of the People of Ireland to their Countrymen and Countrywomen in America." Black abolitionist Charles Lenox Remond brought the document to the United States in December 1841, and the Pennsylvania Abolition Society printed and distributed copies.³⁷

The address emphasized the connections between Irish immigrants in the United States and their native land in hopes that solidarity would convince them to oppose slavery and embrace the cause of black citizenship, urging, "Irishmen and Irishwomen! *Treat the colored people as your equals, as brethren.*"³⁸

The address did not have the desired effect and in fact provoked forceful expressions of Irish American hostility to abolition. The editor of the Democratic *Philadelphia Pennsylvanian* called for an investigation into the veracity of the address and reprinted a memorial from a meeting of Irishmen in Pottstown, Pennsylvania, that called the piece "a hoax." The memorialists insisted that the

Irish in America should be addressed only as "citizens" and not as "a distinct class." A Baltimore gathering termed the O'Connell address "a fraud" and denounced it as "a fire-brand thrown between Irishmen and their native fellow citizens." While many Irish Americans harbored strong feelings for their native land, they also bristled at the assertion that they were anything but fully American and used the occasion vigorously to reassert their allegiance to the United States and to denounce abolition as a monarchical English plot.[39]

Irish immigrants faced questions about their loyalty to their adopted country and had long embraced their whiteness as an argument for their Americanness. Conflict between Irish immigrants and free blacks in Philadelphia, Baltimore, and other cities can to some extent be traced to competition for the low-wage jobs on which both groups depended. Just as important, however, by embracing American racial hierarchies and differentiating themselves from African Americans, Irish immigrants asserted their right to be considered American citizens.[40]

African Americans certainly resented Irish immigrants' invocation of their whiteness in support of their citizenship claims and objected to efforts to use race as a means of building a national political coalition in support of slaveholders' rights. However, free blacks were equally distressed by the frequency with which Irish immigrants joined in the brutal antiblack riots of this period (which is not to say that most white immigrants joined in such mob actions or that antiblack mobs were predominantly Irish). In part, Irish American participation in riots resulted simply from proximity. In Philadelphia as in many antebellum cities, Irish immigrants and free blacks lived in the same neighborhoods, especially the burgeoning districts along the edges of the city proper. Yet proximity and economic competition offer only a partial explanation for Irish involvement in mob violence against blacks. Many antiblack mobs targeted evidence of black economic success and symbols of black refinement and cultivation. In this sense they expressed the fears of poor whites, immigrant and native alike, that whiteness might not guarantee superiority over their black neighbors.[41]

Just as Irish Americans were most vigorously expressing that supposed superiority, James Forten, who posed a formidable and highly visible challenge to this notion, died on March 4, 1842. A crowd estimated at between three and five thousand—roughly half of them white—attended Forten's funeral, held at the African Episcopal Church of St. Thomas. Forten's life had been a rebuke to notions that even the least respectable whites were more deserving of respect than any black person. The public addresses honoring Forten's life challenged Irish American efforts to use their assumed superiority to free blacks as an argument for American citizenship.

Robert Purvis, Forten's son-in-law, delivered his remarks in Mother Bethel Church and emphasized Forten's devotion to the United States. He took as a crucial contribution of Forten's life his leadership in opposing African colonization. Relating Forten's experiences as a prisoner of war during the American Revolution, Purvis highlighted Forten's refusal to accept an offer of transportation to England, quoting him as saying, "I am here a prisoner for the liberties of my country. I *never*, NEVER, *shall prove a traitor to her interests.*" For Purvis, this decision foreshadowed Forten's lifelong commitment to securing his American birthright.[42]

Purvis also pointed to the interracial mourners at Forten's funeral as evidence that "he was a *model*, not as some flippant scribbler asserts, for what is called 'colored men,' but for all men." He continued, "The course pursued by Mr. Garrison he ever thought conformable to the true anti-slavery principles" and emphasized Forten's desire to aid all those in need, "not bestowing nor graduating his gifts by the mere color of his skin."[43]

Stephen Gloucester's address, delivered after Purvis's, placed greater emphasis on Forten's character and piety. Gloucester was speaking in his own church and specifically linked elements of Forten's virtuous personality to early Americans such as Benjamin Franklin and George Washington. Gloucester also highlighted Forten's rejection of colonization and in general his patriotism, yet the pastor was most concerned with Forten as an exemplar of Christian virtue. Gloucester also stressed Forten's service to his home church, the African Episcopal Church of St. Thomas. Not only was Forten a generous patron to his and other churches, but "his attendance at church was regular," and "his seat was not vacant." In keeping with Gloucester's viewpoint, he painted Forten as seeing the church as the locus of black activism. Gloucester also recalled that Forten's last public address was on the subject of "union among ourselves as a people." He thus enlisted Forten among the supporters of black unity yet centered that unity in black congregations within white-controlled denominations.[44]

Both addresses would have inflamed those who resented black success and who hoped to use alleged black degradation as an argument for white solidarity. Both ministers pointed to Forten as the embodiment of black claims to American citizenship, with Purvis depicting Forten as rejecting complexional distinctions, as Purvis did, while Gloucester emphasized Forten's call for racial unity. Both celebrated his virtues and his prosperity and set him up as worthy of admiration by blacks as well as whites. Both addresses celebrated Forten's temperance, though Gloucester placed greater emphasis on it.

A few months later, many white Philadelphians were even more disturbed by a much larger demonstration of black respectability. On August 1, members of the Moyamensing Temperance Society gathered for a procession in honor of the anniversary of West Indian emancipation. Most of the participants were black reformed alcoholics, and the parade route was carefully chosen to pass by a large "proportion of objects needing a temperance reformation," including many Irish-owned liquor dealers. The group proceeded peacefully until it reached Fifth and Shippen (now Bainbridge) Streets, where conflict erupted. According to one report, a white bystander attempted to obstruct the procession and was then pushed aside by one of the black participants. Widespread riot soon erupted, with whites in the mob turning their attention to houses occupied by blacks. Fighting continued for much of the day, though police eventually quieted the disturbance. That night, a large group of citizens met in Independence Square to discuss how to restore peace, but many Philadelphians feared that more rioting would break out.[45]

Shortly before nine o'clock, the recently completed Smith's Beneficial Hall, paid for by black activist and businessman Stephen Smith, erupted in flames. Soon thereafter, Gloucester's Second Colored Presbyterian Church was on fire as well. Firefighters did little to extinguish the flames but focused on preventing them from spreading to additional buildings.[46]

The next day, the fighting resumed, taking on what one observer described as "a more threatening character." The rioters on the second day were "almost to a man, strong, hardy-looking men and were, almost without exception Irishmen." One group of rioters threatened Purvis until a Catholic priest intervened. Scattered violence continued around the city throughout the day, threatening "the destruction of every church, hall, and public edifice belonging to the blacks." The military finally restored order, but the final insult to black Philadelphians came on August 3, when a grand jury declared that a black temperance hall that had survived the riot was a public nuisance. To prevent arsonists from targeting the hall and threatening neighboring buildings, jurors ordered the hall torn down.[47]

Black Philadelphians found the riots shocking and tried to make sense of events. Purvis, Gardner and Payne wrote to various Philadelphia newspapers (including some that did not support abolition) offering their explanations for the riot. They noted that the temperance march had no connection to white abolitionists and blamed the violence on opponents of temperance (especially tavern keepers) who had suffered as a consequence of the reformation of former drunkards. They dismissed the suggestion that the riot had been sparked by certain inflammatory banners carried by members of the procession.[48]

One banner in particular had been singled out as evidence that the black marchers had incited the riot. According to rumors, this banner featured the words "Liberty or Death," alluding to the revolution in Saint-Domingue and depicted slaves massacring their owners. Though these accounts exaggerated the banner's images, it was provocative in its own way. It featured the image of a black man with one hand pointing toward a broken chain and the other pointing toward the word *Liberty* above his head. The background showed a sinking slave ship and a rising sun. The back of the banner bore the words, "The young Men's Vigilant Association of Philadelphia, 'How grand in age, how fair in youth, are holy friendship, love and truth,' instituted July 23d, 1841."[49]

The banner represented the confluence of various streams of black activism, graphically illustrating why many of the white rioters saw that activism as such a threat. The banner's creators intended to show that temperance was not simply a way of helping free blacks but part of a coordinated fight against slavery and in support of black citizenship rights. Anyone who missed the visual metaphor on the front could not have overlooked the inscription on the back, since it connected the Vigilant Committee with temperance reform and British antislavery. Whether or not the creators deliberately sought to bring out the hostility of Irish anti-abolitionists, they could hardly have picked a design that would have caused whites more distress.

Purvis was shocked by these events, writing to Henry Clarke Wright, "I know not where I should begin, nor how, or when, to end in a detail of the wantonness, brutality and murderous spirit of the Actors, in the late riots." But he aimed his most bitter words at those who had abetted the rioters: "Press, Church, Magistrates, Clergymen and Devils are against us. . . . I am sick—miserably sick—everything around me is as dark as the grave." Purvis was so disheartened by what he perceived as Philadelphia's apathy that he moved his family out of the city.[50] He did not, however, turn his back on the activism that tied him to black Philadelphia, and he remained a vigorous defender of the fugitive slave.

Yet withdrawal was not the only option for black Philadelphians in the wake of the riot; if there was reason to despair, there was also reason to hope. Despite Purvis's lament, the city's newspapers expressed considerable sympathy for the plight of free blacks, though some Democratic publications argued that African Americans had brought the situation on themselves. The *Philadelphia Pennsylvanian* lamented the riot as a tragedy but placed much the blame for it on blacks, calling for laws "to prevent their assembling in a way likely to bring about collisions." In contrast, the *Public Ledger*, a penny daily, denounced the decision to tear down the temperance hall as a concession to "mob law."[51] This outrage offered free blacks a crucial opportunity to cultivate sympathy from white Philadelphians, but capitalizing on that opportunity required depicting the riot not as a focused assault on abolition or on free blacks but rather as a violation of property and of respectable members of the community.

Gloucester and the trustees of the Second Colored Presbyterian Church sought to portray the riot in this way. Gloucester sent a letter to the *Public Ledger* in which he outlined the church's history, stressing not only its moral and religious respectability but also its financial independence and rectitude: "In a moment," according to Gloucester, "the result of eighteen years of anxiety and labor, and to secure which has cost near 10,000 dollars, has become a heap of ruins." The minister expected that most Philadelphians (including some of the rioters) would sympathize with him and his congregation if he explained their true nature.[52] Where Purvis despaired, Gloucester saw reason for optimism.

Yet in seeking to appeal to a broader public, Gloucester and the trustees of Second Presbyterian significantly downplayed the church's involvement in the antislavery movement. They insisted that the church had nothing to do with the procession that sparked the riot and declared that "on no occasion has our house been used for the discussion of any of those topics which are so exciting at the present time." This vague language overlooked Second Presbyterian's long history of black activism. Gloucester had chosen a different approach for his activism. At the same time that his church came under attack, he was lecturing on temperance, but he was doing so at a church in Wilmington, Delaware. Many Philadelphians had chosen to celebrate West Indian independence not with a public procession but with sober, reverent church services, as Gloucester and other black leaders pointed out: he had urged his congregants to attend a worship service at Bethel that morning. Moreover, for at least the better part of a decade, some black leaders had counseled against public processions on the grounds that they were counterproductive.[53]

Implicit in Gloucester's letter was an attempt to position his black congregation as a part of a larger coalition in a cultural conflict. The members of the Second Presbyterian Church were on the side of sobriety, order, and religion not simply on the side of African Americans or abolition. The *Emancipator* reprinted his letter alongside one by a white pastor and former resident of Philadelphia, who made this contrast explicit. The Reverend Lucius Matlock blamed the riot on the owners of "groggeries" who had suffered financially as a consequence of black temperance work. Matlock went on to contrast the character of the rioters with that of Philadelphia's free blacks: "These degraded whites, most of them low foreigners, could not endure that the black population should rise above them and therefore conspired to trample them into the dust." "The white laborers, especially the Irish," had "resolved on rooting . . . out" respectable African Americans. Matlock hoped that placing the riot in the context of a larger cultural conflict would help enlist more of the white population in the cause of free blacks. "Will not the friends of temperance, of religion, of moral virtue," he asked, "weigh those things and afford their countenance to their colored fellow-citizens in this day of their calamity?"[54]

Even without such nativist pronouncements by white supporters of black citizenship, many Irish Americans would have seen celebrations of black respectability as a threat. Irish immigrants had long composed a significant portion of Philadelphia's population, and tension between native Protestants and

Irish Catholics had been a consistent undercurrent in city politics. With the increased immigration of the 1840s, however, these conflicts rose to unprecedented heights. Many Irish-born Philadelphians felt that their liberties were under assault.[55]

Of the many ways in which the Protestant majority sought to assert its control over Philadelphia's public culture, among the most upsetting to Catholics was the teaching of Protestant theology in public schools. The central symbol of this practice was the use of the King James Bible as a textbook. In the early 1840s, Catholic Bishop Joseph Kenrick chose to make a stand on this issue, arguing that Catholic students should not be required to read from a version of the Bible of which they did not approve. Many Protestants, in turn, took this insistence as evidence that Catholics were seeking control of the city's schools to keep the light of knowledge and of true religion from Catholic schoolchildren. The Bible issue became a rallying point for nativist and anti-Catholic Philadelphians, and by 1844, nearly all of the city's wards had "native American" associations.[56]

These tensions erupted into violence in May 1844. On April 27, Irish threats forced the postponement of a planned nativist meeting in a private residence. Nativists responded by planning a public meeting in the middle of a heavily Irish neighborhood in Kensington. At first, Irish protesters sought to shout down their native opponents, but the nativists eventually were driven from the stage they had erected, and the crowd dismantled it. A few days later, the nativists returned to the site with a crowd ten times that of the first meeting. Gunfire broke out, and violence persisted for several days. When the dust settled, two Catholic churches and numerous Irish residences lay in smoldering ruins.[57]

Many white observers perceived the riots of 1844 in the context of the antiblack violence of two years earlier. A nineteen-verse song published in 1844 summed up white Philadelphians' attitudes:

> Oh in Philadelphia, folks say how
> Dat Darkies kick up all de rows,
> But de riot up in S'kensin'ton,
> Beats all the darkies twelve to one.
> > An' I guess it wasn't de niggas dis time, etc.
>
> ....
>
> Oh de peaceful Natives go away
> An meet up dar anudder day,
> Den de Irish get *half shot* all round,
> An den de shoot de Natives down.
> > An' I guess it wasn't de niggas dis time, etc.
>
> ....

>   Den for church burners soon de mayor
>   Offered a reward quite rare,
>   But to catch dem dat killed freedoms sons
>   De state couldn't find no laws nor funds.
>   Oh I guess it wan't so in old times, etc.
>   But decent folks am quiet now,
>   Still newspapers keep up a row.
>   De spin long lies about de riot,
>   Because they're makin' money by it.
>   Howebber 'taint de niggas dis time, etc.⁵⁸

The lyrics display obvious sympathy for the nativists, blaming the violence primarily on the drunken Irish but indicting politicians and newspaper publishers as well. Though the stereotyped dialect clearly demonstrates the composer's patronizing impression of black Philadelphians and asserts a certain distance, it also enlists black voices on the side of the nativists.

Using black Philadelphians as a way to denigrate Irish immigrants did not necessarily equate to advocacy of black citizenship, but some abolitionists made this connection. The Pennsylvania Anti-Slavery Society had tended to echo the Garrisonian line, for the most part condemning American churches for their pro-slavery sympathies. The society's 1844 annual report, however, significantly shifted its portrayal of the conflict between native Protestants and immigrant Irish Catholics. The report noted that a significant number of Protestant denominations had taken firmer stands against slavery and celebrated the fact that the past year had brought no new mob violence against black Philadelphians or the abolition movement. The report did, however, comment on the nativist riots of the same year:

> The authors, abettors and palliators of the horrible crimes of 1842 ... the city which looked on with indifference or complacency, and the official authorities who winked at or actually aided in the work of the mob—have begun to see those effects of their folly and wickedness, which we from the first foretold, and to learn by bitter experience how vain is the hope to escape the penalty of that divine law which dooms the transgressor to eat the fruit of his own doings, and be filled with his own devices.⁵⁹

Pennsylvania abolitionists by no means embraced nativist political stances but did recognize some common ground between the two movements or at least the rhetorical value of making such connections.

Nativists' success in parlaying anti-immigrant and anti-Catholic fervor into political success also had implications for antislavery politics. By the time of the Pennsylvania Anti-Slavery Society's 1844 annual meeting, divisions over political questions threatened to rip the organization apart. Delegates rejected a resolution to divide along political lines, and the organization called for members to avoid being drawn into the coming presidential election. At the same time, participants expressed surprising optimism regarding the course of American politics. They credited antislavery's growing influence with causing Whig politicians to oppose the annexation of Texas as well as causing Democrats to seek to make annexation a nonparty issue.[60] While antislavery Pennsylvanians continued to show little interest in the Liberty Party, many of them saw some promise in the two main parties.

Philadelphia Whigs certainly hoped that antislavery voters would remain loyal to the Whig Party. Whig politicians did not explicitly embrace antislavery (a difficult position with Henry Clay at the top of the ticket) but nevertheless wooed antislavery voters with hints that Whigs were the true foes of the Slave Power. They repeatedly denounced Liberty Party presidential candidate James G. Birney as a "locofoco," implying that his true aim was to serve the Democratic Party. They also brought Cassius Clay, an anti-slavery Whig from Kentucky, to Philadelphia to speak on the Whig Party and slavery. Though the Whigs lost both the gubernatorial and presidential elections by slim margins, their efforts helped to prevent the Liberty candidates from winning even 1 percent of the vote.[61]

The Liberty Party's failure in Pennsylvania resulted in part from the continuing salience of other issues as well as from the fact that the two major parties presented a clear contrast on the issues relating to slavery. The Liberty Party made many of its greatest gains in places where the Whig Party had declined significantly. Antislavery Whigs voted for the Liberty Party when Whigs had little chance of winning. In Pennsylvania, however, Whigs remained competitive well into the 1850s, and as historian Leonard L. Richards has argued, Pennsylvania Democrats became some of the most reliable northern defenders of slavery in the 1840s.[62] Antislavery Whigs in Pennsylvania, therefore, saw a significant difference between the two major parties and saw a real possibility of electing Whig candidates.

Unlike the Liberty Party, the newly organized Native American Party made a stunning debut in Pennsylvania, winning two of Philadelphia's three congressional seats and finishing a close second in the city's mayoral election. Nativists did not run a gubernatorial candidate and seem to have voted for the Whig candidate by about a four-to-one margin. The Nativist Party clearly had done what the Liberty Party had not: won over a significant number of Whigs.[63]

Nativists were not abolitionists and some proved themselves opponents of the antislavery cause. But their electoral success and the significant connections between antislavery voters and nativist voters meant that anyone hoping to promote antislavery politics in Philadelphia needed to pay attention to the nativist vote. In addition, for those who saw the Democratic Party as the face of slavery's political power, the frequency with which Irish immigrants voted for Democrats created a natural sympathy between antislavery and nativism. Nativists, in turn, at times backed political abolition. The *National Era*, a political antislavery paper, noted in 1847 that the *Daily Sun*, a Philadelphia nativist publication, "often contains sound anti-slavery articles."[64]

Nativist language provided a way for free blacks to accentuate the injustice of their unequal status. Though Purvis had moved his family out of Philadelphia, he could not escape white prejudice. Some members of the Bensalem Horse Company invited him to join the group, but other members moved to have him expelled after learning that the light-skinned Purvis had "African blood." The *Pennsylvania Freeman* noted the irony that the "prime mover" behind Purvis's expulsion was "a certain Dutchman whose deep mulatto complexion ... would cause him very likely to be taken for one of African blood sooner than" Purvis. Martin Delany's *Pittsburgh Mystery* reprinted this account, using the contrast with the "Dutchman" to emphasize Purvis's elevation: "That Dutchman should have considered it a privilege to belong to a company of which Robert Purvis was a member."[65]

Free blacks had long used such comparisons to illustrate the injustice of their treatment in their native land. The rise of white nativism only made such comparisons more salient. Purvis became interested in breeding livestock and wrote a piece for a local paper about the desirability of emphasizing local rather than imported animals: "Ought we not to make more account of our native breeds, and seek by judicious crossing and care in all other respects, to attain the end we have not yet reached in the matter of stock raising?" In light of the virtues of the fruit native to his region, he asked, "Why can't we therefore, on the same principle, raise native cattle of corresponding excellence?" Purvis's biographer suggests that he intended his comments to apply not just to cattle but also to native-born Americans.[66] Such comparisons held profound meaning to free blacks struggling to assert their right to be seen as American citizens.

In the early 1840s, free blacks in Baltimore and Philadelphia found even their limited citizenship rights threatened. The fight to maintain these limited rights or even to expand them took place at all levels of government. At the same time, they were engaged in a more theoretical struggle to establish themselves as truly American. Some free blacks hoped that the growing white immigrant population could be enlisted in the abolitionist cause, but when this failed, the immigrants' legal and political status became a key element in the case for black citizenship. That struggle became entangled in the region's complex ethnic, racial, and class politics.

PART IV

The Fugitive Slave Law and the Coming of the Civil War

CHAPTER 7

The Tumultuous Politics of the Early 1850s

On the evening of October 14, 1850, a group of black Philadelphians met in Brick Wesley Church, on Lombard Street below Sixth, to attack the recently adopted Fugitive Slave Law. A friendly account in the *North Star* described it as "the recent large Meeting of the colored citizens of Philadelphia"; an openly hostile notice in the *Baltimore Sun* termed it "very largely attended," adding that "several of the colored orators have made flaming speeches against" the law.[1] Organizers intended not merely to rally black opposition to the law but also to make a larger case to the white public.

The resolutions passed by the meeting attempted to place resistance to the Fugitive Slave Law squarely in the tradition of the American Revolution. The law violated both the Declaration's guarantees of "inalienable rights" and the Constitution's provisions for protecting those rights. In particular, according to the resolution, the law conflicted with the Constitution's provision regarding habeas corpus and its provision that "no person shall be deprived of life, liberty, or property without due process of law." Further stressing the analogy between their struggle and that of the Founders, the authors closed the preamble to the resolutions by declaring, "We hereby pledge our lives, our fortunes, and our sacred honor" to resisting the Fugitive Slave Law. The resolutions attacked the measure by appealing to law and morality as well as by painting opposition as defending the family against efforts to tear it apart. One resolution pointed to the hypocrisy of white northerners who applauded and welcomed the refugees from foreign tyranny but spurned people fleeing from domestic tyrants.[2]

The Fugitive Slave Law led some African Americans to despair. It offered evidence that whites would ultimately sacrifice the citizenship rights of free blacks to appease slaveholders, and it spurred many, especially fugitives, to leave the United States.[3] Among those who remained, particularly along the mid-Atlantic border, the law provoked active resistance and an increasing willingness to resort to violence in defending themselves and the targets of slave catchers.[4]

At the same time, the broader response to the law illustrated the continuing importance of the struggle for black citizenship. The law demonstrated not only the Slave Power's political influence but also the limits of slaveholders' ability to control free blacks. Many whites who were willing to abandon some legal protections for free blacks in the interest of easing sectional tensions refused to deny blacks all citizenship rights or to abandon the free black residents of their state to the control of slaveholders.[5] As tepid as this white support may have been, free blacks recognized that cultivating this support was critical. It was delicate work, and many free blacks, especially those in the borderland cities of Philadelphia and Baltimore, engaged in a cautious sort of activism that frustrated some of their allies. Cautious or not, the fight for black citizenship and the limited legal recognition won by that fight helped to make the mid-Atlantic borderlands into a site of intense conflict in the growing national struggle over slavery.

Practical Abolition on the Border

In the late 1840s, African Americans and their allies laid the groundwork for what ultimately became the fierce resistance to the Fugitive Slave Law of 1850. In part, this foundation was legal: black Pennsylvanians worked to ensure that they received legal protection from the state. But African Americans on both sides of the border also labored to establish themselves as citizens, cultivating the sympathy of sometimes ambivalent white allies.

Tensions regarding fugitive slave recovery had long been building, but the passage of the key legal basis for protecting black Pennsylvanians was almost anticlimactic. In February 1847, the Whig majority in the Pennsylvania legislature passed a new antikidnapping bill with very little debate and very little controversy, and Democratic governor Francis R. Shunk signed it into law. At the beginning of February, the Eastern Pennsylvania Anti-Slavery Society, with Robert Purvis as president, had appointed agents to go to Harrisburg to help push the House bill through the Senate. It quickly became clear that the bill would have little trouble passing the Senate, and the agents never left Philadelphia.[6]

This law was one of the new batch of "personal liberty laws" passed in the wake of the *Prigg* decision. It took full advantage of Justice Joseph Story's contention that states could not be compelled to support efforts to reclaim fugitives. In addition to providing penalties for attempting to enslave free citizens, the law prohibited the state government from aiding slave catchers. The courts would not have jurisdiction in such cases, persons claimed as fugitives could not be jailed. Masters had a right, as guaranteed by the Constitution, to reclaim their property, but they had to do so without "illegal violence." Finally, the law repealed an earlier provision that had allowed masters to bring slaves into the state for six months. Unsurprisingly, the antislavery press lauded the bill, but Whig papers also bestowed lavish praise: "Slavery in Pennsylvania has received its deathblow," declared the *Philadelphia North American*. The Pennsylvania Liberty Party passed a resolution praising "the last Legislature of Pennsylvania ... for passing the bill to prevent kidnapping, and to abolish all vestiges of slavery in the State," though the legislature contained no party members.[7]

Though all black Philadelphians could celebrate the political success of antislavery in their state and the strengthening of black citizenship rights, significant disagreement existed over tactics. In early 1847, Stephen Gloucester had traveled to Britain, primarily to raise money to pay for a new church building but also to promote his approach to fighting slavery in the United States. At a May meeting of the British and Foreign Anti-Slavery Society, he declared, "It is time for every man, who respects either humanity or religion, to concentrate his energy for [slavery's] entire destruction." Yet he also suggested that these efforts should proceed "peaceably and quietly," avoiding specifics but noting that "kind language has always accomplished the most good."[8] Gloucester's comments represented veiled criticisms of the Garrisonian approach to abolition, especially its violent denunciations of American churches.

The destruction of Gloucester's church offered only the most vivid evidence that black rights were precarious in Philadelphia and the cultivation of white allies was therefore vital. Among the places where Gloucester appealed for funds were congregations of the Free Church of Scotland. In 1843, Thomas Chalmers had led about one-third of his fellow Presbyterian clergymen out of the established Church of Scotland into a new denomination. Without state support, the Free Church depended on congregants' voluntary weekly offerings, and to place the church on firmer financial footing, Chalmers had sought support from American congregations. Much of that support had come from congregations in the South, especially South Carolina. Chalmers denounced slavery as "a great evil" and "inimical to Christianity" but refused to cut off slaveholding Presbyterians despite calling on antislavery churchmen to "bring direct influence to bear on the American legislature." Garrisonian abolitionists (as well as many British abolitionists) denounced this position, just as they denounced American churches for compromising with slavery. Frederick Douglass had visited Great Britain during 1845 and 1846 and had campaigned vigorously against the Free Church for its acceptance of slaveholder money.[9]

Many American abolitionists, including some from his native city, criticized Gloucester, with the *Pennsylvania Freeman* labeling him "the Betrayer of the Cause of his Enslaved Fellow Men." Abolitionist Henry C. Wright declared that Gloucester had not only accepted the tainted funds of the Free Church but had used the opportunity to denounce American abolitionists by name. Wright insisted that Gloucester had "repudiate[d] American abolitionism" and declared his sympathy for American slaveholders by stating, "A man may be a slaveholder innocently." This account of Gloucester's speech was contradicted by at least one person in the audience, but many American abolitionists were outraged by the seeming betrayal of the antislavery cause. A group of black Philadelphians protested at a Masonic hall in September, declaring that Gloucester was "not a fair representative of the colored people of the city and county of Philadelphia."[10]

Many abolitionists, among them Douglass, denounced Gloucester when he returned to the United States in early 1848, but he insisted that he had not abandoned the fight against slavery. In 1848, black abolitionist speakers William Wells Brown and Charles Remond joined Robert Purvis in addressing a large audience regarding the black church's failure adequately to embrace the fight against slavery. The meeting was held at the Philadelphia Institute after several of the city's large churches had declined to host it. After the main speakers had finished, they invited to the stage anyone who wished to defend the church's actions. Daniel Scott, a pastor of the Union Baptist Church, rose and began speaking. Remond evidently heard Gloucester voicing his approval of Scott's words and invited Gloucester to the platform. Gloucester declined the invitation to speak but agreed to debate Remond at a future date, when he would "prove that the churches of Philadelphia were anti-slavery."[11]

The two met four days later at the Little Wesley Church, where each was allotted twenty minutes to speak. Gloucester used his time to defend the antislavery character of his church as well as other black congregations. James J. G. Bias, who disagreed with Gloucester's position, granted that he "did as well as men generally do when contending against the right." Remond then attempted to refute Gloucester's claims, and the audience voted Remond the victor, though Gloucester also received significant support.[12] Though much of the black community of Philadelphia rejected Gloucester's tactics as a compromise with slavery, his approach also received considerable backing.

Many black abolitionists found this seeming caution a distressing sign of malaise among the city's leadership. In October 1848, Douglass visited Philadelphia, in part to raise support for his journal, the *North Star*. To his dismay, he found many of the city's churches closed to him: "The churches most hostile to the Anti-Slavery movement, and bitterly opposed to opening their doors," wrote Douglass, "are Stephen Gloucester's, St. Thomas's, and Large Bethel." Douglass singled out Gloucester as "a viper" and contended that he and other church leaders were thwarting the will of their congregants who were genuine enemies of slavery.[13]

Douglass's supporters responded by organizing a three day antislavery convention at the Brick Wesley Church, hailing it as "the commencement of better days" for Philadelphia's antislavery movement. The convention, Douglass noted, was filled to overflowing by a crowd that included not just supporters of his approach to antislavery but also its critics. In particular, Isaiah Wears and John C. Bowers disagreed with the convention's attitude toward the black church: "It sounded rather strange, however, to have colored men preferring the old mad-dog charge of Infidelity, Anti-Sabbath, Anti-Church, Anti-Ministry, &c., against the abolitionists," lamented Douglass. "These stale charges, caught from the lips of their evangelical oppressors, were blown into our ears by a Mr. Wears and Bowers, with all the enthusiasm of newly discovered truth."[14]

Wears and Bowers defended their somewhat more cautious brand of antislavery. On one hand, these stalwarts of the black antislavery movement were supporting their own congregations. Wears was a member of Mother Bethel, and Bowers was a member of the African Episcopal Church of St. Thomas, both of which Douglass had criticized. However, they also challenged the whole tenor of the convention. Douglass may have dismissed Wears and Bowers as the unfortunate "echo" of "the stale slang of slaveholders," but they spoke for many black Philadelphians who were active in the fight against slavery but disagreed with Douglass's attitude toward the black church.[15]

Despite Douglass's criticism, Wears, Bowers, and other black Philadelphians remained committed to the fight against slavery and the struggle for black citizenship rights. Two months later, those two men found themselves in Harrisburg, where Wears served as vice president and Bowers as recording secretary at a conference calling for black enfranchisement. Black Philadelphians had positioned themselves as potentially virtuous voters who could help to bring order to an unruly political system. "Now that the 'noise and confusion,' incident to an electioneering campaign, is subsiding," wrote one black Philadelphian, "permit me to call your attention to another, and to at least a portion of the community, a much more important matter, than that of a partisan election, because the principle involved should have precedence."[16]

The convention drafted "An Appeal to the Voters of the Commonwealth of Pennsylvania" and "An Appeal to the Colored Citizens of Pennsylvania." The first made the case for black voting by appealing to American institutions. It nodded to the "soul stirring appeals in behalf of republicanism in foreign lands" as a means of channeling Americans' zeal for republican revolutions in Europe into the cause of black suffrage. Yet as had long been the case in black political rhetoric, comparisons to foreign events needed to be balanced by assertions of blacks' Americanness: "We make no foreign issue with you—we place ourselves on your own declaration of rights and principles. On these hang our future hope, and with them we will stand or fall." The appeal to black citizens made this point even more directly: "If we are asked what evidence we bring to sustain our qualifications for citizenship, we will offer them certificates of our BIRTH and NATIVITY."[17]

While some black Philadelphians pressed for an end to Pennsylvania's voting restrictions, others, including those whom Douglass had dismissed as insufficiently committed to the antislavery cause, continued to work to advance black citizenship rights within the major Protestant denominations. In the spring of 1843, William Douglass, the pastor at St. Thomas, renewed his congregation's petition to participate in the state convention of the Protestant Episcopal Church. A 1795 rule had declared that St. Thomas could not send a delegate to the convention, and Douglass's petition prompted the church not only to reaffirm the rule but also to broaden it to include any church "in like peculiar circumstances," citing "the color and other physical properties of the parties, their political and social condition—and their consequent unfitness, from all of these causes, for the situation of legislators and rulers in the church planted in Pennsylvania." The church's report also suggested that agitation by the "colored race" might well produce political and denominational turmoil.[18]

A minority report by the committee that rejected William Douglass's petition disputed these assertions and defended African Americans' right to be full citizens within the church. It applauded the congregation's improvements in such areas as "literary qualifications": though such deficiencies would previously have prevented St. Thomas from participating in the convention's decisions, this was no longer the case. The report also denied that allowing black congregations a voice in the convention would produce turmoil. Perhaps most importantly, it reminded the convention that "God has made of one blood all nations of men." The convention as a whole voted to accept the majority report, though the representatives of St. Thomas may have been encouraged that the clergy supported the report only by a forty-four to forty-two margin, although the laity vote, fifty-one to sixteen, was much more lopsided.[19]

Black Baltimoreans also devoted themselves to religious organizing. On October 13, 1849, black clergymen and lay delegates gathered for the first Maryland State Convention of the Colored Protestant Methodist Churches, chaired by Nathaniel Peck, the pastor of Israel Colored Protestant Methodist Church, which had recently seceded from the African Methodist Episcopal Church. Organizers intended the meeting to organize the different black Protestant Methodist churches and to "unite in one inseparable interest all the colored Protestant Methodist churches in the United States." To that end, the meeting called for a national convention, to be held in Philadelphia the following summer. These Baltimore men saw themselves as leaders of a national black-controlled organization but recognized that any such organization needed to have strong roots in Philadelphia. They also saw their organization as extending beyond strictly doctrinal boundaries, with black Presbyterians, Zion Methodists, and even Quakers included as corresponding members. Organizers' larger ambitions were reflected by their decision to print their proceedings not only in the *Baltimore Sun* but also in the *North Star*, the *National Anti-Slavery Standard*, and the *Pennsylvania Freeman*.[20]

While black Philadelphians continued their struggle for citizenship rights by a variety of means, some outsiders viewed their efforts as a disappointment. A New Yorker writing to Frederick Douglass's *North Star* noted with disgust the "sad failures" he had witnessed on a recent trip through Philadelphia. Despite the promise of the Harrisburg meeting, he lamented, little of its program was put into place, and black Philadelphians focused on the things that divided them rather than on those that brought them together.

> Let the quiet of the church, the stability of ordinary societies among us, the accumulation of dollars and cents, the anniversaries of Odd Fellow societies, the display of Free Masons, the levees of Sons and Daughters of Temperance, the suppers of Good Samaritans and Fancy Balls and parties, be made subordinate for the time being, to the great and true idea of our moral, social, political and religious recognition.[21]

The most prominent source of this criticism was Douglass himself, who was hardly a disinterested observer. The objects of his scorn certainly rejected the notion that they had turned their backs on the antislavery cause. While Douglass may have believed that fraternal orders constituted a distraction from political engagement, many black Freemasons, for example, saw the order as offering them a means of participating in American politics and a forum for asserting their right to American citizenship. More broadly, black associations of all sorts, including black churches, served as a way for free blacks to experience the "full duties, rights privileges, and pleasures of American life"—that is, of enacting black citizenship.[22]

Moreover, white Baltimoreans also did not perceive black organizations as a distraction from the real struggle. In 1848, black residents of Baltimore had formed the Philanthropic Order of Sons of Temperance. Under pressure from whites, spearheaded by deputy attorney general of Maryland, Frederick Pinckney, the group disbanded. Whites both decried the supposed degradation of the free black community and recognized that such organizations had significance far beyond promoting temperance.[23]

Black Philadelphians and black Baltimoreans embraced a kind of practical antislavery uniquely suited to their region. While some black churches avoided certain types of antislavery meetings and thus drew the ire of abolitionist critics, many of those churches served as critical points along the Underground Railroad. Baltimore constables frequently searched black churches in hopes of apprehending runaways. In response to Frederick Douglass's claims that the African Episcopal Church of St. Thomas supported slavery, pastor William Douglass joked that southern masters ought to bring their "property" into St. Thomas or one of the other maligned "triune band of pro-slavery brothers." Such "pro-slavery" churches remained safe havens for fugitive slaves.[24]

Black Citizenship and the Politics of Union

In January 1850, Senator James Mason of Virginia introduced a new fugitive slave bill on the floor of the Senate. Many slaveholders had grown increasingly distressed by northern resistance to the existing laws. Supporters claimed that the new law was needed to guarantee that northerners would fulfill their constitutional obligation to return fugitive slaves. Slaveholders sought to remedy federal weakness in such matters by increasing penalties for those convicted of aiding fugitives, by expanding the number of federal officials to whom slave catchers might turn for adjudication, and by requiring northern whites to serve in slave posses.[25]

Henry Clay, the Great Compromiser, was willing to seek middle ground on certain issues that divided the union, but on this matter he was unwilling to compromise. He declared that he would support "the furthest Senator from the South in this body to make penal laws, to impose the heaviest sanctions upon the recovery of fugitive slaves, and the restoration of them to their owners." New York senator William H. Seward countered southern extremism with an amendment to grant accused fugitives the right to a trial by jury, but the Senate dismissed this proposal out of hand. As the bill took shape, it came to embody what historian Thomas D. Morris has called the "radical proslavery position."[26]

The measure faced serious opposition in the North. Antislavery senators were infuriated by the proposed legislation, but even many northerners less devoted to antislavery found the bill distasteful. Various senators attempted to reintroduce some sort of jury trial component during discussions on the measure during the first half of 1850. The author of one letter printed in the *Philadelphia Inquirer*, a Whig paper, explained the importance of such a provision: slave owners, he argued, would be satisfied only if the federal government set up a line of troops along the northern edge of the South to "watch for the runaway niggers." He admitted that the Constitution required all northern states to "deliver up fugitives from labor" but noted that difficulty arose "in proving that the parties claimed as fugitives are really such" and questioned whether southern jurisdictions could be trusted to make this determination. Only by placing such determinations in the hands of northern juries could "the rights of the free colored citizens" be preserved. "I do not think," continued the writer, "any measure which does less than this, even if passed, can be successfully administered."[27]

The Fugitive Slave Act of 1850 passed on September 18 as part of the package of five bills known as the Compromise of 1850 and made few if any concessions to northern concerns. Northern politicians denounced the bill as violating the rights of northern whites and coercing reluctant northerners into versions of southern slave patrols. Northerners feared not only the potential encroachment on white liberties but also threats to free black rights. But slave owners still remained dependent on the cooperation of northern whites. The law had been written to facilitate the return of fugitives, but without northern support, the measure would be difficult to enforce. "Where slaves are disposed to escape, and a vast community of allies are on their borders," noted the *Washington Southern Press*, "no law can be effectual."[28] Slaveholders sought assurances from the northern public as well as the legal right to recover their property.

If border-state slaveholders hoped for signs of reassurance from their neighbors to the north, the reports of free black reaction to the new law were ominous. "The passage of the fugitive slave bill, or some other cause," reported the Philadelphia correspondent for the *Baltimore Sun*, "has thrown our colored population into a state of feverish excitement, which I fear may cause some difficulties." About ten days later, he reported that "the colored people are holding a meeting tonight in one of their churches, in opposition to the fugitive slave law. It is very largely attended." The correspondent counseled that "it would be well to put a stop at once to such meetings of the colored people and their abettors." The following night, he reported on another meeting with both black and white participants.[29]

The first case brought in Philadelphia under the new legislation indicated that difficulties might arise in enforcing it. The presiding judge decided that the claimant failed to present adequate evidence of his ownership of the accused, but the large multiracial crowd that gathered outside the courthouse made it clear that a different verdict would have been difficult to enforce. Newspapers both to the north and to the south reprinted local accounts of these events, asking how the white masses would treat the new legislation.[30]

For slaveholders, their legislative victory represented but the first step in stemming the flow of runaways from the Border South. Though die-hard abolitionists would oppose both the law and any attempts to recapture fugitives, such opponents remained a small minority. More important was how nonabolitionist whites would regard the legislation. To reassure slaveholders that the union was sound, northerners needed not simply to repudiate those who would assist fugitives but also to demonstrate that the vast majority of northerners would vigorously defend slaveholders' rights. In this case, language and the accompanying public performance proved a crucial battleground in determining whether a piece of legislation would accomplish its supporters' goals.[31]

The *Inquirer* sought to steer a moderate course between sectional extremists. It admitted that some features of the Fugitive Slave Law conflicted "with the popular sentiment of freemen" but argued that these flaws could best be addressed "peaceably, quietly and if not without excitement, at least without any attempt at the nullification of an act of Congress." Calm administration of the law was key to averting the danger of disunion. The paper even suggested that southern fire-eaters hoped that the Compromise of 1850 would fail, so northern moderation was needed to teach these extremists a lesson.[32]

Whether such "moderation" was intended as a means of isolating southern extremists or as a way to assuage slaveholders' concerns, many white Philadelphians looked to publicly express their support for adherence to the Compromise of 1850. On November 21, a large group of Philadelphians met at the Chinese Museum to declare their "allegiance to the CONSTITUTION and the LAWS of OUR COUNTRY." Friendly accounts estimated the crowd in the thousands, with thousands more denied entry to avoid overcrowding. The meeting itself constituted a carefully orchestrated expression of the "honest feelings of the citizens of Philadelphia." The gathering took place "without distinction of party," and speakers were carefully chosen to provide a partisan balance. Published accounts of the meeting sought to emphasize participants' strong support for the Compromise of 1850 and in particular for the Fugitive Slave Law. According to one newspaper story, the resolutions passed by the meeting were "frequently and warmly cheered, particularly those sustaining the Fugitive Slave Law."[33]

Despite organizers' efforts to create a pageant of unanimity and nonpartisanship, fault lines emerged. Aged Whig John Sergeant opened the meeting in the chair and issued brief remarks. He denied the presence of a single "disunionist or secessionist" within Pennsylvania's borders; since all Pennsylvanians were devoted to the union, as long as a law was constitutional, Pennsylvanians would support its enforcement. He echoed the *Inquirer*'s suggestion that the law or even the Constitution might at some point need to change, but his remarks emphasized loyalty to the union and respect for the laws.[34]

Former U.S. vice president George M. Dallas then took over as chair. The longtime Democratic politician also offered an extended celebration of the union and the "ripe fruits" it had bestowed on the American people but then launched into a comprehensive defense of the Fugitive Slave Law. He not only called for adherence to the law and respect for the Constitution but praised the measure's specifics: "This Fugitive Slave Bill is *just*:—just to the fugitive, just to the claimant of his service, and just to the public." Furthermore, it was, "*expedient*," putting down "an imported fanaticism" that had stirred up slaves in the Border South and had brought them to the border North. Pennsylvania's public opinion had for too long remained "injuriously inert." The time had come for the people to reassure the slaveholding South by "showing that we deeply and sincerely sympathize in the sufferings and wrongs to which they have been subjected."[35]

Whigs walked a tightrope, hoping to position themselves as moderate defenders of the Constitution and to avoid seeming like servile defenders of the Slave Power or being manipulated by Democratic puppet masters. One Whig paper, the *North American*, refused to endorse the meeting for just this reason, claiming that it was a "locofoco" plot intended to benefit the Democratic Party. The Whigs who spoke at the meeting were careful not to paint abolitionists with too broad a brush. Though he criticized anyone who harbored fugitive slaves, Whig Josiah Randall admitted that "among the few Abolitionists in our community are to be found the most exemplary men in private life." Arguing that the Fugitive Slave Law would not lead to the kidnapping of legitimately free blacks, Randall leaned on the authority of antislavery lawyer David Paul Brown, calling for a repeal of the 1847 antikidnapping law while offering reassurances that free black Pennsylvanians would be safe.[36]

Black Philadelphians were locked out of legislative political maneuvering and excluded from the voting places where political parties struggled for supremacy, but they could and did work to shatter the perception of public support for the Fugitive Slave Law that its supporters had worked so hard to create. Compromisers hoped that public spectacles could demonstrate the good faith of the vast majority of Pennsylvanians and the willingness of this majority vigorously to support the recovery of fugitive slaves. But such public gatherings also opened the door for opponents of the Fugitive Slave Law, including free blacks. Challenging the illusion of popular support for the Compromise of 1850 became one of the great political tasks of the ensuing decade.

Just as black Philadelphians negotiated between an ominous threat and political leverage, black Baltimoreans, too, faced a challenge to their existing rights and demonstrated surprising power. In 1850, Maryland voters had approved a call for a convention to revise the state constitution. While the convention mainly addressed issues of representation, pro-slavery zealots under the leadership of Curtis W. Jacobs pushed for measures to eliminate the state's free black population. Jacobs, a wealthy Eastern Shore slave owner who also had significant slave holdings in Alabama, chaired the "committee on colored population." Convention delegates initially approved Jacobs's motion to appoint a committee to "devise for some plan for the ultimate riddance of free colored persons and their colonization," adopting a resolution in favor of the taxation of free blacks to support colonization. However, when Jacobs's committee submitted its recommendations months later, the majority of the convention balked at the harsh measures suggested. In addition to general efforts to remove the free black population, the committee's official report advocated specific measures to deny free blacks the right to acquire real estate, a total ban on manumission (unless accompanied by departure from the state within thirty days), registration of free blacks, and a ban on free black immigration. The convention voted forty-two to thirty-three against even discussing Jacobs's proposals.[37]

But delegates had no disagreements on the question of the Fugitive Slave Law. In December 1850, the convention unanimously approved and distributed a report "On the Late Acts of Congress Forming the Compromise, etc." Though the document ostensibly commented on the compromise measures, it focused on the Fugitive Slave Law, denouncing northerners who refused to aid the return of fugitive slaves and declaring the legislation "but a tardy and meager measure of compliance with the clear, explicit and imperative injunctions of the Constitution." Nevertheless, the convention insisted, the new law provided northerners with an opportunity to demonstrate their patriotism through their support for the "officers of the Government in the execution of the laws."[38] Marylanders understood, perhaps better than anyone else, that the Fugitive Slave Law could be effective only if white Pennsylvanians backed its enforcement.

Christiana and the Limits of Violent Resistance

This willingness was put to the test on September 11, 1851, in the small town of Christiana, which lay between Philadelphia and Lancaster, Pennsylvania. Two days earlier, Edward Gorsuch, a slaveholder from Baltimore County, had traveled to Philadelphia and obtained warrants under the new Fugitive Slave Law for four individuals who he believed were his slaves. Gorsuch; a deputy marshal, Henry Kline; and two Philadelphia police officers whom Gorsuch had hired then set out for Christiana, where he had heard the fugitives were living. Gorsuch's group planned to meet up with other men from Maryland, including Gorsuch's son, Dickinson. Despite their efforts to travel inconspicuously, a black tavern keeper, Samuel Williams, who was connected to the Vigilant Committee of Philadelphia, got wind of Gorsuch's plan and shared the information with African Americans living near Christiana.[39]

The police officers quit after learning that Christiana's African Americans had been warned, but early on the morning of September 11, the rest of the posse arrived at the home of William Parker, where a guide informed them that two of the fugitives were to be found. According to historian Thomas P. Slaughter, the guide "delivered his employers, as if on a silver platter to the very seat of Lancaster's anti-slavery resistance." Parker himself was a fugitive from slavery and was committed to resisting the efforts of slave catchers with force if necessary. He knew that Gorsuch was coming, and his household, which indeed included two of Gorsuch's fugitives, was ready.[40]

Gorsuch and Kline approached the house and called to those inside to surrender peacefully. While the two sides exchanged words, one of the inhabitants of the house blew a horn, which was a signal of distress. According to some reports, the slave posse then began firing. Both sides exchanged fire as both blacks and whites who had heard the horn rushed to the scene. Castner Hanway, a white miller, urged the slave catchers to leave, telling them that they would not be able to recapture the fugitives. Hanway's efforts proved unsuccessful, and after some more gunfire, the slave posse had been chased off and Edward Gorsuch lay dead, possibly shot by one of his former slaves.[41]

The Christiana riot and especially its aftermath reveal that while free blacks were often willing to defend themselves by force, their armed resistance formed part of a complex strategy whereby African Americans exploited white Pennsylvanians' distaste for the actions of slave owners like Gorsuch. Parker and the fugitives from Gorsuch's farm fled north, ultimately escaping to Canada. Soon after, a force of around forty-five Marines and another forty Philadelphia police officers descended on the area, rounding up people suspected of involvement in the riot.[42]

The struggle shifted from the bloody ground around Parker's house to the courts and to the ballot box. Pennsylvania governor William Johnston, a Whig, had opposed the Fugitive Slave Law and refused to support a repeal of the 1847 antikidnapping law. Even before the Christiana incident, his Democratic opponents had tarred him as a friend of "disunionist" abolitionists. Though this charge exaggerated the governor's antislavery sentiments, he clearly opposed the Slave Power's efforts to extend its authority onto Pennsylvania soil. Yet he also recognized that many Whigs in his state hated abolitionists and were willing to acquiesce in the enforcement of the Fugitive Slave Law in the interest of sectional comity. Pro-Compromise Whigs were troubled by Johnston's abolitionist leanings, and in March 1851, Josiah Randall privately expressed his unwillingness to support Johnston in the upcoming election. Johnston happened to be journeying to Philadelphia on the day of the riot, and his train had stopped in Christiana hours after the fighting had subsided. The governor did not get off the train, apparently wanting nothing to do with the explosive situation. Not until two days later did the governor issue a statement on the riot and offer a reward for those responsible. His political opponents depicted his delay as an expression of sympathy for the fugitives and their allies.[43]

Democrats sought to exploit the riot for political gain but ran the risk of overplaying their hand. Southern newspapers called for decisive action and looked for evidence that the people of Pennsylvania repudiated the bloody work of Christiana. "The event cannot be passed over with an indeterminate result," warned the *Baltimore Sun*, "without greatly impairing the confidence of the southern people." The paper also expressed cautious optimism based on the Philadelphia press's response. A month after the riot, Governor Johnston lost his bid for reelection; newspapers attributed his defeat to Pennsylvanians' desire to demonstrate support for slaveholder rights. Yet only by bringing the participants to justice could the state and people of Pennsylvania demonstrate their devotion to the union, so the district attorney decided that the accused needed to be tried for treason. This move brought the possibility of overreaching if the prosecution failed to win a conviction.[44]

The prosecution decided to try each of the thirty-eight defendants individually, beginning with Hanway. His trial opened on November 24, 1851, with the prosecution facing an uphill battle. Prosecutors worried that they were at a disadvantage in selecting a jury, and the defense seemed to have much better knowledge of which prospective jurors were friendly to its case. Both black and white opponents of slavery as well as the Vigilant Committee of Philadelphia had raised money to pay for defense lawyers and to provide for the families of the defendants. Perhaps most ominous in the eyes of southern newspaper editors, the crowds overflowing the courthouse included blacks as well as whites.[45]

In both the court of law and the court of public opinion, the defense turned on the definitions of kidnapping and legal fugitive slave recovery along the border. Like vigilance committees throughout the North, the Christiana network that rallied to Parker's house made little distinction between aiding fugitives from slavery and protecting free blacks from kidnappers, just as kidnappers often failed to distinguish between alleged fugitives and legitimately free blacks. Free black Philadelphians tried to demonstrate for the white public that slave catching and kidnapping differed little in practice. During the buildup to the trial, a county convention of black Philadelphians called both for the specific support of the Christiana defendants and for the general resistance to ongoing efforts for the "further *enslavement* of the *nominally free colored population*." Inside the courthouse, the defense sought to portray Southeast Pennsylvania as a place where kidnappers frequently abducted free blacks and sold them into slavery. In this light, the rioters did not constitute traitors attempting to undermine federal law but rather were reasonable defenders of the rights of free blacks. Perhaps to underscore their status as American citizens, the black defendants wore red, white, and blue scarves.[46]

The jury accepted this argument, acquitting Hanway in just fifteen minutes. Prosecutors subsequently decided not to press charges against the other prisoners. Maryland attorney general Robert Brent attributed the jury's decision to conditions in the court, especially the presence of numerous black spectators. He alleged that "free negroes were admitted through the Marshal's office into the courtroom, while crowds of white citizens were kept outside the door." Brent worried that if northerners believed the defense's argument that kidnapping was rampant on the border and that resistance to slave catchers thus constituted a reasonable defense of black rights, not an unlawful attack on legitimate agents of the state, Maryland might well be "powerless to protect her citizens."[47]

Many white Pennsylvanians grudgingly accepted the abstract principle that they were obliged to return fugitives from slavery but also harbored serious doubts about slave catchers and balked at putting that principle into practice. Johnston had lost his reelection bid at least in part because "moderate" members of his Whig Party wanted to show their respect for southern rights, yet the Christiana trial had indicated that this bipartisan consensus was shaky.

Black Philadelphians had helped show that concerns about the rights of free blacks could be used to challenge border whites' willingness to support the Fugitive Slave Law. Such challenges could be used both to defend those who were legally free and to provide cover for efforts to aid fugitives. Shortly after the Christiana trial, William Still suggested that the accompanying publicity shined light on kidnappers "who under shelter of the brutish Fugitive Slave Law, manage to acquire the title of 'Marshal,' whereby they have felt they were authorized to commit all manner of outrage upon colored people with impunity."[48] Doubts about kidnapping could undermine northern willingness to uphold the Fugitive Slave Law and trust in the good faith of slaveholders and their agents.

By this time, Still had quietly established himself as one of Philadelphia's most dedicated enemies of slavery. Born in 1821, the youngest child of two former slaves, Still grew up in rural New Jersey. In 1844, he moved to Philadelphia, where he worked a number of low-paying jobs. He had received little formal schooling, but he took advantage of the city's intellectual resources to improve his reading and writing skills. In 1847 he took a job as a janitor for the Pennsylvania Abolition Society but soon took a more active role. He subsequently dedicated himself to aiding fugitive slaves.[49]

William Still, ca. 1870.
Courtesy of the Charles L.
Blockson Collection, Temple
University, Philadelphia.

Rethinking Black Connections to the United States and the Politics of Vigilance

Historians have long recognized that the passage of the Fugitive Slave Law of 1850 prompted many free African Americans to rethink their relationship to the United States. Some northern free blacks began to reconsider their opposition to emigration, considering the possibility that African Americans' future lay outside the United States. Martin Delany's 1852 work, *Condition, Elevation, Emigration, and Destiny of the Colored People of the United States* is the best-known expression of this reconsideration.[50] Yet for all the soul-searching that the Compromise of 1850 provoked, the Fugitive Slave Law refocused many African Americans on the struggle for black citizenship within the United States.

Though many of those newly considering various emigration plans remained skeptical of Liberian colonization, supporters of the idea hoped to capitalize on the reaction to the new law to change the situation. Benjamin Coates, a Philadelphia Quaker, hoped that African colonization could lead to the ultimate extinction of slavery in the United States. He often criticized American Colonization Society leaders for their reluctance to offend southern supporters by openly opposing slavery, and he backed efforts to promote black uplift. Prior to 1851, however, his efforts to secure black allies had produced little success.[51]

In January of that year, he reached out to the most famous black American, Frederick Douglass, a staunch opponent of colonization. "I have intended subscribing for the North Star for some time," began Coates, "and have been prevented from doing so earlier, by the accumulation of newspapers that I already receive." He complimented Douglass on the paper's efforts to demonstrate the potential of free African Americans. Coates subsequently went on to make the case that black emigration to Liberia was a crucial means of undermining slavery.[52]

Douglass continued to oppose colonization, but he also printed Coates's correspondence, adding commentary that poked holes in his arguments. Douglass continued to dispute the idea that free blacks would be better off in Africa but praised Coates as "a humane and benevolent man, a sincere philanthropist." Douglass did not believe that all colonizationists intended to strengthen slavery. In Douglass's view, Coates and others who coupled their belief that blacks would be better off in Africa with calls for better treatment of blacks in America were merely misguided.[53]

Other Pennsylvania advocates for colonization also hoped that the Fugitive Slave Law would reignite blacks' interest in African colonization, but not all backers of emigration shared Coates's humanitarian sensibilities. The Pennsylvania Colonization Society sent two agents to the State House in Harrisburg to persuade the legislature to appropriate funds for colonization. Before an audience that included members of both houses of the legislature as well as the governor, John Durbin argued that African colonization offered a "safe, equitable and peaceful solution of the only real danger that threatens our glorious Union." He included among his arguments the potential that colonization would lead to emancipation, though he dwelled more on the need to separate the black and white races. Durbin anticipated his critics: though some would say that "it is impractical to transport to Africa three millions of men women and children... what do we see before our eyes?" European immigrants "are now coming to our shores at an average of a thousand a day." If such numbers could flow in one direction, they could do so in the other. The legislature responded by appropriating two thousand dollars to support colonization, stipulating that the funds could be used only to transport black Pennsylvanians.[54]

Not long thereafter, a large group of black Philadelphians assembled to express their objection to this specific legislation as well as to reassert their general opposition to African colonization. Meeting at the Philadelphia Institute on April 16, 1852, many of the city's leading black activists joined others in approving resolutions against the appropriation and declaring their attachment "in common with other American citizens... to this our native land." The meeting also denounced the American Colonization Society as "the great enemy to the cause of impartial freedom in our land" and recommended that "our brethren ... stand firm," remaining and fighting "in this, the land of our birth." The meeting was chaired by Delany, who the same month published *Condition, Elevation, Emigration, and Destiny of the Colored People of the United States*.[55]

Delany's book contended that black elevation could best be achieved outside the United States though still in the Americas. Yet as Robert S. Levine has argued, Delany's work is more conflicted than it is often perceived to be. Much of the book argues that African Americans have a right to equality in their native United States and that such equality is indeed possible. However, Delany signals a shift in the middle of the work by bringing up the Fugitive Slave Law, which has "disenfranchised" African Americans. The remainder of the book argues in favor of black emigration to Central and South America. Like Durbin, Delany points to European immigration as a means of understanding the potential for black emigration, but in this case, the argument is that just as Irish and German immigrants had elevated their condition by emigrating, so too could African Americans.[56] Yet despite his evolving willingness to entertain the idea of voluntary emigration, Delany's participation in the Philadelphia meeting helps demonstrate that opposition to African colonization and its implications of coerced removal remained a powerful symbol around which a diverse coalition of African Americans rallied.

Still shared Delany's willingness to consider the idea that emigration outside the United States was an appropriate tool for African Americans. Like most black Philadelphians, Still continued his denunciations of African colonization in the wake of the new Fugitive Slave Law. He had cosigned a call for an 1851 meeting that linked the law and the resurgence of the colonization movement as parts of a larger pro-slavery conspiracy. Still resolved to remain in the United States to continue his fight against slavery, but he recognized that for many African Americans, especially fugitives, emigration offered an appealing option. After editor Henry Bibb fled to Canada in response to the Fugitive Slave Law, he and Still corresponded, and the Philadelphian's letters appeared in Bibb's *Voice of the Fugitive*. In 1852, Still signed a call for a North American black convention in Toronto.[57]

Still maintained his vehement opposition to the "poisonous doctrines" of African colonization while neutrally mentioning the growing black interest in emigration to Canada and the British West Indies. Still's work with the Vigilant Committee of Philadelphia had brought him into contact with many fugitives who ultimately found their way to Canada, so he understood the larger, black network that stretched north from the slave states across the Canadian border. Yet Still also wrote glowingly to Bibb of efforts to establish a "Colored

Mechanics Institute" in Philadelphia to improve the condition of free blacks who remained in the United States.⁵⁸ Still saw emigration not as the sole way to improve black conditions but rather as one of many tactics for achieving that goal. Emigrants to Canada could remain part of the struggle against slavery in the United States.

Just as Coates had hoped that the Fugitive Slave Law would renew black Philadelphians' interest in colonization, white colonizationists in Baltimore hoped that their city's free blacks would warm to the idea of Liberian emigration. In January 1850, Baltimore Quaker Moses Sheppard wrote, "I believe the colored people of Baltimore are less averse to colonization in Africa than they were formerly." However, he feared that their hopes of "acquiring equality" might prevent them from understanding their true interests.⁵⁹ Whatever encouragement free black Baltimoreans took from the Maryland Constitutional Convention's rejection of Jacobs's plan was tempered by the fact that it represented a continuation of the status quo rather than an improvement.

Sheppard's letter implied that small gains might actually work against free blacks' interests in the long term by giving them false hope for equality in their native land. Writing shortly before the Jacobs committee made its recommendations to the Maryland convention, Maryland colonizationist John H. B. Latrobe declared that all emigration was driven by the forces of "repulsion and attraction." Latrobe recognized the need to drive consensual emigration by making it clear to free blacks that "when two races live together, one will dominate the other. '*The two can never be upon equal footing as regards social and political rights and privileges.*'"⁶⁰

Latrobe made his case publicly later that year in a response to French novelist Victor Hugo, who had written a letter in support of abolition. Latrobe's letter, published in the *Maryland Colonization Journal*, began by refuting the idea of immediate emancipation but then argued for the necessity for free blacks to emigrate. Latrobe repeated his belief that the two races would forever remain distinct and that history had shown that wherever two distinct races remained in close proximity, one would be inferior to the other. Only in Africa could the black man "escape the white man's power." Free black recognition of this fact would spur their emigration. In addition, Latrobe argued, the growth of the white population, "by native birth and from foreign countries," would prove the decisive factor in "repelling" blacks from the United States, and he echoed the point that immigration illustrated the practicability of noncoercive removal of a massive population: "Where the Irishman and German has one motive to leave Europe," he wrote, "the free black man has ten to leave America."⁶¹

While white supporters might depict colonization as a natural, inevitable process, free blacks would have a say in the success or failure of any colonization plan. On July 7, 1852, the *Baltimore Sun* advertised,

> THERE WILL BE A PUBLIC MEETING held on THIS (Wednesday) EVENING at 8 o'clock in the school house attached to Asbury chapel, for the purpose of electing delegates to represent the colored people in the Convention. The public are respectfully invited to attend.

Similar advertisements appeared throughout the month. In June, a group of free black men led by Baltimoreans James Handy and John H. Walker had called for a statewide convention to consider strategies for bettering Maryland's free blacks. The group's circular both alluded to the principles of the Declaration of Independence as an inspiration to American free blacks and indicated that Liberian emigration would be the central topic of discussion.[62]

The Baltimore press noted the impending convention with approval. The *Daily Times* saw it as "evidence of a new and generally unexpected change of sentiment on the part of the colored population," which was finally turning its back on the false promise of "equality in social and political rights with the whites." For his part, Frederick Douglass wrote, "We did not venture to hope that such a meeting could be held in Baltimore."[63] Douglass, it seems, recognized that a meeting would provide a broad forum for discussion among the city's black population.

White Baltimore likely allowed the meeting only because it promised to promote African colonization, but the convention ultimately became a catalyst for the expression of opposition to African colonization plans. A crowd of African Americans gathered outside the convention and harassed the delegates as they entered. Some of the throng found their way into the meeting hall as spectators and expressed their opposition to Liberian colonization. In response, the Dorchester County delegation announced its withdrawal from the convention, prompting applause and cheers from the spectators. One delegate, Darius Stokes, was assaulted by men who claimed that he was a paid agent of the American Colonization Society. Some of the disapproving spectators even reached the convention floor.[64]

The delegates themselves had significant differences of opinion regarding Liberian emigration. Some wholeheartedly embraced colonization as the best course of action, while others were more cautious and sought additional information. Delegates also attempted to dispel the idea that they were tools of the American Colonization Society, a notion to which they attributed much of the black public's opposition to the meeting. Resolutions passed by the convention offered reassurances that Liberian emigration should be but one option among many and echoed white colonizationists' argument that European immigration was driving black interest in colonization.[65]

Though Walker had been among those who called for the convention, he emerged as something of a voice of opposition within the gathering, expressing concerns that the convention was coming too close to endorsing the position that free blacks had no place in the United States. In his initial remarks, Walker stated his hope that the convention would seek generally to improve African Americans' condition, considering Liberia as well as all other options. He closed by announcing that he personally "intended now to remain where he was," a statement that earned applause from the crowd. The convention's official resolutions reiterated Walker's viewpoint: "It is not our purpose to counsel emigration as either necessary or proper in every case."[66]

Earlier in the convention, Walker had proposed a petition to the state government to "obtain a change of legislation in reference to the colored people." Another delegate opposed the suggestion on the grounds that it was contrary to "the spirit of the circular which called them together." On the meeting's final day, still another delegate called for the drafting of a memorial to the state legislature "praying for more indulgence to the colored people," couching the request as a means of preparing free blacks for emigration. If such proposals did not go anywhere, they do indicate that some of the delegates sought to use the convention for broader purposes than simply the promotion of Liberian emigration. And even the most devoted supporters of emigration believed that free blacks should have control of any plan and that full knowledge of conditions in Liberia was necessary before free blacks would consent to emigrate.[67]

Still a firm opponent of colonization, Douglass nevertheless praised the Baltimore convention: "Yes!" he wrote, "the free colored people of a slave state have been permitted, with comparative safety under official protection, to meet like men."[68] Whereas black Philadelphians of divergent political instincts continued to rally around opposition to colonization, Baltimore's free African American community turned a meeting ostensibly organized to promote Liberian emigration into a forum for both a robust expression of opposition to colonization and a general display of black political expression. In both cities, even free blacks who did not reject emigration out of hand sought to make clear their rejection of the colonizationist position that free blacks could not remain in the United States and that African Americans could never be American citizens.

As the passage of the Fugitive Slave Law put some wind back into the colonization movement's sails, opponents launched a rhetorical struggle in the public sphere and worked to aid fugitives in more concrete ways. By the early 1850s,

Vigilant Committee of Philadelphia: (top, L to R) James Miller McKim, N. W. Dupee, Charles Wise; (center, L to R) Thomas Garrett, Robert Purvis; (bottom, L to R) Jacob C. White, Passmore Williamson, William Still, ca. 1852. Courtesy of Boston Public Library.

some abolitionists had come to believe that the Vigilant Committee of Philadelphia existed more in name than in practice. In December 1852, therefore, a group of black and white residents of the city met to reorganize the group. The new organization would be as pared-down as possible, with few officers, and they would have clear responsibilities. In addition to a chairman and a treasurer, the Acting Committee of four men would "have the responsibility of attending to every case that might require their aid." Robert Purvis became the new group's chairman, while William Still served as the first chairman of the Acting Committee, whose members also included Jacob C. White, N. W. Dupee, and one white man, Passmore Williamson. Though much of its work was clandestine, the group itself and the membership of the Acting Committee were quite public: their addresses appeared in the *Pennsylvania Freeman*, ostensibly so that potential donors could find them but also so that fugitives could locate them.[69]

Over the next eight years, this Vigilant Committee aided more than eight hundred fugitives from slavery.[70] The broader public clearly acquiesced in this work, since the committee made no attempt to hide its existence. Just over a decade earlier, a white mob had burned Pennsylvania Hall to the ground; in contrast, the Vigilant Committee acknowledged contributions in the newspaper. The public's willingness to accept the committee's operation resulted in large part from continued concerns about the kidnapping of free blacks. Fears that the Fugitive Slave Law gave appointed commissioners too much power were exacerbated by high-profile kidnapping cases, including one in which a free black man, Adam Gibson, was seized on a Philadelphia street by a notorious slave catcher, George Alberti. When Gibson was taken before commissioner Edward Ingraham, he declared that Gibson was actually a fugitive slave, Emery Rice. Gibson was taken to Maryland as a slave, but he later returned to freedom, and Alberti was tried and convicted in Pennsylvania as a kidnapper. The case provoked outrage, and not simply among abolitionists. Declared the *Philadelphia Daily News*, "We have no idea of sustaining U.S. Commissioners who chose to convert themselves into willing kidnappers of free negroes."[71] Concerns about kidnapping could undermine confidence in the operation of the "legitimate" work of recovering fugitives.

Despite Democrats' calls for repeal, the 1847 antikidnapping law remained on the books as a threat to those who sought to seize free blacks and perhaps as a deterrent to legal slave catchers. The Pennsylvania House had voted strictly along party lines for repeal even before the Fugitive Slave Law was enacted, but the measure failed in the Senate. In April 1851, however, it passed both houses. After Governor Johnston refused to sign the bill, repeal became an issue in the fall election: Johnston's Democratic opponent, William Bigler, declared his intention to repeal the law. After his election, one of Bigler's first moves was to call for repeal, and he subsequently pardoned Alberti. Despite these victories for the supporters of slavery, black Philadelphians continued to rally white support by emphasizing the threat of kidnapping.[72]

The Fugitive Slave Law had set back the cause of black citizenship, but the reaction to that law showed that white opinion remained mixed. Philadelphia's free blacks rededicated themselves to cultivating moderate white allies, recognizing that even tepid white support could be a valuable tool. The failure of radical pro-slavery measures in Maryland reassured Baltimore's free blacks about the existence of opportunities in their state. In both places, free blacks remained committed to the fight for citizenship rights, limited though they might be.

CHAPTER 8

African Americans and "Political Insubordination"

The new principal of the Institute for Colored Youth, Charles L. Reason, was a native New Yorker, but he immersed himself in the activist milieu of black Philadelphia. He overhauled the institute's already rigorous curriculum, molding it into an unparalleled school for the city's black children, and made the school an intellectual focal point by attracting speakers from across the nation. Yet like many of Philadelphia's black activists, Reason coupled his fairly genteel educational and cultural work with other, more radical actions. In New York, he had worked to secure political rights for African Americans, and he continued that struggle when he moved south. He protested vigorously when white abolitionist Lucy Stone agreed to lecture in a hall that barred black attendees. Most important, he became active in the Vigilant Committee of Philadelphia, both publicly as a member and less publicly by helping to forward fugitives to William Still and the other members of the Acting Committee.[1]

These were auspicious times for the antislavery cause. Many activists saw the collapse of the Whig Party as a great opportunity to push for a more vigorous antislavery politics. Even political setbacks were deemed to be minor and temporary obstacles on the road that inevitably led to abolition. On November 25, 1852, the *Pennsylvania Freeman* warned slavery's defenders not to take the decline in the vote for the Free Soil Party in the recent presidential election as an accurate reflection of the country's antislavery sentiment: "Unseen and silently, like the deep forces of Nature it is working in thousands of hearts." Directly below this column the paper printed an account of how Kentucky slaveholders who had thought that the Compromise of 1850 had solved all of their problems were now finding that fugitives continued to stream across the Ohio River.[2]

While Still, Reason, and other black abolitionists had cause for optimism, it was tempered by recognition that black freedoms remained precarious. Even if they shared the *Freeman*'s confidence in the eventual success of the antislavery cause, short-term political setbacks had real consequences, especially for free blacks living on the border between freedom and slavery. For all of the national Whig Party's failings, many elected Whig officials at the state level had supported at least some black citizenship rights, and these rights, in turn, had offered a critical means of defending free blacks from kidnapping and slave catchers. Democratic victories placed free blacks at risk.

Moreover, the parties that replaced the Whigs had yet to take positions on the issue of black citizenship. Many free blacks saw antislavery sentiments behind much of the support for the new ambiguously antislavery political parties but needed to make sure that they remained true to those sentiments. Black abolitionists also worried that the even the more explicitly antislavery Republican Party might seek to widen its electoral appeal by downplaying or even abandoning the cause of black citizenship. Thus, free blacks on both sides of the mid-Atlantic border found themselves defending their limited citizenship rights and reasserting their ideological claims on their American birthright.

Fighting for Black Citizenship in Pennsylvania

Black Philadelphians had long engaged in a wary courtship of the Whig Party. They often denounced Whigs, especially at the national level, as at best the dupes of slave masters and at worst as willing supporters of the Slave Power. At the state and local levels, however, Whigs were critical allies in the fight for black citizenship. As the Whig Party disintegrated in the 1850s, black Philadelphians surveyed a new political scene, seeking to find another party that would remain committed to the fight for black citizenship.

The 1852 elections had proven disastrous for the Whigs of Pennsylvania as well as throughout the United States. In the October state elections, the Democratic candidate for canal commissioner (the race at the top of the ticket) slightly increased his percentage of the vote, while the vote for the Whig candidate declined from 48.6 percent to 45.2 percent. The Native American Party was the chief beneficiary of this decline, increasing its share of the statewide vote from 0.5 percent to 2.4 percent, while the Free Soil Party (which had not run a candidate in 1851) received 1.1 percent of the vote. Turnout dropped across the board, and Whigs attributed their loss to this decline, promising that their voters would turn out for the presidential election the following month. Turnout for the November election was indeed significantly higher, but the Whig presidential candidate, General Winfield Scott, increased Pennsylvania vote totals from four years earlier by only 1 percentage point, while Democrat Franklin Pierce won the state handily and the election. The Free Soil presidential candidate, John P. Hale, took 2.2 percent of the Pennsylvania vote.[3]

The Whig decline resulted at least in part from the disillusionment of antislavery supporters. Earlier in the year, James Buchanan had predicted to Governor William Bigler, a Democrat, that Whigs would conduct their campaign on three issues: "1. Tariff, 2. Free Banking Bill, 3. The modification of the Fugitive Slave Law as intimated in Governor Johnston's message, for the purpose of obtaining votes from the Democratic Free Soilers in the Northern Part of the State" In fact, Buchanan had overstated the Whigs' determination to run on the issue of the Fugitive Slave Law. Whigs in Philadelphia not only emphasized economic issues but sought to depict themselves as members of the party of the union and to suggest that the men "of the most rabid Free-soil and Disunion school" were actively supporting the Democrats.[4]

Despite their disappointment with the outcome of the election, many Whigs hoped to bide their time and exploit Democratic officeholders' missteps. But the Whig vote again declined in 1853. Pennsylvania Whigs sought to rally their base by calling for the privatization of the Mainline Canal, but the issue failed to capture the minds of voters as traditional Whig economic issues had often done. Perhaps just as disturbing to the Whig faithful, their party's failure was accompanied by a proliferation of smaller parties contesting various issues. As in many northern states, temperance arose as a pressing political issue, and in places where Whigs refused to endorse the prohibitionary Maine Law, independent temperance tickets cut into the Whig vote. Candidates from the Native American Party won four seats in the State House from Philadelphia County, where the waters were further muddied by the presence of "consolidation" candidates who advocated the merger of the city and county into one municipality. The Whig vote declined to an all-time low in the state, and the party held just twenty-six of the one hundred seats in the State House.[5]

Philadelphia's antislavery press praised what the *Pennsylvania Freeman* termed "Political Insubordination." Abolitionists had for years denounced the major parties and suggested that political wire-pullers had used the national parties to thwart the antislavery will of the people of Pennsylvania. Now, however, citizens showed an "increasing disposition to break from the lead of political managers and caucus dictation and begin to do their own thinking."[6] Yet Pennsylvania abolitionists must also have seen that voters' independent thinking had led them not to antislavery candidates but to temperance, nativist, or reformist "consolidation" candidates. Further, slavery's opponents had often maligned the Whig Party for its subservience to the Slave Power, but they also knew that they had at times found allies among Whigs, as when Whig governor William Johnston had refused to sign the repeal of the antikidnapping law. When they looked at this new political landscape, then, black Philadelphians undoubtedly felt a mixture of anxiety and possibility.

National events eventually brought more focus to the political confusion of the early 1850s. In January 1854, Stephen Douglas, a Democratic congressman from

Illinois, introduced a bill to pave the way for the creation of two new states from the Nebraska Territory north of the Missouri Compromise line. The new states would be permitted to determine for themselves whether to permit slaveholding. Douglas knew this bill would "raise a hell of a storm in the North." Opposition to the Kansas-Nebraska Bill and its repeal of the Missouri Compromise galvanized northern antislavery sentiment and proved a crucial factor in solidifying the Republican Party.[7]

Black Philadelphians shared white northerners' outrage at this proposed expansion of slavery and were determined not only to speak out against it but also to keep the issue of black citizenship a vital part of any antislavery coalition. Their attacks on the Kansas-Nebraska Bill demonstrated their take on the matter. In March 1854, prominent black Philadelphians organized an "Anti-Colonization and Anti-Nebraska Meeting." Joining together opposition to African colonization with their criticism of the expansion of slavery, these men painted a picture of a larger pro-slavery plan to undermine the African Americans' rights. The gathering's organizers made it clear that they did not oppose the Kansas-Nebraska Bill because it violated the Missouri Compromise; rather, they argued, any expansion of slavery was unacceptable. They also denounced the Homestead Bill, which excluded free blacks, pointing out that "color was not thought of as a hindrance to their suffering in two wars to maintain the rights of the American people."[8] Black Philadelphians resisted attempts to expand the antislavery electoral coalition through concessions to white racism.

The Philadelphia District Annual Conference of the African Methodist Episcopal Church established a committee to address the Kansas-Nebraska Bill, attempting to frame it as an assault on black citizenship rights. The committee's report, signed by black activists William Catto and James J. Gould Bias, denounced the bill not on the specific grounds that it expanded slavery but as a representative example of all the legislation that denied African Americans' equality. The report also alluded to the Kansas-Nebraska Bill as an expression of Slave Power aggression, "another stretch of that power which, like the horse-leech still cries 'Give, give!' or like the grave, 'is never satisfied.'" The committee was ultimately less concerned with the potential expansion of slavery into the new territories than with convincing white neighbors that any concession to the Slave Power would lead to demands for further concessions.[9]

At least one observer noted that the Kansas-Nebraska Bill rendered white Philadelphians less willing to acquiesce in the recovery of fugitive slaves and more supportive of black citizenship rights. A correspondent for the *National Anti-Slavery Standard* wrote,

> The passage of the Nebraska Bill has operated as a practical repeal of the Fugitive Slave Law. Even here in Pennsylvania, the favorite hunting ground of

slaveholders—made such by our geographical position and political subserviency—it is now next to impossible to execute this infamous statute. The people have for some time only wanted a pretext for open hostility to it, and now one is afforded them in the outrage that has been perpetrated in the passage of the Nebraska Bill.[10]

Even the explosive issue of slavery's expansion, therefore, was channeled through local issues as a means of shattering white Pennsylvanians' willingness to make sacrifices to the Slave Power in defense of the union.

Yet northern outrage at these aggressions of the Slave Power did not necessarily translate directly into political gains. During the spring and summer of 1854, the nativist (but especially anti-Catholic) Know-Nothing movement emerged from the shadows to win stunning political victories across the nation, in many places appealing to antislavery voters alongside those more concerned about immigrants or temperance.[11] In June, the Whig/Know-Nothing candidate, Robert Conrad, became the first mayor of the consolidated city of Philadelphia. After assuming office, Conrad appointed a police force composed exclusively of native-born officers and set about aggressively enforcing the Sunday liquor laws.[12] Some Whigs reached out to this politically potent movement, hoping to ride it to victory. Others refused to embrace nativism and instead sought to emphasize the issue of slavery, which had been made more immediate by the passage of the Kansas-Nebraska Act in May. Further complicating the situation, the Democratic governor, Bigler, had enraged some members of his own party by appointing a Catholic, James Campbell, as postmaster general.[13]

Antislavery politicians were divided on how to approach this chaotic political environment. Pennsylvania Free Soilers initially spurned the Whig gubernatorial candidate, Judge James Pollock, hoping that David Wilmot might be convinced to run instead. In his nomination speech, Pollock had only vaguely alluded to the slavery issue. While his guarded comments failed to excite antislavery activists, temperance and anti-Catholic forces saw Pollack as a clear contrast to Bigler. Free Soilers nominated a separate candidate, David Potts, in May, but eventually withdrew his nomination and backed Pollock after the judge issued a strongly worded letter denouncing the Kansas-Nebraska Act and calling for trial by jury for those accused as fugitives from slavery. During the summer, Pennsylvania Whigs moved to head off any antislavery voters who might be wavering: "The Whig candidates talk as strongly against the aggressions of the South as the genuine Abolitionists themselves," noted the *National Anti-Slavery Standard*, "but the game has been so often played by political parties that they will need to be on probation a long time." Antislavery voters backed Pollock as the most likely option to win but remained skeptical about his real commitment to their cause.[14]

Pennsylvania Whigs' newfound zeal for antislavery may have won them votes among some Pennsylvanians, but their waffling on the issue of temperance cost them among others. Pollack remained popular among dry voters, but many Whigs running for offices down the ticket faced independent Maine Law candidates. Other Whigs failed to reach out to nativists and consequently faced Democratic and Native American challengers who were endorsed by the Know-Nothing movement. Pollock had joined the Know-Nothing order and consequently received its nod even though the Native American Party also ran a candidate. He won the election handily, receiving a larger percentage of the vote than any other Whig in the state's history. But his victory clearly resulted from Know-Nothings' support, since the Whig candidate for canal commissioner lost overwhelmingly to the Democrat who also received Know-Nothing support. While abolitionists often claimed that antislavery sentiment lay behind electoral success, the Philadelphia correspondent for the *National Anti-Slavery Standard* admitted that Pollock's sizable victory could not be attributed to his belated opposition to the Kansas-Nebraska Bill.[15]

Some black Philadelphians embraced these divergent political issues, seeking to link them to the struggle for black citizenship. In March 1854, Jacob C. White Jr., whose father and namesake was also an activist and member of the Vigilant Committee of Philadelphia, penned an essay, "What Rum Is Doing for the Colored People." On a certain level, White's essay fit into a long tradition of black racial uplift. He argued that only by abstaining from drink could blacks demonstrate their fitness in the eyes of whites. Yet White also stated that the consumption of alcohol was not merely a lower-class vice: "The *Respectable Groggeries* are ruining the very class of people to whom we are to look as warriors who are to fight for our liberty and our rights." Even more important, White explicitly placed his call for abstention in the larger context of the political temperance movement: "If there are any people who have a good reason for advocating the passage of the '*Maine* Liquor Law,' or some other kind of prohibitory liquor law, it is the Colored people of this country."[16] White looked to connect the cause of black rights to the ascendant political temperance movement.

Though many antislavery voters hailed the victory of Know-Nothing candidates, the new party's role in antislavery politics was not entirely clear. In February 1855, *Fredrick Douglass' Paper*, which had previously complimented the Know-Nothings, began to warn of the party's "inevitable drift in a pro-slavery direction." Indeed Pollock sought to use the Know-Nothing Party as the foundation of a new national party. Just a few weeks after his election as governor, Pollock wrote, "We have the material for a 'liberal, tolerant, high-minded, and truly American party' and it will be used."[17] Whatever doubts black Philadelphians harbored about the Know-Nothings' devotion to antislavery, African

Americans knew that they needed to appeal to party supporters' opposition to slavery and relatively pro-black sentiment.

Political nativists, too, had reasons to appeal to antislavery voters. On May 24, 1855, Pollock visited Philadelphia's Institute for Colored Youth. Although the governor was interested in forging a national political party that might transcend the slavery issue, he was willing to reach out to free blacks in his own state. Jacob C. White Jr., who had previously distinguished himself through his advocacy of the temperance cause, delivered the welcoming address. According to White, the Institute's teachers and students were glad that Pollock had chosen to visit their school and given them the opportunity to demonstrate their successes. White noted that "this great Commonwealth" did not yet grant free blacks the full rights of citizenship, but he assured the governor that the school was preparing its students for the day when it would. White recalled Pollock's "noble sentiments" regarding "Common School Education" and stated his hope that the Institute's students would prove themselves "useful, worthy and respected citizens in this country of our birth and affection" and thus demonstrate that African Americans "may advance without an alienation from the land of our nativity." White's words constituted a thinly veiled reference to both African colonization and Philadelphia's nativist politics. The *National Anti-Slavery Standard* reported that Governor Pollock "seemed especially pleased with the Coloured High School, and said that his visit to no other in the city had afforded him such satisfaction."[18] White and his allies hoped that the governor's "satisfaction" might eventually translate into support for the cause of black citizenship.

While White carefully cultivated political allies, other black Philadelphians pressed the cause of black citizenship more directly, even attempting to extend citizenship rights to slaves brought onto Pennsylvania soil. On July 18, 1855, a young black man he had never seen before placed a hastily written and unsigned note into William Still's hand: "Mr. Still—Sir: Will you come down to Bloodgood's Hotel as soon as possible—as there are three and they want liberty. Their master is here with them, on his way to New York."[19]

Still immediately found the sole white member of the Acting Committee of the Vigilant Committee of Philadelphia, Passmore Williamson, and the two hurried to the hotel. After discovering that the people mentioned in the note had left, the abolitionists headed for the ferryboat landing, where they had been told they would find a woman and her two sons. Learning that the passengers had already boarded the vessel, Still and Williamson pushed their way aboard and found the woman on the top deck. Williamson took the lead, striding up to her and informing her that if she wished to be free, she was—she merely needed to walk to shore with her children. Her elderly master at first insisted that she had no desire to leave him, but when Johnson rose to go with the abolitionists, he attempted to stop her. Williamson restrained the man while Still and a few black men who had witnessed the scene spirited away the woman and her children. The woman, the activists soon learned, was Jane Johnson, and her master was John Wheeler, the U.S. minister to Nicaragua.[20]

After Johnson and her children had escaped, Williamson introduced himself to Wheeler and then returned to his office before setting out for Harrisburg, where he had a previously scheduled business engagement. Wheeler was on his way back to Nicaragua and had dined with President Franklin Pierce at the White House the previous night. The diplomat found the federal marshal for the Eastern District of Pennsylvania, who sent Wheeler to another Democratic ally, Judge John Kane. Kane issued a writ of habeas corpus requiring Williamson to appear in court. He did so after his return from Harrisburg but denied any knowledge regarding the whereabouts of Johnson and her children. Judge Kane declared Williamson to be in contempt of court, and he was taken to the Moyamensing Prison. The five black dockworkers who had helped Johnson escape were also taken into custody, and they and Still later faced charges.[21]

The case was politically charged from the start. Kane apparently was concerned that the incident and the attention it almost immediately received would prove politically troublesome for Democrats in the coming elections. The judge's efforts to soften the political damage had the opposite effect, and Williamson became a martyr for abolition. A stream of well-wishers visited his cell, and most observers agreed that sympathy for Williamson significantly broadened opposition to slavery. The Quaker lawyer embodied the fear that slave owners' political power threatened not only slaves but also white men and women. The nonabolitionist press, particularly the nativist *Philadelphia Sun*, depicted Williamson sympathetically, though Democratic papers denounced him and his antislavery allies. The newly organized Republican Party initially nominated Williamson as its candidate for canal commissioner (the highest state office contested in 1855), though his nomination as well as that of the Whig candidate ultimately were withdrawn in favor of unified support for Know-Nothing Thomas Nicholson. The fusion attempt failed, however: Nicholson lost, and Democrats retook the state House of Representatives.[22]

Black Philadelphians recognized Williamson's usefulness as a symbol but also struggled to make sure that the emphasis on the white Williamson did not erase the contributions of his black allies or eclipse the issue of black citizenship. The Colored National Convention met in Philadelphia in October 1855 and sent a committee headed by Robert Purvis to pay respects to Williamson, but the convention also passed a resolution reminding the public of the conduct of John Ballard, William Custis, John Braddock, James Martin, Josiah Moore, and William Still, the black men who had aided Jane Johnson's escape. Purvis also participated in a September meeting just north of Philadelphia that issued a similar dual celebration of blacks' and whites' struggle against slavery. That meeting also praised the *Sun*'s coverage of the incident, continuing black abolitionists' long-standing practice of reaching out to potential political allies, even those, like the nativist *Sun*, that had not always supported the cause.[23]

Pennsylvania's antislavery voters worried not only about the danger that the Slave Power posed to white liberties but also about the expansion of slavery into the Border North and the violation of free blacks' rights. Williamson sued Judge Kane for damages, and the legal maneuvering accompanying the case eventually led the state legislature to weigh in on the matter. The Democratic majority declared that "the right of transit through Pennsylvania with their slaves is already secured to the citizens of the slaveholding States by the law of Nations, and the Federal Constitution." Still published a letter in the *Provincial Freeman* in which he cited this language as evidence of the legislature's subservience to slavery, though he hoped that Governor Pollock would prove less servile. In Still's view, the Williamson case demonstrated that the Slave Power not only was willing to sacrifice the rights of white northerners but also sought to make slavery legal in Pennsylvania again.[24]

Still and many other black Philadelphians recognized that antislavery activists walked a fine line between steadfast commitment to principle and willingness to compromise in the interest of electoral success. Following the failure of the fusion candidates in 1855, antislavery voters rallied to the Republican presidential candidate, John C. Frémont, in 1856, yet Frémont received a mere 32 percent of the vote in Pennsylvania. Almost 18 percent of the opposition to the Democratic administration voted for the American Party candidate, former president Millard Fillmore. Before the election, Still had written that substantial benefits would result from the establishment of a large, strong antislavery party, even if that party failed to win this election. "Even if the Republican party should not succeed in electing their candidates," he wrote in June 1856, "they will most assuredly succeed in establishing a strong Northern party; in exposing the infamy of slaveholding doughfaceism, &c."[25] For Still, such a party, even if unsuccessful in the short run, would yield long-term dividends for the cause of antislavery.

Soon after the election, however, black Philadelphians faced the consequences of the Republicans' failure in Pennsylvania. Although they had demonstrated that a broad-based antislavery party could win throughout much of the North, their failure in the Keystone State had helped throw the presidential election to Democrat James Buchanan and had enabled the Democrats to hold on to the state legislature. Soon after the new legislature was seated, a Democratic state senator presented a memorial from citizens of Philadelphia and neighboring Bucks County asking for a law "prohibiting negroes and mulattoes from coming into our State, with view of acquiring residence." This proposal no doubt disturbed black Pennsylvanians, but they must also have been encouraged by the opposition the idea generated, especially when a handful of Democratic legislators expressed embarrassment at the memorial's "vulgar party cant."[26] The incident possessed an immediacy that the discussion of the extension of slavery may have lacked.

Similarly, Pennsylvanians saw the U.S. Supreme Court's March 6, 1857, ruling in *Dred Scott v. Sandford* not just in the national context of a struggle over slavery in the western territories but in the local context of the Border North. While the case itself concerned the legal status of an enslaved man who had been brought by his master into free territory, Chief Justice Roger Taney's "goals in Dred Scott were more political than legal." Rather than writing a narrow legal decision, Taney took the opportunity to attempt to resolve the thorny issues of slavery and states' power to legislate it. Taney's decision declared that Congress had no authority to ban slavery in the territories and that African Americans could not be citizens of the United States. By implication, it also declared that free states did not have the power to emancipate slaves brought into their territory, affirming Judge Kane's position in the Williamson/Johnson case. The pro-southern Supreme Court had called into question the existence of "free" states.[27]

When black Philadelphians met to express their outrage at the decision, they emphasized the Supreme Court's denial of the right of African Americans to be citizens rather than the decision's implications for the extension of slavery into the West. In a "spirited meeting" at Israel Church, Purvis blasted the idea that free blacks should take comfort in Republican declarations that the decision was unconstitutional. "The Supreme Court," Purvis reminded his listeners, "is the appointed tribunal, and what it said is constitutional, is constitutional to all practical intents and purposes." He saw no point in denying, as some abolitionists did, the fact that the Constitution defended slavery. The meeting declared that "no allegiance is due from any man, or any class of men, to a Government founded and administered in iniquity." Furthermore, under such a Constitution and government, African Americans could only ever be "an alien, disfranchised and degraded class."[28]

Such language might have indicated a retreat by Purvis and other black Philadelphians who had refused to relinquish their claims to American citizenship. Mary Ann Shadd Cary, a free black woman who had moved to Canada in the wake of the passage of the Fugitive Slave Law and who later edited the *Provin-*

cial Freeman, called on the meeting's participants to go beyond the rhetoric that denounced the pro-slavery government. "Do the Purvises, Remonds, and others, who took part in the meeting intend to stay in the U. States?" she asked. "If so, the resolutions amount to nothing, if not why not say so friends? Your national ship is rotten sinking, why not leave it, and why not say so boldly, manfully?" Yet Purvis did not abandon his native country and in fact remained a strong critic of those who did. Still maintained a close relationship with those who had emigrated to Canada, but he, too, remained in the United States.[29]

At least part of their reasoning emerges in a hopeful resolution passed by the Philadelphia meeting:

> *Resolved*, That we rejoice that slave holding despotism lays its ruthless hand not only on the humble black man, but on the proud Northern white man; and our hope is that when our white fellow slaves in these so-called free states see that they are alike subject with us to the slave oligarchy, the difference of our servitude being only in degree, they will make common cause with us.[30]

The resolution distinguishes between the American nation and the American government. The latter is dominated by the Slave Power, but attendees at the meeting hold out hope for the former and see promise in the awakening of white northerners to the threat to their liberties. Black Philadelphians hoped that the emergence of this sort of criticism of the Slave Power would not lead white northerners away from the abolitionist defense of black rights but would instead lead them to make common cause with free blacks. To this end, Purvis, Still, and others worked to make sure that the rights of free blacks remained bound up with the rights of white northerners.

Nevertheless, Taney's decision caused Still to have serious doubts about the possibility of achieving significant progress in the United States. He shared his disillusionment in a published letter to Cary, written just over a week after the decision's publication. He noted that Isaiah Wear and some of Philadelphia's other black leaders saw the decision as further evidence that no man could be spared from the fight against slavery and racial prejudice. Others even argued that the decision was good because it laid bare the ambitions of the Slave Power, thereby hastening the day when the North would stand united against slaveholder aggression. But Still admitted, "I am not of the number any longer to subscribe to the above 'staying' &c. doctrine," and he wrote approvingly of emigrants to Canada. Still might change his mind if free blacks vigorously engaged in the effort to change the United States, since "it would then seem imperative duty to submit to existing circumstances." But he saw little evidence of such an effort. His disillusionment, then, arose both from the decision itself and from the seeming lack of active resistance to it and was likely reinforced by the results of the fall 1857 elections in Pennsylvania. The antislavery Democrat turned Republican, David Wilmot, received only 40 percent of the vote in his campaign for governor. A significant number of nativist voters could not bring themselves to vote for Wilmot, and the American Party candidate received almost 8 percent of the vote. Democrats expanded their share of the one-hundred-seat legislature from fifty-three to sixty-eight.[31]

Still's letter constituted a call to action. It was printed in the *Toronto Provincial Freeman*, and Canadian readers might have read his words and felt justified in their decision to emigrate. But those who had remained in the land of their birth might well have felt themselves challenged to do more to fight against slavery and for black equality, just as Still did.

Still's work remained simultaneously secretive and public. The Vigilant Committee of Philadelphia continued its work unabated through the 1850s, and though much of it was clandestine, the committee's position as the organizational heart of the Underground Railroad meant that it also could be a weapon in the broader fight against slavery. Carefully considered publicity formed a crucial part of that effort. Still's public references to the committee's work tended to be vague: "P.S. Just had, this evening, a fine arrival, per underground," he wrote in one letter to the *Provincial Freeman*. Yet he and other members of the Vigilant Committee released just enough information to feed the legend of the Underground Railroad. In a letter printed in the *Liberty Bell* in late 1857, committee member James Miller McKim noted that fifty men, women, and children had "passed through the hands of our Vigilance Committee in the last fortnight." They came "from every part of the border States," he noted, and as a result of their actions, "the tenure by which slave property is held all along our borders is greatly weakened." Magnifying the Vigilant Committee's effectiveness required that large numbers of slaveholders, especially along the border, knew of its activities and feared that their slaves would find their way onto the Underground Railroad.[32]

The Dred Scott decision caused some disillusioned African Americans to reconsider their attachment to the United States, and white colonizationists again sought to seize the opportunity to soften free blacks' aversion to African colonization. Benjamin Coates, a white Philadelphia Quaker, had for years been intrigued by the idea of cultivating cotton in West Africa. He hoped that the crop would prove an economic boon for Africa, simultaneously attracting black immigrants from the United States and undercutting the profitability of cotton cultivation in the slaveholding South. In 1858, he published his argument in a pamphlet sent to numerous prominent abolitionists. He also suggested the creation of the African Civilization Society to promote these goals, though he admitted that many free blacks would see this new organization as "only African Colonization under another name, which it really is." While some free blacks remained resistant to anything that smacked of colonization, others expressed support. Former Philadelphian William Whipper, for example, responded positively to Coates's plan.[33]

Many free blacks supported emigration to Africa out of a growing sense of black nationalism, but as historian Wilson Moses has demonstrated, black nationalism was a complex phenomenon. Some advocates of emigration cited their devotion to the establishment of a black nation, but many proponents of black nationalism never made a serious effort to settle outside of the United States. Black nationalism could even be used as a tool for assimilationist ends as part of the fight for black citizenship in the United States. Many advocates for emigration emphasized it as a practical measure rather than as the fulfillment of an ideological commitment.[34]

Similarly, interest in African colonization appears to have undergone a resurgence among whites for a variety of reasons. Some, like Coates, advocated it as a means of undermining slavery. Others, driven by the idea that blacks and whites could never live together peacefully in the United States, hoped that colonization would ultimately remove the entire black population. Still others had more modest aims. An editorial in the *Philadelphia Inquirer*, which now supported the Republicans, advocated colonization as a means of removing the "low and abandoned class of men and women of African descent"—but not all free blacks. "There are good and bad of all kinds of the human family," and the editor insisted that most free blacks were productive members of the communities in which they lived.[35]

Pennsylvania colonizationists recognized that though many free blacks spoke the language of black nationalism while remaining in the United States, others hoped to find a better life in Liberia, even while maintaining their claim on American citizenship. White Pennsylvanian Charles Brown hoped that even those who remained committed to the goal of black citizenship in the United States could be induced to support colonization and offered a resolution:

> While we have no sympathy with those who would deny to the colored man his rights on American soil, and who advocate African Colonization merely as a means of removing from this country the descendants of Africa, we do feel a warm interest in what our brethren are doing in Liberia.... When, therefore, the Pennsylvania Colonization Society will assure us that it is *not expatriation* which they desire, but the happiness and usefulness of colored persons in Liberia... we will cordially lend our influence to carry forward, with them, the same benevolent enterprise.[36]

As a consequence of some combination of disillusionment with black progress in the United States, a shift in the rhetoric of colonization, the failures of antislavery politics, and other factors, emigration to Liberia boomed in the wake of the Dred Scott decision. Between 1858 and 1860, about as many free blacks left Pennsylvania for Liberia as had done so in the previous twenty years.³⁷

At the same time, however, the 1858 elections offered cause for optimism. In the spring municipal elections, People's Party candidate for mayor of Philadelphia Alexander Henry soundly defeated the incumbent Democrat. And in the fall, Pennsylvania Republicans routed their opponents, who had been splintered by Buchanan's support of Kansas's fraudulent pro-slavery Lecompton government. Democrats in Pennsylvania also shouldered much of the blame for a national financial crisis beginning in late 1857. The Republican share of the state legislature jumped from thirty seats in 1856 to sixty-seven seats two years later, though these gains apparently resulted from Democratic voters' disillusionment with their party rather than from a dramatic increase in the number of Republican voters. It remained to be seen whether these antislavery victories would translate into progress for the cause of black citizenship.³⁸

Fighting for Black Citizenship Rights in Maryland

Maryland politics proved just as tumultuous as those of its northern neighbor. In October 1854, Baltimore elected the relatively unknown Samuel Hinks, a Know-Nothing, as mayor. In 1855, the American Party swept the state, electing four of six congressmen, fifty-four of seventy-four members of the House of Delegates, and eight of the eleven contested State Senate seats. In 1856, Maryland was the only state to cast its U.S. presidential electoral votes for Millard Fillmore, and in 1857, the state elected a Know-Nothing governor. Little distinguished the legislature's Know-Nothings from its Democrats on issues relating to slavery or free blacks, but the state Democratic Party continued to insist that the Know-Nothings were controlled by antislavery northerners. According to Baltimore Know-Nothing congressman Henry Winter Davis, the party needed to hold its "tongue on the negro issue," but reticence opened members up to Democratic attacks. Perhaps just as disturbing to defenders of slavery was the emergence in Baltimore of northern-style urban politics, with ethnic conflict, machine politics, and violent mobs.³⁹

Whites found these developments even more alarming in light of free blacks' increasing political assertiveness, particularly in Baltimore. The free black convention held there in 1852 (ostensibly in support of colonization) had stunned even northern observers. Further evidence that Baltimore's African Americans were becoming increasingly attuned to electoral politics came in the fall 1856 when a group of free blacks returning from a picnic engaged in an altercation with a group of Irish immigrants. Such skirmishes were fairly common, but in this case, after driving off the Irishmen, the African Americans spied "a political liberty pole, erected by Democrats of that vicinity, ... gave three cheers for Frémont and immediately attempted to pull the pole and the flag down."[40] The incident not only illustrated an increasingly assertive black population's interest in the Republican Party but also bore what southern Democrats saw as ominous overtones regarding the connections between the Republicans' explicit antislavery sentiment and the nativist issues that had broad appeal.

As free black Marylanders awakened to their potential political influence, many whites, especially slave owners, remained fearful of the free black population. In February 1858, the state legislature passed a bill tightening restrictions on the manumission of slaves, a move that received notice in the northern press. Maryland slaveholders also remained concerned about the numbers of slaves who fled their masters, and a Kent County meeting of owners warned that abolitionists who helped encourage slaves to escape would be tarred and feathered. A series of county meetings called for a larger meeting of residents of all of the Eastern Shore in the fall. This meeting, organizers hoped, would help to end what one Philadelphia newspaper termed the "Slave Stampedes in Maryland."[41]

The convention's initial goals—greater control of the free black population and greater efforts to prevent abolitionists from influencing slaves—were unsurprising, but the gathering took an unforeseen and ominous turn. Several delegates, most prominently Curtis W. Jacobs, a radical pro-slavery voice at the 1850 constitutional convention, contended that the only solution to the problems posed by free blacks was their reenslavement. According to Jacobs, "Restoring the free negroes to servitude should at once be avowed as the only remedy to the evils complained of." The convention did not support these drastic measures but did call for a statewide convention to be held the following year in Baltimore, where organizers hoped that even the representatives of the parts of the state where slavery was less common could be persuaded to join the effort to fight antislavery forces.[42]

If the prime movers behind the convention hoped that holding the meeting in Baltimore would convince the city's whites of the importance of their goals, they were mistaken. When the gathering opened, not a single Baltimore delegate was in attendance, though a few attended later. Led by Jacobs, the convention's minority called for legislation to give free blacks two options: leave Maryland or return to slavery. He also argued that the state should sell reenslaved blacks at low prices and allow payment in installments, dramatically increasing the number of whites with a direct stake in slavery. The overwhelming majority of the delegates, however, generally agreed with the notion that free blacks were detrimental to the institution of slavery but pushed for more moderate measures, such as the more rigorous enforcement of laws requiring the removal of emancipated slaves from the state. Some delegates opposed Jacobs on the grounds that free blacks were essential to the state's economy, but others denounced the morality of reenslavement. Returning to slavery those who "have acquired by our laws and the tenderness of their masters" their freedom would be akin, declared one delegate, to "the highwayman who demands of the traveler his money or his life."[43] Even slaveholders mustered little support for the drastic Lower South remedies proposed by Jacobs.

Those views changed after John Brown's October 16, 1859, attack on the federal arsenal at Harpers Ferry, Virginia, which he hoped would lead to a rebellion by slaves and poor whites. Brown's rebellion was quickly put down, but it provoked hysteria throughout the South, including in neighboring Maryland, which had been Brown's base of operations.[44] The fact that free blacks had been among Brown's initial band stoked white Marylanders' fears concerning the state's large free black population. Less than a month later, on November 6, 1859, Marylanders went to the polls. The *Baltimore Sun* cast the election as an explicit defense of southern "rights and institutions." The American Party had enjoyed significant majorities in the previous legislature, but both houses now flipped to the Democratic column, with the party holding an eighteen-seat margin in the House and a two-seat edge in the Senate.[45] Jacobs was among the newly elected legislators, and they proved much more open to his reenslavement plan.

White Marylanders were not alone in the attention they paid to the events at Harpers Ferry. Early on the morning of December 13, 1859, Baltimore police broke up the annual ball of the "association of colored caulkers" as a result of some sort of disturbance. White Baltimoreans were appalled to learn that on one part of the floor was a chalk picture of John Brown bearing the inscription "The martyr—God bless him," while another part of the room featured a picture of pro-slavery Virginia governor Henry Wise, "and near it one of a huge Ethiopian, with inscriptions unfit for publication."[46] Free blacks not only admired Brown but placed his raid into the larger political context. The attack on Harpers Ferry was not simply a slave rebellion; it was a part of a larger political assault on slavery and proslavery politicians, and Baltimore's free blacks hoped to join that assault.

In his position as the chair of the legislature's Committee on the Colored Population, Jacobs helped push for a stringent new law to solve the "blighting influence of free negro-ism." Jacobs's committee proposed placing drastic new restrictions on free blacks in the state, banning future manumissions, and requiring that free blacks who remained in the state be hired out for ten-year labor contracts. The bill also created a sizable bureaucracy tasked with enforcing these measures. Though white Marylanders remained concerned about their free black population, the committee's solution went too far even for the Democrat-controlled legislature. It passed a milder version of the bill that barred manumission and allowed each county to vote on whether to create a board of commissioners to make sure that free blacks who did not own property were hired out for one-year terms. This vote would be held in the fall, at the same time as the presidential election.⁴⁷

From the start, black Baltimoreans had rallied to oppose the reenslavement campaign. Black Methodists helped to persuade the church's white pastors to submit a memorial to the legislature declaring their rejection of this or any other "oppressive and vexatious changes in existing laws." Andrew B. Cross, a white clergyman and member of the Baltimore City Council, wrote an open letter to Jacobs, denouncing the "monstrous propositions before the legislature." Black churches held days of prayer and hosted prominent black speakers who railed against reenslavement. Thousands of free blacks signed a petition urging voters to reject the bill when it was placed before the electorate. In November 1860, more than 70 percent of Maryland voters rejected the reenslavement bills, with Baltimoreans opposing the measures by a margin of nearly eight to one. By Pennsylvania standards, the state's failure to reenslave free blacks might not have looked like a victory for the cause of black citizenship, but black Marylanders, particularly those in Baltimore, could take heart from the fact that an overwhelming white majority had rallied to the defense of at least some measure of black citizenship rights.⁴⁸

Africa, "Foreigners," and Black Citizenship

Many white opponents of slavery continued to see African colonization as the key to expanding antislavery's popular appeal. In 1851, the Washington-based *National Era* had begun publishing installments of a sentimental novel by Harriet Beecher Stowe. Published in book form the following year, *Uncle Tom's Cabin; or, Life among the Lowly* became an instant best seller. Abolitionists recognized that the book's popularity offered a tremendous opportunity to widen the antislavery circle, but many veterans of the fight, especially free blacks, were disturbed by the book's closing chapters. What many abolitionists perceived as the book's most heroic character, the self-emancipated George Harris, decides that even though he is light-skinned enough to "mingle in the circles of the whites," he will instead embrace his "mother's race." Harris's yearning for "an African nationality" then leads him to conclude that he must leave the United States. He rejects "worn out" and "effeminate" Haiti as a destination unsuitable for a proud nation before casting his lot with Liberia, declaring, "On the shores of Africa I see a republic."⁴⁹

Robert Purvis found Stowe's endorsement of colonization particularly painful. In a letter to Oliver Johnson, the editor of the *Pennsylvania Freeman*, Purvis lamented the novel's Liberian turn, especially since he saw in the rest of the book the potential to produce "a speedy and mighty change in the nation's sentiment toward the cause of freedom." The conclusion, therefore, hit him as "a terrible blow." Johnson printed Purvis's letter and expressed his sympathy with Purvis's view yet maintained that on balance, the work was likely to further abolitionists' work. Purvis, however, saw any attempt to widen antislavery's appeal by embracing colonization and its implicit denial of a place for blacks in the United States as ultimately harmful to African Americans.[50]

Purvis remained one of the most outspoken and unbending critics of any thaw in the relationship between abolitionists and colonization. He spoke in favor of the anticolonization resolution adopted by the American Anti-Slavery Society meeting in May 1852 and took the opportunity to malign what he saw as Frederick Douglass's increasingly conciliatory stance on colonization, which Purvis attributed to a bribe paid to Douglass by Benjamin Coates. Douglass dismissed this accusation and denied that he was friendly to colonization, but the split between the two black abolitionists continued to widen. A year later, Douglass explained Purvis's hostility as a consequence of his "blood stained riches" (an allusion to his white cotton-merchant father).[51]

Purvis no doubt exaggerated Douglass's sympathy for African colonization, but it was true that few could match Purvis in his denunciations of the American Colonization Society. In 1853, black Philadelphians met to collectively express their opposition to colonization. This time, the gathering was prompted by several days of "warm public discussion" of colonization in West Chester, not far from Philadelphia. A group of black Philadelphians led by William Still once again met at Brick Wesley Church, where speakers expressed their outrage at the "absurd notion that Africa alone is their 'Fatherland'" and the only place where they were entitled to be "free and elevated." Also among the speakers was Mary Ann Shadd. Once again, opposition to colonization brought together those who supported voluntary emigration and those who felt that even consensual colonization constituted an admission that blacks could not be American.[52]

African Americans countered the abstract claim that people of African descent could not be Americans by commemorating the contributions that free blacks had made to their nation's history. On November 25, 1852, the *Pennsylvania Freeman* printed a review of Boston-based black abolitionist William Cooper Nell's book, *Services of Colored Americans in the Wars of 1776 and 1812*. According to the review, the volume reminded Americans "of the loyal devotion of the people of color to their country in the hour of danger and disaster." Furthermore, "The impartial foreigner who reads this page of our country's history cannot but be indignant at our aggravated and repeated injuries to men who have imperiled their life in defense of our freedom and rights." Nell's work has been read as a demonstration of black capabilities, refuting claims of racial inferiority, but the *Freeman* pointed explicitly to it as an argument that African Americans had earned American citizenship, underlining this assertion by using a "foreigner" as a reader.[53]

This tactic for pushing the cause of black citizenship was not new in the 1850s, but it acquired a new resonance in the decade's political context. William Lloyd Garrison had invited Purvis to speak at the May 1854 meeting of the American Anti-Slavery Society on a topic of his own choosing, "colonization, colorphobia, the claims of the colored population to freedom and equality in the land of their birth." Purvis offered a resolution in which he praised the progress "in public sentiment on the subject of the colored man's rights." Rather than pointing to Whig efforts to assume the mantle of antislavery in Pennsylvania, Purvis chose to celebrate the public denunciation that had greeted statements made by New York–based printer John Mitchel, an Irish nationalist. In his journal, *The Citizen*, Mitchel had denied that owning slaves was immoral, invoking the authority of Moses, Socrates, and Jesus Christ. Mitchel continued, "We, for our part, wish we had a good plantation, well stocked with healthy negroes, in Alabama." The northern public response, Purvis declared, had led to Mitchel's "defeat, disgrace and moral death," evidence that such servile defenses of slavery would no longer be tolerated.[54]

Purvis went further, however, calling attention not just to Mitchel's words but to the man himself and specifically his Irish origins. The public's rejection of this "Irish miscreant," Purvis predicted, would become "a warning to any unprincipled foreign adventurer who may hastily prostrate their servile souls to the slaveholding spirit of our land." He contrasted black Philadelphians' support for Irish Repeal with this Irishman's treatment of African Americans and pointed out the irony that such foreign-born defenders of slavery might become American citizens while Purvis could not. "In other words," continued Purvis, "this liberty-loving patriot shall decide whether his influence shall be for or against native born Americans, many of whom are descendants of those who shed their blood in the Revolutionary struggle."[55]

Purvis viewed the northern public's rejection of Mitchel's pronouncements as the most important aspect of the incident but highlighted Mitchel's foreign birth to implicitly reassert African American claims on American nationality. Purvis might have pointed simply to northern outrage at the Kansas-Nebraska Bill, but just as the Know-Nothing Party merged antislavery with fear of immigrant political influence, so Purvis depicted Mitchel's proslavery writings as not just wrong but as fundamentally un-American. By emphasizing Mitchel's foreignness, Purvis provided an unexpected counter to those who had come to see American politics and American society as irredeemably hostile to African Americans.

In the mid-1850s, the *Christian Recorder*, the newspaper of the African Methodist Episcopal Church, also took up the cause of black citizenship. The journal's stated mission was to publish material on "1. Religion, 2. Morality, 3. Science and Literature," but politics, too, became an important subject. A letter published under the heading "Our Political Rights" exhorted readers to sustain the political efforts that arose during times of crisis and to continue to petition the state legislature for black political rights. If black Pennsylvanians had "expended half the zeal in the right direction that has been lost in denouncing the oppressors and each other, we would, long since have reaped the benefit in the amelioration of our condition." But such political optimism did not go unchallenged. A month later, Johnson Woodlin, a black Philadelphian and activist, challenged the efficacy of such tactics, suggesting that the achievement of full citizenship in the United States was unforeseeable.[56]

Just as Purvis had used the foreignness of his opponent to highlight his own Americanness and to link the antislavery cause to American patriotism, so, too, the *Christian Recorder* used what it depicted as the foreignness of Catholicism to highlight the Americanness of the publication's form of black Protestantism. The *Recorder* frequently printed strikingly anti-Catholic rhetoric, often featuring stories warning of the international threat posed by the Catholic Church. According to a typical piece from August 1854,

> Rome works insidiously among us, as she does everywhere else. Our people must be made acquainted with her subtleties and plans if we would defeat them. . . . It is only by enlightening the people on the nature and objects of Rome's movements that we can hope to save our country from the dangers which threaten it from that quarter.

The editors refrained from endorsing the Know-Nothing Party but printed letters from readers who supported Know-Nothings. "I would rather be with the Know Nothing party," wrote church member William Moore in September 1854, "than stay with the Do Nothings."[57] Moore implied that he believed that the Know-Nothings would do something to advance the antislavery cause, but he also engaged in the rhetorical mingling of nativism and antislavery.

Some African Americans sought to emphasize their Americanness by depicting white immigrants' antiblack prejudice as fundamentally foreign; however, far more blacks saw white supremacy as the product not of foreign prejudice but of American slavery. In September 1854, free black orator and former slave William Wells Brown returned to the United States after a sojourn in Great Britain. He disembarked in the city of Philadelphia, only weeks before the Know-Nothings' Pennsylvania electoral triumph. The Vigilant Committee of Philadelphia welcomed him at the Brick Wesley Church, and after a month in the city, Brown traveled to West Chester to address the annual meeting of the Pennsylvania Anti-Slavery Society. Brown began by denouncing slavery as a "great mistake" of the American founders, but he urged his audience to look around to see slavery's consequences: northern free blacks were suffering from the degradations wrought by the Peculiar Institution.[58] Like so many proponents of political antislavery, Brown focused on slavery's effects on the North rather than on the evils of slavery. By focusing on the plight of free blacks, he resisted attempts by some political opponents of slavery to emphasize the danger that the Slave Power presented to white northerners. Free blacks, he insisted, must be among those defended from the encroachment of aggressive slavery.

In addition to depicting slavery as the root of northern race prejudice, Brown also stressed the injustice of the fact that foreign-born whites received rights denied to American-born blacks. When Brown and two of his foreign-born shipmates disembarked after landing in Philadelphia, they

> started to walk up the streets of Philadelphia together; we hailed an omnibus; the two foreigners got in; I was told that "niggers" were not allowed to ride. Foreigners, mere adventurers, perhaps, in this country, are treated as equals, while I, American born, whose grandfather fought in the revolution, am not permitted to ride in one of your fourth-rate omnibuses. The foreigner has a right, after five years residence, to say who shall be president, as far as his vote goes, even though he cannot read your Constitution or write his name, while 600,000 free coloured people are disfranchised.[59]

By focusing on his companions' foreignness, ignorance of American culture, and their illiteracy, Brown highlights his own claims for American citizenship and perhaps even taps into nativist whites' anxieties.

Another black Philadelphian, Frank Webb, drew on the more negative aspects of political nativism to make a different sort of case for black citizenship. Webb had connections to prominent black Philadelphians and seems to have been something of an activist. In 1854, he delivered a lecture at the black Banneker Institute on "The Martial Capacity of Blacks." In the wake of the failure of his business, he wrote a novel, *The Garies and Their Friends*, and accompanied his wife, a respected actress, on a tour to Great Britain. Set in Webb's native Philadelphia, the novel was published in London in 1857.[60]

The novel, the second one to be published by an African American, centers on a Philadelphia riot (based in part on the actual riot of 1842) in which Irish immigrants terrorize the city's free blacks. The riot results from the machinations of the novel's villain, Stevens, a lawyer. Incensed that the amalgamationist

Garie family has moved in next door to him, Stevens concocts a plan to murder Garie and to drive the black residents out of his neighborhood (and to buy up their property for a song). Stevens hires some Irish thugs to start the riot. When they express concern about the legal consequences of their actions, Stevens assures them that he will use his political influence to protect them. He also uses these men to deliver the Irish vote in his district on Election Day: "I'm all right down here, you know," he brags to a potential officeholder. "I own the boys in this district; and if you say you put some little matters through for me after you are elected, I'll call it a bargain." The Irish thugs carry out their assignment, resulting in Garie's murder.[61]

Webb uses Irish immigrants to illustrate the injustice of denying native-born African Americans the rights of citizenship and depicts white immigrants as a crucial means by which unscrupulous northern politicians oppress free blacks. Webb wrote just as Know-Nothing politics was ascendant, and his book embraces the Know-Nothing assertion that ignorant immigrant voters were the tools of the Slave Power. Though the Irish rioters bear no particular hatred for their free black neighbors, they are easily manipulated by the oily Stevens. Just as Know-Nothings had warned, demagogues easily manipulate (Catholic) Irish immigrants with no real appreciation for U.S. republican institutions. Webb transposes the 1842 riot into 1850s political culture. Similarly, he takes longstanding abolitionist suspicions of electoral politics and places them in the different but related political culture of the Know-Nothings, who also expressed profound suspicion of political wire-pullers.[62]

If Webb saw immigrant whites as the enablers of a political system that had denied black Pennsylvanians the rights of citizenship, he may well not have been surprised in January 1855 when a Know-Nothing legislator from western Pennsylvania introduced a bill "to confer upon Colored Persons the Right of Citizenship." The measure would have granted free black residents of the state the same "civil, religious and political rights" as other citizens of the commonwealth. In support of this bill, a group of black Philadelphians drafted a *Memorial of Thirty Thousand Disfranchised Citizens*, which they published and presented to the state legislature.[63]

The memorial drew on the long tradition of black political discourse, but befitting its political context, it is suffused with a sort of black nativist rhetoric. It criticized the injustice of granting citizenship to white immigrants while denying it to native born blacks and depicted white immigrants as key participants in the political disfranchisement of free blacks. The first section offered a litany of the abuse suffered by black Pennsylvanians: "Assaulted on public streets . . . dragged before a magistrate, incapable of speaking our language correctly . . . Forced from our places of business by a population incapable of comprehending the freedom of our institutions." Such offenses, the memorial declared constituted an " imitation of that tyranny from which [immigrants] have but recently escaped." In contrast to their oppressors, blacks "are native Americans, and since allegiance is due from us, protection and equal rights are due from the Government." The memorial subsequently shifts to demanding citizenship as a right: "Return to us those rights of which we are deprived, and which you have so freely given to the sons of men who fought against your independence." The authors also invoked Crispus Attucks, a former slave slain in the 1770 Boston Massacre who had emerged in the 1850s as a powerful symbol of the black contribution to the American Revolution, reminding readers that "the first blood shed upon the altar of American Republicanism" was that of "a colored man." Despite black activists' efforts, the bill failed to pass. Sympathy for black voting rights was outweighed by the political risks and by continuing fears of racial amalgamation.[64]

Over the 1850s, more and more voters became willing to support the antislavery cause. Some contemporaries observed this trend, but even optimistic free blacks living on the border did not have the luxury of waiting out this progress. Their liberties remained precarious, and they needed to appeal to whatever allies could be found. Often they looked to political parties that were not explicitly antislavery but that nonetheless possessed significant sympathy for antislavery and even for black citizenship rights. In addition, while free blacks applauded the antislavery progress of the 1850s, they justifiably worried that antislavery politicians might abandon the cause of black citizenship while searching for a larger share of the voting public. Slavery loomed as a national issue, while black politics continued to focus on African Americans' citizenship rights: protections from kidnapping, free states' treatment of accused fugitive slaves, whether African Americans were really Americans, should all African Americans be reenslaved? These questions continued to roil the politics of Maryland and Pennsylvania as the United States marched toward Civil War.

CHAPTER 9

The End of the Border
Black Citizenship, Secession, and the Civil War

Like their counterparts in Baltimore, many black Philadelphians applauded John Brown's efforts. Some did so in private. William Still apparently knew of Brown's plans prior to the attack, and after the assault, three black pastors from Philadelphia wrote to Virginia governor Henry Wise asking that the bodies of two of the men who fought with Brown at Harpers Ferry be transferred to their care. Others expressed their support in public. Black Philadelphians draped their homes in black in Brown's honor and held public prayer meetings. Robert Purvis spoke at a large meeting in National Hall whose attendees included both supporters of Brown and "union" counterprotesters. Purvis denounced the "trembling despots of Virginia" and warned that Brown's execution "marks the beginning of the end." He continued, "I thank God for this unmistakable sign of the times which indicates a deeper feeling for the irrepressible conflict." This remark drew both cheers and hisses from the audience. Baltimore newspapers expressed shock at the level of support for Brown but also reported considerable outrage in Philadelphia at Brown's actions.[1]

Some black Philadelphians agreed with Purvis regarding the growing antislavery tide, but the mixed response that such claims received surely reminded them that many white Philadelphians remained willing to sacrifice black citizenship rights in the interest of defending the union. Despite Purvis's rhetorical optimism, black Philadelphians understood that the political successes of the late 1850s were tenuous. They certainly worried that the ascendant Republican Party remained too willing to abandon even its limited support for black citizenship rights in the interest of electoral success or sectional comity. Most of all, they recognized that the liberties of free black Pennsylvanians continued to face threats from the existence of slavery to the immediate south. True, Maryland had rejected the Deep South measures advocated by Curtis W. Jacobs, but slavery remained.

As long as slavery remained in Maryland and as long as Pennsylvania denied black residents' citizenship rights, black Pennsylvanians lived in a precarious borderland. On April 2, 1859, slave catchers seized a black man known as Daniel Webster near Harrisburg. They alleged that he was in fact Daniel Dangerfield, who had run away from his owner in Virginia seven years earlier. He was taken by train to Philadelphia and brought before the U.S. commissioner. A large, antislavery crowd gathered almost immediately, with some cramming themselves into the small room where the hearing was held and most, among them Purvis, remaining outside. Fearful that they would attempt to rescue the man, police pushed back the assembled crowd with "an unusual degree of roughness." Inside, the spectators cheered each move by the defense. The commissioner decided that the claimants had not adequately demonstrated that the accused had been enslaved; when word of the verdict leaked out, the massive crowd burst into cheers "so great that the proceedings inside could not have been heard." Webster emerged and was carried down the street in triumph "upon the shoulders of a colossal colored man."[2] Many of the gathered crowd surely remembered when the Philadelphia police had failed to defend abolitionists from proslavery mobs. They must have marveled at this turn of events, as the city's police force restrained this antislavery mob.

Whatever optimism prevailed among black Philadelphians, they remained cognizant of the threat that slavery posed to them. In an 1860 celebration of West Indian emancipation, Still used the border as a call to arms: "Let us fancy ourselves just across Mason Dixon's line, only a few hours ride from this spot—regarded there as property—as belonging if you please to the most pious and kindhearted slaveholder that could be found—deprived of all rights, liable to all outrages." He again called for renewed efforts at black self-improvement, but he also laid out a larger plan that continued his active support for fugitives. He coupled a hope for and reliance on white benevolence with a more active and confrontational assault on slavery, noting that this strategy was particularly important in Pennsylvania "because we are bordered by three slaveholding states." In Still's view, black Pennsylvanians geographic position not only meant that they had a particular responsibility to aid their fugitive brethren but also forced them to recognize that whites from free as well as slave states were watching. Black Pennsylvanians needed to show themselves in the best possible light and use what influence they had with "those friendly to us in legislative halls, editorial chairs and places of power." Still held out hope that white politicians were becoming increasingly receptive to such claims.[3]

Yet underneath the optimism remained the conviction that white Philadelphians' latent support must not be taken for granted; it needed to be cultivated.

Still provided an anecdote illustrating the antislavery potential of such work. The editor "of an influential and popular journal" had been a staunch supporter of full enforcement of the Fugitive Slave Law but was nevertheless curious about the workings of the Underground Railroad. After promising to remain silent, he was permitted to witness the "arrival of fifteen passengers," a sight that so moved him that he donated money to the cause on the spot. The editor and other white Philadelphians might have been willing to sacrifice black Philadelphians on the altar of the Fugitive Slave Law but nevertheless retained sympathy for black rights. Still continued his clandestine work in support of fugitives, and in December 1860, he provided aid to the members of a fugitive family who had escaped with Harriet Tubman on her last trip into Maryland.[4]

The outbreak of the Civil War threatened to remake the mid-Atlantic borderland, but in the early months of the war, the Lincoln administration did its best to reassure nervous Border State slaveholders. In response to pressure from a Maryland congressman, Lincoln urged General-in-Chief Winfield Scott to allow Maryland masters to recover fugitives who had fled to Union lines. Most Republicans recognized that whatever the case in the states that had seceded, in Maryland and the other slaveholding states that had remained loyal to the Union, the Fugitive Slave Law remained in effect and should be enforced.[5]

But who would enforce this law remained to be determined, and masters increasingly found their efforts to recover their property thwarted. Republicans may have given lip service to support for the Fugitive Slave Law, but many believed that local governments bore responsibility for enforcement. Historian James Oakes has argued that however eager Lincoln was to appease Maryland slaveholders, he regretted his early concession to their "property" rights, and he and Republicans in Congress soon made it clear that Union soldiers were not as a matter of policy to participate in the return of fugitive slaves. From the outset of the war, Maryland had been flooded by Union troops, and they thus became de facto emancipators. Maryland slaveholders who entered Union camps to claim fugitives alleged that they were ridiculed and threatened with violence. Some units were more amenable to slave catchers than others, but Maryland frequently complained that despite its loyalty to the Union, its citizens' rights were being denied.[6]

African Americans applauded the Union Army's role in promoting emancipation: "There are upwards of two hundred fugitive slaves hovering around this camp," reported black Philadelphian George Stephens, who was traveling with the army in Maryland. "When this division moves, if it ever does, a black army will move with it."[7] Whatever the public pronouncements of the Lincoln administration, Stephens was sure that the Union Army would protect the rights of these black contraband of war.

While the Fugitive Slave Law still technically threatened black liberties, many of those who had previously been involved in aiding fugitives now shifted to providing aid for this new wave of men, women, and children fleeing from slavery. Still headed an "Office for Obtaining Employment for Colored Persons," which assisted former slaves not only with finding work but also with locating lost relatives and finding housing. The office coordinated its work with the newly established Freedman's Relief Association in Washington, D.C.[8]

Black Philadelphians gradually found the border region less and less threatening, though Maryland slaveholders clung tenaciously to the institution of slavery. Despite Lincoln's warning that the "friction and abrasion" of warfare would be the end of slavery in their state and the growing numbers of slaves fleeing north, Marylanders rejected the president's offer of compensated emancipation.[9]

The Civil War transformed the context of the struggle for black citizenship in Pennsylvania, but even before the collapse of the mid-Atlantic border, black Philadelphians had begun pushing more aggressively for citizenship rights. In the spring of 1857, the *Provincial Freeman* had printed a letter in which Still expressed skepticism about the possibility of achieving any measure of black equality in the United States in the near term and implied support for Canadian emigration. Just over two years later, Still presented a very different face in a letter to a conservative newspaper, the *North American*. Identifying himself as "a colored man and constant reader of your paper," he offered to share the grievances of "genteel colored people" regarding their exclusion from the city's streetcars.[10]

The letter demonstrates that by 1859, Still saw the possibility of ending some of the legal and customary discrimination faced by black Philadelphians. However, it also shows that Still recognized the political reality that this struggle could not be won on the pages of the *Liberator* or the *National Anti-Slavery Standard*. The *North American* had been a Whig journal before leaning to some degree toward the Native American and Know-Nothing Parties. Though critical of slavery at times, it would hardly have been considered an antislavery paper. Still tailored his appeal specifically to the paper's conservative readers. He noted that throughout the North and even in New Orleans, African Americans were permitted to ride on streetcars, hoping to shame white Philadelphians by pointing out that even free blacks in the Deep South enjoyed some rights still denied to black Philadelphians. Still blamed whatever degradation existed among black Philadelphians on "groggeries," which "low and degrading as they may be, are not licensed by colored men." Still not only painted degraded blacks as the victims of white rum sellers but implicitly differentiated respectable blacks who avoided these establishments from their lower-class brethren. He sought to create a political coalition between white and black supporters of temperance. Still's letter was not successful in the short run, but it did hint at the sort of strategies that would ultimately bring positive results.[11]

Black Philadelphians seemed increasingly confident in their strategy of stressing respectability. On March 2, 1860, while addressing the Colored Evening School, Still called for a renewed devotion to education among black Philadelphians. As befit the occasion, he exhorted his listeners to strive for self-help, but he was also realistic about the barriers that remained for free blacks in the North. And he reiterated the note of optimism that was present in his letter to the *North American*: "Some of the opposite race have always sympathized with us."[12]

This optimism carried over to black opponents of African colonization, who were increasingly confident that the argument in favor of black citizenship in the United States had won. Asked his opinion of the African Civilization Society in the spring of 1860, Purvis responded,

> The best judgment of the colored people today is to remain in this country, for reasons as good—nay, better, than that of any other class—remain. The past and present inspire a faith that no far-off future will bring with it a practical acknowledgment of our just claims to a perfect equality of rights in this our native land.[13]

Black Philadelphians saw that antislavery politics were on the rise not only in their state but throughout the North and hoped to make sure that antislavery politics remained joined to the push for black citizenship.

Despite this public optimism, Purvis remained suspicious of many Republican politicians. He recognized the party as a vital force in the struggle against slavery yet worried about its members' moderation and willingness to abandon a more radical embrace of black equality. In the spring of 1860, he told the American Anti-Slavery Society, "I could not be a member of the Republican Party if I were so disposed. I am disfranchised; I have no vote; I am put out of the pale of political society." He railed against the party's willingness to support colonization and the refusal of even its most radical members to deny the legality of "slavery where it exists." He would not, therefore, have joined the Republicans even if he did receive the vote.[14]

A few months later, at the meeting of the Pennsylvania Anti-Slavery Society, Purvis renewed his criticism of the Republican Party at the same time that he insisted that he supported its prospects. His denunciations constituted an effort to influence the party rather than to dissuade white voters from supporting it. Purvis saw himself as a political outsider and his role not as drumming up support for the Republican Party but as shaping it. On the same page on which the

New York Herald gleefully reported Purvis and other Pennsylvania abolitionists' opposition to the Republicans, expressing hope that that it would lead to Lincoln's defeat, the paper also printed an article hinting at black Pennsylvanians' true feelings toward the Republican Party: "We understand that among the most liberal contributors" to the Pennsylvania Republican election fund "were the negroes of the city of Philadelphia, who handed over some fifteen thousand dollars to their white brethren of the black republican stripe."[15] Despite the party's shortcomings, black Philadelphians supported it.

Once the Civil War began, African Americans retained this mix of suspicion and support for Lincoln and his party, but they believed that black military service was the key to pushing the nation toward the cause of black liberty. Free blacks throughout the North demanded that they be allowed to fight. On April 20, 1861, just a week after the fall of Fort Sumter, black schoolteacher Alfred M. Green rose to address a meeting of African Americans in Philadelphia: "The time has arrived when we may again give evidence to the world of the bravery and patriotism" of African Americans. He acknowledged that black service in previous conflicts had failed to secure full citizenship and admitted the great failings of the United States. Yet Green nevertheless insisted that African Americans were devoted to their native land and would defend it against "the howling leaders of Secession and treason." Green also insisted that black patriotism could help transform the conflict into a war against slavery and for black equality, "creating anew our claims upon the justice and honor of the Republic." At the same time, northern black troops would "inspire your oppressed brethren of the South with zeal for the overthrow of the tyrant system."[16] Black troops would transform the war as well as the nation.

Such sentiment was not unanimous, however. In September 1861, "R.H.V." wrote to the *Weekly Anglo-African* that "the raising of black regiments for the war would be highly impolitic and uncalled for under the present state of affairs, knowing, as we do, the policy of the government in relation to colored men." He argued that black soldiers should not be willing to fight on behalf of a government that still defended slavery, though he recognized that the alternative was worse. He argued, therefore, that black service would prove a political liability for the current administration and would help to bring into power its opponents.[17]

The *Anglo-African* published Green's reply to this letter. Though Pennsylvania, like most northern states, still refused to enlist black troops, Green noted that black men in Philadelphia and the surrounding area had organized into companies and were drilling in anticipation of the day when they would be able to fight. In so doing, Green argued, northern blacks were demonstrating themselves to be a fighting force that the Lincoln administration would eventually recognize it could not do without. And when Lincoln reached that realization, blacks would have strengthened their position, and "our favor would be more courted ... and our dictation received with more favor and regard." As a result, Green contended, blacks would possess a much more powerful means of influencing the government than "our weak, effeminate pleadings for favor on the merits of our noble ancestry."[18] For nearly half a century, black arguments for citizenship had centered on just such invocations of nativity and past service to the nation, but Green's assessment was correct: black service in the Union Army would ultimately prove a much more powerful lever of influence.

Yet African Americans' claims on the United States continued to be called into question. On August 14, 1862, President Lincoln met with a group of black pastors from the District of Columbia. "You and we are different races," he informed them. "We have between us a broader difference than exists between almost any other two races. Whether it is right or wrong, I need not discuss; but this physical difference is a great disadvantage to us both, as I think your race suffer very greatly, many of them, by living among us, while ours suffer from your presence." The only answer, he insisted, was for free blacks to consent to leave the United States and settle elsewhere. Lincoln went further, informing the members of the delegation that African Americans who refused to leave the land of their birth were "selfish." "For the sake of your race," he lectured, "you should sacrifice something of your present comfort." African Americans across the North were outraged, both at the renewal of calls for colonization and at the president's insulting rhetoric.[19]

Later that month, Purvis drafted a response to this renewed colonization movement, addressing it to Senator Samuel Pomeroy, a Kansas Republican who served as the government's agent in organizing the plan. Purvis lamented the fact that colonization had once again reared its head, and he dutifully recalled the long history of free black opposition to it, quoting the January 1817 words of his father-in-law, James Forten. The opinion of the vast majority of free blacks, he insisted, had not changed. He closed, "Sir this is our country as much as it is yours, *and we will not leave it*." Though he continued to champion the notion that black nativity was a sufficient reason for black citizenship, Purvis also embraced the enlistment of black Union troops as a new, powerful argument for black equality.[20]

Despite his public castigation of the delegation of black pastors, the president's support for colonization was waning. Lincoln had hoped that his advocacy of emigration would soften opposition to the Emancipation Proclamation, the preliminary version of which he announced on September 22, just over a month after his meeting with the pastors. Lincoln continued to work with colonizationists even after issuing the final Emancipation Proclamation on January

1, 1863, but colonization clearly had not won over its opponents. In addition, the final Emancipation Proclamation authorized the enlistment of black soldiers, and in early 1863, Purvis agreed to serve as a recruiter for black regiments.[21]

The enlistment of black men further undermined Maryland's support for the institution of slavery. The state had the largest pool of potential free black soldiers outside the Confederacy as well as a large population of contraband fugitives who might also contribute to the Union cause. The War Department initially permitted the enlistment only of black Marylanders who were already free, hoping to assuage the fears of slaveholders and their sympathizers. This restriction upset the delicate balance between slaveholding and nonslaveholding whites, since those who relied on the labor of free blacks saw the policy as an unfair concession to slaveholders. Fugitives continued to stream in, and the War Department ultimately expanded the enlistment of fugitives. Even conservative politicians who had previously been strong supporters of slavery began to see little reason to continue to support the disintegrating institution.[22]

The effort to press for black citizenship did not await the end of the war. In mid-April 1863, the National Union League met in Baltimore and called for the enlistment of black troops to put down the rebellion. On May 1, Alexander T. Augusta, a black surgeon and commissioned officer, purchased a ticket in Baltimore and was preparing to take the train to Philadelphia when he was assaulted by two white men. With the help of a police officer, Augusta tracked down one of his attackers, who was taken into custody. Another group of whites later attacked Augusta, but police defended him. The *Baltimore Clipper* chastised Augusta for showing himself in uniform on the streets of Baltimore, and he responded with an account published in the *Christian Recorder*: "While I have always known Baltimore as a place where it is considered a virtue to mob colored people, still, I had a right to expect a safe transit through there, after the resolution passed only two weeks before, at the National Union League." In Augusta's view, the enlistment of black troops and, just as important, whites' recognition of the need to enlist black troops had transformed conditions in the state. The next year, during a state constitutional convention, black Baltimoreans announced that they would not be satisfied with the abolition of slavery: only complete equality of citizenship would be acceptable. The "Loyial Colard men of Baltimore Citey" also drafted an address to the president in which they demanded that their government reward their loyalty.[23] Black Marylanders continued to lack many citizenship rights, but they were increasingly unwilling to accept this injustice.

As Robert Purvis rose to address the thirtieth annual meeting of the American Anti-Slavery Society on May 12, 1863, he found himself in a nation in the midst

"A guard of colored soldiers," possibly from Fort William Penn, ca. 1863. Courtesy of the Library Company of Philadelphia.

of profound changes. "Mr. Chairman," announced Purvis, "this is a proud day for the 'colored' man. For the first time since this Society was organized, I stand before you a recognized citizen of the United States." Once the applause died down, he continued. Some of his colleagues in the antislavery movement had warned him to be cautious since the war was not yet won and slavery was not yet dead: many people certainly still did not see black men as equal to white men. Yet Purvis, who had been as harsh a critic of the U.S. government as anyone, refused to be a skeptic: "The good time which has so long been coming is at hand."[24]

"Sir, this is a glorious contest," continued Purvis. "It is not simply and solely a fight about the black man. It is not merely a war between the North and the South. It is a war between freedom and despotism the world over." The Union Army, he insisted, was fighting not merely the Confederacy but "a pro-slavery Europe and a pro-slavery England." Purvis recalled that when he visited Britain years earlier, Irish abolitionist Daniel O'Connell had stated that he would not shake an American's hand until he had been assured that he was an abolitionist. Now Purvis saw the tables turned: though he had often denounced the government of the United States "as the basest despotism the sun ever shone on," he had refused to renounce his claims on America and on citizenship in the land of his birth. But now he could say, "I consider it an honor to be a citizen of this republic," and the British citizen, "be he Saxon or Celt," would have to prove that he was an enemy of slavery.[25]

As Purvis continued, it became clear that he was not simply there to celebrate. "Mr. Chairman, I had intended to say something about the Copperhead Democrats, but these dastards don't trouble me now. They are as malignant, as venomous, as traitorous as ever, and perhaps more so, but their power is gone and their days are numbered." These traitors might continue to "denounce the black man as inferior," and they might "hound on an Irish mob . . . but their power is done." African Americans' service in the Union cause presented a powerful new weapon in the fight for black citizenship, but that weapon had to be used. Purvis's speech, then, was also a call to action.[26]

African Americans in both Philadelphia and Baltimore responded to that call. Black veterans returned home to Philadelphia after the war and found that their service to the nation had failed to win them full citizenship rights. Still, Purvis, and other longtime antislavery activists joined with members of a new generation to make the case that both the North and the South needed reconstruction. Black Philadelphians were no longer vulnerable to kidnapping or reenslavement and were now free to turn their attentions to broader ambitions for black equality that had at times been sacrificed in the interest of more modest but essential gains. The struggle for black suffrage, always important but sometimes inconsistent, took on renewed vigor. The fight for equal public accommodations became critical. Both fights ultimately succeeded despite ongoing white resistance and its sometimes bloody consequences. But many white Philadelphians remained vehemently opposed to the notion that their black neighbors deserved the rights of citizenship. As historian Matthew Countryman has noted, many twentieth-century African Americans encountered enough racism in Philadelphia that they referred to it as "up South."[27]

In Baltimore, too, white resistance to full black citizenship remained strong. As historian Barbara Jeanne Fields has pointed out, the loyal slave state of Maryland had a far shorter experience of Reconstruction than its disloyal brethren. Maryland abolished slavery on its own, though only a few months before the passage of the Thirteenth Amendment. However, white Marylanders made few other concessions to African Americans' demands. The state constitution of 1864 abolished slavery but restricted suffrage to white men. A handful of white Republicans supported full citizenship rights for African Americans, but most Maryland party members competed with Democrats to denounce black citizenship. Many black children were bound into a system of apprenticeship with the aid of courts that generally sided with former masters and were largely unsympathetic to parents' claims. The state legislature eventually repealed some of the elements of the antebellum Black Codes, but many racially specific laws remained.[28]

At base, many whites continued to reject black claims of Americanness, increasingly framing this argument in the language of Darwinian evolution, and cloaking old claims that Africa was the rightful place for African Americans in pseudoscientific language. Even the most powerful argument that African Americans could muster in defense of their right to full citizenship—African Americans' loyalty to and military service in the Union cause—was increasingly forgotten as Americans came to remember the Civil War as a conflict fought only by white men.[29] The battle for full black citizenship had just begun.

Yet although the struggle for black citizenship did not succeed in all it set out to accomplish, it did not fail. Emancipation did not equal the end of white supremacy, but it did equal the end of slavery. As free blacks in the mid-Atlantic borderlands in the decades before the end of slavery pushed and pushed for even limited citizenship rights, they helped to protect whatever liberties free blacks had acquired, and they had helped to create a legal space in which African Americans could build lives. This was no small feat.

NOTES

INTRODUCTION

1. Leslie, "Pennsylvania Fugitive Slave Act"; Child, *Isaac T. Hopper*, 208–9.
2. See Richard S. Newman, *Freedom's Prophet*.
3. William Meredith to William Morris Meredith, February 13, 1826, Richard Allen to Jacob S. Waln, William Lehman, and William Morris Meredith, February 14, 1826, both in Meredith Family Papers, Series 7.
4. Jonathan Roberts and Klein, "Notes and Documents."
5. Jonathan Roberts to Eliza Roberts, February 19, 1826, Box 7, Roberts Papers.
6. Ibid.
7. Leslie, "Pennsylvania Fugitive Slave Act," 445.
8. *FJ*, July 6, 1827; *Register of Debates*, Senate, 19th Cong., 2nd sess., 289–90.
9. *FJ*, July 6, 1827.
10. Ibid.
11. Historical Census Browser, University of Virginia, Geospatial and Statistical Data Center, http://fisher.lib.virginia.edu/collections/stats/histcensus/index.html. I use population figures for Baltimore City and Philadelphia County. While the city of Philadelphia remained legally distinct from the rest of the county until the 1850s, the city had already spilled over its borders by the early nineteenth century and the urban districts bordering on the city were very much a part of it in the minds of many Philadelphians, black and white.
12. Taylor, *Transportation Revolution*, 78; McFeely, *Frederick Douglass*, 71; Eric Foner, *Gateway to Freedom*, 1–2.
13. Harford (14.3 percent) and Cecil Counties (13.9 percent) in Maryland, New Castle County in Delaware (17.8 percent), and Chester County in Pennsylvania (7.9 percent) all possessed significant numbers of free blacks in 1850 (Historical Census Browser, University of Virginia, Geospatial and Statistical Data Center, http://fisher.lib.virginia.edu/collections/stats/histcensus/index.html). I am building on Harrold's framework in *Border War*.

14. Nash, *Forging Freedom*; Hahn, *Political Worlds*, 24–49; Winch, *Philadelphia's Black Elite*. In *Freedom's Port*, a study of the free black community of Baltimore, Christopher Phillips largely eschews this declension narrative, as does Dunbar in her study of black women in Philadelphia, *Fragile Freedom*. Rael notes this emphasis on withdrawal in his introduction to *African-American Activism*, 7–9.

15. Kantrowitz, *More Than Freedom*, 6. See also Horton and Horton, *In Hope of Liberty*, esp. 237–68; Hodges, *David Ruggles*; Washington, *Sojourner Truth's America*. Both Hodges and Washington note the importance of "practical abolition" among free blacks. Indeed, while "practical abolition" was appealing to New York–based abolitionists such as Ruggles and Truth, it was absolutely essential in the mid-Atlantic borderland, where the legal and political rights granted free blacks were always tenuous and where radical abolitionism had limited appeal (for whites at least).

16. Hämäläinen and Johnson, *Major Problems*, xvii. See also Hämäläinen and Truett, "On Borderlands"; Truett, *Fugitive Landscapes*; Adelman and Aron, "From Borderlands to Borders"; Reséndez, "National Identity."

17. Salafia, *Slavery's Borderland*, argues that the region around the Ohio River was a site of borderland "compromise and accommodation," setting it apart from regions further from the border, while Harrold, *Border War*, makes the clearest case for a borderland as a site of conflict over slavery. I generally find Harrold's case more persuasive, though my arguments concerning the mid-Atlantic borderland should not be applied to the very different context of the Ohio Valley. In general, scholars who have examined issues related to fugitive slaves have emphasized the border as a place of conflict. See Blackett, *Making Freedom*; LaRoche, *Geography of Resistance*; Lubet, *Fugitive Justice*; Wong, *Neither Fugitive nor Free*; Maltz, *Fugitive Slavery on Trial*; H. Robert Baker, *Prigg v. Pennsylvania*.

18. As Rockman notes, the resistance of many white Marylanders to the most extreme proposals to restrict the legal rights of free African Americans were rooted in a recognition of the economic value of free black labor (*Scraping By*, 13).

19. Novak, "Legal Transformation"; Kettner, *Development of American Citizenship*. Discussing Lincoln's attitude toward black rights, Oakes, "Natural Rights," notes that nineteenth-century Americans often distinguished among natural rights, citizenship rights, and rights that were assigned by states. As useful as this distinction is, it often broke down in practice, and rights that Lincoln might have placed under all three of these categories were referred to as "citizenship rights," especially by African Americans. In "Leave of Court," a study of African Americans in antebellum Baltimore, Martha S. Jones points out that most poor people, especially those of color, are likely to encounter the law in everyday cases in trial courts; thus, we must look to those courts, not simply to the better-known high court cases, to understand the citizenship rights of free African Americans.

20. Sinha, "Alternative Tradition of Radicalism," contends that black activists created a radical counternarrative of the American revolutionary tradition that emphasized the centrality of slavery and racial oppression to the American nation. I agree that this

was an important dimension of African American thought and activism in these years, though it is not an emphasis of this book since it tended not to be the most practical means of advancing the cause of black citizenship.

21. See Kettner, *Development of American Citizenship*, 287–333. This dimension of the struggle for black citizenship resembles what Kantrowitz terms "a citizenship of the heart" in which African Americans "established their place among their white countrymen" ("More Than Freedom," 6). On the Americanness of African Americans, see Bay, "See Your Declaration Americans!!!" Bradburn argues that white Americans in the revolutionary period tended not to consider free blacks citizens but instead to perceive them as "denizens," a separate legal category borrowed from British law. He notes, however, that significant disagreement existed on this matter. By the mid-nineteenth century, this category seemed to become less important as a way of understanding the legal status of African Americans (*Citizenship Revolution*, 235–71, 356 n. 10). Isenberg illuminates the complexity of women's claims on American citizenship, including their invocation of "birthright citizenship" (*Sex and Citizenship*, xi–xvii).

22. In this regional emphasis, it complements recent work on the politics of slavery and on black intellectual history, which has often been national in focus. On the national politics of slavery, see Mason, *Slavery and Politics*; Forbes, *Missouri Compromise*. For a strong example of how intensely local the struggle over slavery often was, see Hammond, *Slavery, Freedom, and Expansion*. Crucial works in this black intellectual history include Rael, *Black Identity and Black Protest*; Bay, *White Image*; Rita Roberts, *Evangelicalism and Politics*; Ernest, *Liberation Historiography*.

23. On the importance of colonization in the mid-Atlantic, see Tomek, *Colonization and Its Discontents*; Campbell, *Maryland in Africa*.

24. On the importance of slave resistance, see Freehling, *Road to Disunion*, vols. 1, 2; Oakes, "Political Significance." On the neglect of free African Americans in recent antebellum political history, see Wilentz, *Rise of American Democracy*; Earle, *Jacksonian Antislavery*; Morrison, *Slavery and the American West*. For an example of political history that highlights free African Americans in the antebellum period, see Varon, *Disunion!*

CHAPTER 1. THE DIALECTIC OF COLONIZATION

1. *PADA*, December 7, 23, 30, 1816.
2. Ibid., December 27, 1816, January 2, 1817.
3. Ibid., January 10, 1817. The account of the anticolonization meeting is James Forten's from eighteen years later (*Emancipator*, June 30, 1835).
4. See, for example, Staudenraus's account of the origins of the ACS (*African Colonization Movement*, 12–35). For a good overview of the African colonization movement, see Burin, *Slavery and the Peculiar Solution*, 6–33.
5. *PADA*, January 2, 1817.
6. "The First Annual Report of the ACS," in American Colonization Society, *Annual Reports*, 1–11; Staudenraus, *African Colonization Movement*, 27.

7. Guyatt, *Providence*, 183–94. For evidence that some Philadelphians rejected this argument and saw the ACS emphasis on evangelizing Africa as partisan, see *Philadelphia Weekly Aurora*, October 27, 1817.

8. "The First Annual Report of the ACS," in American Colonization Society, *Annual Reports*, 8–9. On Mercer's role in the early colonization movement, see Egerton, "Its Origin Not a little Curious."

9. *PADA*, December 27, 1816. Consent also lay at the heart of slaveholders' depiction of the consistency between republicanism and human bondage. As Freehling has pointed out, "Consent to be governed was the first requirement of American republican legitimacy, and few slaveholders could respect themselves if they altogether embodied the antithetical despotic creed: that the governed must be terrorized into subjection." As a result, they demanded that their slaves participate in the "charade" of consent (*Reintegration of American History*, 257). More recently, Furstenberg has argued that early American "civic texts," such as Washington's Farewell Address, helped Americans to see both citizenship and slavery as consensual (*In the Name*, 13–23, 187–222). Onuf has demonstrated that Jefferson also saw the colonization of African Americans as the key to assuring that the nation would be held together by consent rather than coercion (*Jefferson's Empire*, 15–16, 147–88).

10. "The First Annual Report of the ACS," in American Colonization Society, *Annual Reports*, 9; *PADA*, January 2, 1817.

11. Fredrickson, *Black Image*, 12–21; Tomek, *Colonization and Its Discontents*, 37–42. On Ralston and his support for the black church, see Winch, *Philadelphia's Black Elite*, 10. For colonizationist appeals in Philadelphia newspapers, see, for example, *PADA*, December 30, 1816, August 11, 1817.

12. Sidbury, *Becoming African in America*, 80–90, 148–50; Cuffe, *Captain Paul Cuffe's Logs and Letters*, 45–56.

13. Cuffe, *Captain Paul Cuffe's Logs and Letters*, 252–53; Miller, *Search for a Black Nationality*, 44.

14. Winch, *Gentleman of Color*, 8–52.

15. Winch, *Philadelphia's Black Elite*, 32–34; James Forten to Paul Cuffe, October 10, 1815, in Cuffe, *Captain Paul Cuffe's Logs and Letters*, 385–86. On the African Institution of Philadelphia's support for colonization, see "Letter from the Philadelphia African Institution," *Boston Recorder*, March 18, 1817.

16. On the importance of the British in early black rhetoric, see Gosse, "As a Nation."

17. Absalom Jones, "Thanksgiving Sermon."

18. Parrott, *Two Orations*; Parrott, "Oration."

19. Forten, "Series of Letters."

20. Sidbury, *Becoming African in America*, 1–15, 131–55.

21. Paul Cuffe to Robert Finley, January 8, 1817, Paul Cuffe to James Forten, January 8, 1817, both in Cuffe, *Captain Paul Cuffe's Logs and Letters*, 492–93, 493–94; Floyd Miller, *Search for a Black Nationality*.

22. John James to Paul Cuffe, June 7, 1816, James Forten to Paul Cuffe, January 25,

1817, both in Cuffe, *Captain Paul Cuffe's Logs and Letters*, 48, 501–3; "A Voice from Philadelphia," in Garrison, *Thoughts*, 9.

23. Historians have tried to explain the black elite's shift from support for colonization to staunch opposition. Floyd Miller points out that while many scholars have depicted Forten's and Parrott's backing of Cuffe's colonization plan as the anomaly, they demonstrated a long-term commitment to "Christian humanism and racial awareness" that explains their support of Cuffe (*Search for a Black Nationality*, 49–50). Winch argues that the black elite turned against the ACS when it became clear that white colonizationists would be in control. Just as important, she argues, in light of the broad opposition to colonization in Philadelphia's black community, these leaders recognized that their status would be compromised if they persisted in advocating colonization (*Philadelphia's Black Elite*, 38). Tomek echoes Winch's argument (*Colonization and Its Discontents*, 132–62). While I agree that this was a significant motivation, concerns about the implications of the rhetoric of colonization for black citizenship rights were equally important.

24. James Forten to Paul Cuffe, January 25, 1817, in Cuffe, *Captain Paul Cuffe's Logs and Letters*, 501–3.

25. See, for example, *PADA*, August 12, 1817; *Lexington Western Monitor*, August 30, 1817; *Leesburg Genius of Liberty*, October 17, 1817; *Alexandria Gazette*, August 23, 1817; *New York National Advocate*, August 14, 1817; *Chillicothe Weekly Recorder*, September 18, 1817; *Wilmington American Watchman*, September 20, 1817.

26. "A Voice from Philadelphia," in Garrison, *Thoughts*, 9.

27. Ibid.

28. Nwankwo, *Black Cosmopolitanism*, has traced the development of "black cosmopolitanism" during the nineteenth century as people of African descent came to define themselves "through the world beyond one's own origins." In Nwankwo's view, individuals did not embrace black cosmopolitanism for its own sake but rather sought to use it to advance claims on membership in the nation. Similarly, Bolster points out that black sailors in early America often hoped to use the expanded freedom afforded them not as a means of asserting membership in a transnational community but rather as a way to claim American citizenship (*Black Jacks*, esp. 113–17, 144–53). Waldstreicher makes a similar point, while noting that African Americans also appropriated the practices and forms of white nationalism for the purpose of fighting slavery and promoting "cultural autonomy" (*In the Midst of Perpetual Fêtes*, 323–25).

29. James Forten to Paul Cuffe, January 25, 1817, in Cuffe, *Captain Paul Cuffe's Logs and Letters*, 501–3. There are clear parallels here to the way black nationalism later could be used to strengthen black claims to full citizenship in the United States. See especially Moses, *Golden Age*; Rael, *Black Identity and Black Protest*, 216–20.

30. Nwankwo, *Black Cosmopolitanism*, 14; Richard S. Newman, *Freedom's Prophet*, 204; James Forten to Paul Cuffe, October 10, 1815, in Cuffe, *Captain Paul Cuffe's Logs and Letters*, 385–86.

31. Finkelman, "Problem of Slavery," 146–49. As Waldstreicher has shown, both Re-

publicans and Federalists denounced their opponents in the late eighteenth century by linking them with African Americans (*In the Midst of Perpetual Fêtes*, 231).

32. Rogers M. Smith, *Civic Ideals*, 162–63; Cotlar, "Federalists' Transatlantic Cultural Offensive." Stressing the American birth of African Americans turned this cultural offensive on its head.

33. Rogers M. Smith, *Civic Ideals*, 1–39.

34. *New York Christian Herald*, April 5, 1817; Isaac V. Brown, *Biography*, 121–24.

35. *New York Christian Herald*, April 5, 1817; *Washington Daily National Intelligencer*, December 30, 1816.

36. *BP*, July 8, 11, 1817; *Wilmington American Watchman*, July 16, 1817.

37. Phillips, *Freedom's Port*, 83–113; Fields, *Slavery and Freedom*, 23–39; Rockman, *Scraping By*, 41.

38. Browne, *Baltimore in the Nation*, 70–89, 96–101; Hickey, *War of 1812*, 59–60; Graham, *Baltimore*, 71.

39. *NWR*, October 4, November 8, 15, 1817.

40. Ibid., November 8, 1817; *Baltimore American Commercial Daily Advertiser*, July 8, 1817.

41. *NWR*, November 8, 1817; Robert G. Harper to Elias Caldwell, August 20, 1817, in "The First Annual Report of the American Colonization Society," in American Colonization Society, *Annual Reports*, 14–28.

42. Nash, *Forging Freedom*, 213–14.

43. *PADA*, July 10, 19, August 11, 12, 18, 1817. On African colonization as a reenactment of the colonization of North America and of New England in particular, see Guyatt, *Providence*, 191–92.

44. *PADA*, August 12, 18, 1817.

45. Ibid., August 12, 1817. This address is also reproduced in Garrison, *Thoughts on African Colonization*, 10–13. On the importance to the ACS of the idea that color posed an insurmountable obstacle, see Rael, *Black Identity and Black Protest*, 163, 180.

46. *PADA*, August 12, 18, 1817.

47. Forbes, *Missouri Compromise*, 33–50; *Annals of Congress*, House of Representatives, 15th Cong., 2nd sess., 1205.

48. Forbes, *Missouri Compromise*, 33–68; Mason, *Slavery and Politics*, 177–212; William Rawle Journals, November 23, 1819, Rawle Family Papers, Series 1, Box 2.

49. *Philadelphia Franklin Gazette*, February 11, 14, 17, 1820; Sergeant, "Speech on the Missouri Question."

50. *PADA*, February 8, 1820; Forbes, *Missouri Compromise*, 75–81; Jonathan Roberts to Matthew Roberts, January 27, 1820, William Jones to Jonathan Roberts, February 13, 1820, Jonathan Roberts to Matthew Roberts, February 25, 1820, all in Roberts Papers, Box 3, Letters 1815–32.

51. Burin, *Slavery and the Peculiar Solution*, 15.

52. *NWR*, November 27, 1819, March 4, 1820; *Philadelphia National Recorder*, November 27, December 4, 1819.

53. *St. Louis Enquirer*, February 12, 1820.

54. Forbes, *Missouri Compromise*, 108–20; *NWR*, December 23, 1820; *BP*, December 15, 1820.

55. *NWR*, August 14, 1819; *Philadelphia National Recorder*, November 27, 1819; William Rawle Journals, November 18, 1819, Rawle Family Papers, Series 1, Box 2; *Washington African Intelligencer*, July 1820; "The Third Annual Report of the American Society for the Colonization of the Free People of Color of the United States," in American Colonization Society, *Annual Reports*, 46–49.

56. Berlin, *Generations of Captivity*, 161–63.

CHAPTER 2. AMERICA, AFRICA, HAITI

1. Winch, *Philadelphia's Black Elite*, 14–15.

2. Jeremiah Gloucester, *Oration*, 9–10.

3. Ibid., 11–14.

4. For a general account of African American interest in Haiti, see Power-Greene, *Against Wind and Tide*, 17–45.

5. For a comparative context for African American diaspora studies, see Hine and McCloud, *Crossing Boundaries*.

6. Coker, *Journal*, 9–10; Graham, *Baltimore*, 72–75; Payne, *History*, 13; Coker, "Dialogue." Sidbury makes the case that Coker's vision of African colonization remained within the tradition of Cuffe (*Becoming African in America*, 172–73).

7. Phillips, "Resistance to Colonization"; Payne, *History*, 14–15, 28; Graham, *Baltimore*, 75; Coker, *Journal*, 42–43.

8. Coker, *Journal*, 3–8, 22–23, 43–44; *Providence Religious Intelligencer*, August 26, 1820; Floyd Miller, *Search for a Black Nationality*, 55–68.

9. Staudenraus, *African Colonization Movement*, 86–87; "Fifth Annual Report," in American Colonization Society, *Annual Reports*, 1–26, 47.

10. Staudenraus, *African Colonization Movement*, 53–54; Burin, *Slavery and the Peculiar Solution*, 14–15.

11. Mouser, "Baltimore's African Experiment"; *GUE*, May 8, 1823.

12. Ronald Angelo Johnson has shown that white Americans, even slaveholders, had previously celebrated certain aspects of the Haitian Revolution. But Haiti's geographic proximity to the United States now meant that the idea of free Africans in the island nation posed a far more disturbing prospect than the idea of free Africans on the other side of the Atlantic ocean (*Diplomacy in Black and White*, esp. 169–74). For an illuminating account of the response to the Haitian Revolution among slaveholders in another part of the Atlantic world, see Ferrer, *Freedom's Mirror*.

13. Hunt, *Haiti's Influence*, 164–65; Staudenraus, *African Colonization Movement*, 82–83; Arthur O. White, "Prince Saunders"; *Amherst Hillsboro Telegraph*, March 10, 1821.

14. Dewey, *Correspondence*, 3–11; Staudenraus, *African Colonization Movement*, 82–83; Hunt, *Haiti's Influence*, 164–66.

15. Winch, *Philadelphia's Black Elite*, 56–57; Richard S. Newman, *Freedom's Prophet*, 238–39; Winch, *Gentleman of Color*, 216–17.

16. *New Bedford Mercury*, August 20, 1824; Richard S. Newman, *Freedom's Prophet*, 238; *Trenton Federalist*, September 6, 1824.The exact number of black Philadelphians who emigrated to Haiti is difficult to ascertain (Winch, *Gentleman of Color*, 217).

17. Richard S. Newman, *Freedom's Prophet*, 245–58. See also Rael, *Black Identity and Black Protest*, 223–26.

18. Saunders, "Address"; Richard S. Newman, *Freedom's Prophet*, 246–47, 257–58; Dewey, *Correspondence*, 10. On American perceptions of the links between Protestant Christianity and political liberties in this period, see Billington, *Protestant Crusade*, 1–31.

19. Winch, *Gentleman of Color*, 215–16; *GUE*, November 1824. Northern white evangelicals shared these concerns, as did members of the PAS. See for example, *New Hampshire Observer*, December 27, 1824; PAS Papers, Reel 1, Minutes of the General Meeting, August 30, 1824.

20. *GUE*, October 1824.

21. Lundy, *Life, Travels, and Opinions*, 21–22; *GUE*, October 1824; *Independent Chronicle and Boston Patriot*, July 31, 1824; *GUE*, November 1824.

22. Staudenraus, *African Colonization Movement*, 87–89; "Eighth Annual Report," in American Colonization Society, *Annual Reports*, 15.

23. *NWR*, July 3, 17, 1824; *ARCJ*, July 1825.

24. *GUE*, August 1825.

25. *Windsor Vermont Journal*, May 9, 1825; *Salem Gazette*, January 17, 1826.

26. *Richmond Enquirer*, March 14, 1826; *GUEBC*, July 4, 1825, June 24, 1826.

27. *Boston Missionary Herald*, April 1825, 128–29.

28. Charles C. Harper to Ralph Gurley, September 11, 1826, ACS Papers, Reel 1, 25–26; Winch, *Gentleman of Color*, 218–19; Richard S. Newman, *Freedom's Prophet*, 261; *USG*, April 19, June 14, 1825.

29. *Washington African Repository and Colonial Journal*, April 1829, 61–62.

30. *FJ*, February 15, 1828.

31. Staudenraus, *African Colonization Movement*, 94–103, 119; *ARCJ*, August 1825.

32. *GUEBC*, July 4, 1825.

33. Graham, *Baltimore*, 93–94.

34. *GUE*, August 1825.

35. Remini, *Henry Clay*, 276; Baxter, *Henry Clay*, 57–59.

36. Van Buren, "Autobiography," 199–202; Cole, *Vindicating Andrew Jackson*, 43; *Register of Debates*, Senate, 19th Cong., 1st sess., 165–66.

37. *Register of Debates*, House of Representatives, 19th Cong., 1st sess., 2232; Pamela Baker, "Hemphill, Joseph," in *American National Biography Online*; *Philadelphia North American and Daily Advertiser*, May 30, 1842; Andrew Jackson to Samuel Houston, April 15, 1826, in Jackson, *Papers*, 6:104–5.

38. Andrew Armstrong to Henry Clay, February 12, 1826, in Clay, *Papers*, 5:60–61; Joseph Grist (South Carolina), Circular Letter, May 8, 1826, in Cunningham, *Circular Letters*, 3:1321–23; *Register of Debates*, Senate, 19th Cong., 1st sess., 285–86; Remini, *Henry Clay*, 297.

39. Watson, *Andrew Jackson vs. Henry Clay*, 143–51.
40. John H. Kennedy to R. R. Gurley, November 27, 1827, ACS Papers, Reel 3, 174–75; Turnbull, *Crisis*.
41. *GUE*, November 1824; *GUEBC*, September 24, October 1, 1825; Whitman, *Price of Freedom*, 152–57.
42. Teilhac, *Pioneers*, 26; *GUEBC*, September 30, 1826; *Richmond Enquirer*, August 26, October 7, 1825.
43. *ARCJ*, August 1826; *BGDA*, October 3, 1826; Ralph G. Gurley to John Kennedy, October 14, 1826, ACS Papers, Reel 1, 129–30.
44. Ralph R. Gurley to John Kennedy, October 19, 30, 1826, William B. Davidson to Ralph R. Gurley, December 2, 1826, all in ACS Papers, Reel 1.
45. Charles C. Harper to Ralph R. Gurley, January 3, 1827, ibid.; *GUEBC*, February 25, 1827; Phillips, "Resistance to Colonization," 189.
46. *ARCJ*, December 1826.
47. *Register of Debates*, Senate, 19th Cong., 2nd sess., 289–90; Staudenraus, *African Colonization Movement*, 176–77; *ARCJ*, April 1827.
48. *GUEBC*, February 24, 1827.
49. Ibid., March 3, 1827; Phillips, *Freedom's Port*, 221.
50. *FJ*, May 18, July 27, 1827; *BGDA*, February 2, 1827. See also *PADA*, March 21, 1827.

CHAPTER 3. INTERSTATE DIPLOMACY AND FUGITIVE SLAVES

1. Breck, "Diary," 505; Winch, *Gentleman of Color*, 292–94.
2. Keyssar, *Right to Vote*, 16–17, 20, 26–52; Klein, *Pennsylvania Politics*, 34–35; Phillips, *Freedom's Port*, 60.
3. Klein, *Pennsylvania Politics*, 106–9; William Rawle Sr. Journals, October 1, 5, 1819, Rawle Family Papers, Series 1, Box 2; *Pennsylvania Election Statistics*.
4. Novak, "Legal Transformation," 98.
5. Ibid., 98–99; Richard S. Newman, *Freedom's Prophet*, 159–60.
6. Winch, "Philadelphia."
7. See, for example, *Philadelphia Weekly Aurora*, November 27, 1820; Meaders, "Kidnapping Blacks."
8. PAS Acting Committee Minutes, December 11, 1817, PAS Papers, Series 1, Reel 5; Winch, "Philadelphia," 7.
9. PAS Minutes, December 3, 1818, January 5, 1819, PAS Papers, Series 1, Reel 5. For an excellent discussion of the PAS's efforts to fight kidnapping, see Richard S. Newman, *Transformation of American Abolitionism*, 60–85.
10. Winch, "Philadelphia," 6; *Annals of Congress*, 14th Cong., 2nd sess., 36, 58, 65, 87, 96, 311. The quotation is from a December 1816 resolution that originated from the Quaker meeting in Baltimore.
11. *Annals of Congress*, 15th Cong., 1st sess., 513; Leslie, "Pennsylvania Fugitive Slave Act," 431–32.
12. PAS Minutes, January 5, 1819, PAS Papers, Series 1, Reel 5; Leslie, "Pennsylvania

Fugitive Slave Act," 433; *Philadelphia Franklin Gazette*, January 13, August 28, November 10, 1820; *West Chester Village Record*, December 6, 1820.

13. Leslie, "Pennsylvania Fugitive Slave Act," 433; *BP*, July 10, December 18, 1821.

14. *NWR*, December 1, 1821; Leslie, "Pennsylvania Fugitive Slave Act," 434–36; *Easton Gazette*, December 22, 1821. This is an early example of what Harrold has termed "interstate diplomacy" (*Border War*, 72–93).

15. Minutes of General Meeting, February 28, 1823, PAS Papers.

16. *BP*, September 7, October 17, 1822; *Alexandria Herald*, October 30, 1822. On Vesey, see Egerton, *He Shall Go Out Free*. The *Democratic Press*'s description is mentioned in *BP*, October 17, 1822.

17. Richard S. Newman, *Freedom's Prophet*, 243–45, 241.

18. Forbes, *Missouri Compromise*, 155.

19. Linebaugh and Rediker, *Many-Headed Hydra*, 241; Forbes, *Missouri Compromise*, 155–56.

20. Forbes, *Missouri Compromise*, 155–56.

21. *Baltimore Chronicle* reprinted in *Trenton Federalist*, March 31, 1823. On southern use of the hypocrisy of northerners as a critique of antislavery, see Litwack, *North of Slavery*, 37–40.

22. Forbes, *Missouri Compromise*, 156–58.

23. *BP*, April 22, 1823; Fields, *Slavery and Freedom*, 17; Whitman, *Price of Freedom*, 61–92; Phillips, *Freedom's Port*, 46–47.

24. Whitman, *Price of Freedom*, 72–73; Fields, *Slavery and Freedom*, 34.

25. Fields, *Slavery and Freedom*, 35–36; Phillips, *Freedom's Port*, 182–83.

26. Leslie, "Pennsylvania Fugitive Slave Act," 436–37; *GUE*, February 4, 1826; *Philadelphia Democratic Press*, January 30, 1826; *Philadelphia Aurora and Pennsylvania Gazette*, February 3, 1826. On Chambers and Goldsborough's connections with colonization, see Staudenraus, *African Colonization Movement*, 176; *ARCJ*, October 1827.

27. *Philadelphia Democratic Press*, February 9, 1826; *Philadelphia Aurora and Pennsylvania Gazette*, February 11, 1826.

28. See for example, *PADA*, February 10, 13, 16, 17, 1826.

29. Ibid., February 14, 1826; "Memorial to House and Senate of Pennsylvania," Minutes of the General Meeting, February 11, 1826, PAS Papers, Reel 2.

30. Jonathan Roberts to Eliza Roberts, February 17, 1826, Roberts Papers, Box 7; *GUE*, February 18, 1826.

31. Roberts Vaux to William Morris Meredith, February 14, 1826, Richard Allen to William Morris Meredith, February 14, 1826, William Rawle to William Morris Meredith, February 14, 1826, all in Meredith Family Papers.

32. William Meredith to William Morris Meredith, February 13, 17, 1826, both in ibid.; William Morris Meredith to Roberts Vaux, September 12, 1826, Vaux Family Papers.

33. *NG*, January 19, 1826; *PADA*, January 16, 17, February 3, 1826; Livingwood, *Philadelphia-Baltimore Trade Rivalry*, 91.

34. Livingwood, *Philadelphia-Baltimore Trade Rivalry*, 1–24; Larson, *Internal Improvements*, 162–65; *Register of Debates*, 18th Cong., 2nd sess., 216–20.

35. Livingwood, *Philadelphia-Baltimore Trade Rivalry*, 84–86; *Register of Debates*, 18th Cong., 2nd sess., 216, 294.

36. *Easton Gazette*, March 11, 1826.

37. Francis Helminski, "Howard, Benjamin Chew," in *American National Biography Online*; *BP*, January 7, 1826. Howard's speech advocating the connection of these two issues apparently was not recorded.

38. *NG*, April 29, 1826; *Augusta Chronicle and Georgia Advertiser*, May 17, 1826; *New Hampshire Gazette*, June 6, 1826; *Newport Mercury*, September 16, 1826.

39. *NWR*, October 14, 1826; *NG*, October 6, 1827; *GUE*, October 20, November 17, 1827; William Rawle Journals, October 9, November 10, 1827, Rawle Family Papers.

40. James Buchanan to Andrew Jackson, September 21, 1826, in Jackson, *Papers*, 6:212–13; *Philadelphia Democratic Press*, October 14, 1828, quoted in Klein, *Pennsylvania Politics*, 248–49; "Extract from a Letter from a Member of the Philadelphia Jackson Committee of Correspondence," *Augusta Chronicle and Georgia Advertiser*, August 16, 1828. For a broadside printed in Tennessee making this claim, see http://hdl.loc.gov/loc.rbc/rbpe.17401600.

41. *Washington Daily National Journal*, October 17, 1828.

42. *FJ*, July 20, 1827.

43. Davison, "E. W. Clay," especially 20–21. The Library Company of Philadelphia has a set of these prints.

CHAPTER 4. BLACK CITIZENSHIP IN THE AGE OF NAT TURNER

1. *BL*, January 22, February 12, 1831. Though neither letter is signed by Forten, the first is obviously his based on the biographical detail. The second is signed "A Colored Philadelphian," one of his usual pen names, and Winch attributes it to Forten (*Gentleman of Color*, 242–43).

2. *BGDA*, August 25, 1831; *BP*, August 29, 1831; *NG*, August 30, 1831.

3. *BP*, September 19, 1831; *NG*, September 17, 1831.

4. *NG*, September 20, 1831; *BL*, October 8, October 15, 1831; Phillips, *Freedom's Port*, 191–92; Rockman, *Scraping By*, 246–52.

5. *MG*, November 10, December 1, 1831; *Easton Republican Star and General Advertiser*, March 6, 1832.

6. *MG*, March 22, 1832; Freehling, *Road to Disunion*, 1:202–4.

7. *BGDA*, March 17, 1832; *MG*, March 22, 1832. As Evitts has noted of a somewhat later period, most Marylanders did not want to make a choice between the "North" and the "South" but worked desperately to maintain connections and allegiances with states to the north and to the south (*Matter of Allegiances*).

8. *MG*, March 22, 1832.

9. *Journal of the Proceedings*, 342–59; *MG*, March 29, 1832; Campbell, *Maryland in Africa*, 35–37.

10. *MG*, March 29, 1832; Freehling, *Road to Disunion*, 1:205. Between 1830 and 1840, Maryland's free black population increased from 52,938 to 62,078, growing from 11.8 percent to 13.2 percent of the total (Historical Census Browser, University of Virginia,

Geospatial and Statistical Data Center, http://fisher.lib.virginia.edu/collections/stats/histcensus/index.html).

11. Campbell, *Maryland in Africa*, 10–13; *Address to the People of Maryland*.

12. *GUE*, December 18, 1829; *BL*, April 2, 1831.

13. *GUE*, July 1831. Watkins was quite likely drawing on Walker's *Appeal* in this address. Walker also balanced an abstract, cosmopolitan worldview with concrete claims for black rights in the United States. Walker, like Watkins, focused on the ACS as the enemy of African Americans and as the ally of slaveholders.

14. Charles C. Howard to R. R. Gurley, November 15, 1831, ACS Papers, Reel 12; Campbell, *Maryland in Africa*, 23–29.

15. *Address to the People of Maryland*; Maryland, Board of Managers, *News from Africa*, 16.

16. *PADA*, September 2, 1831; *Philadelphia Inquirer*, reprinted in *Easton Gazette*, January 28, 1832.

17. *USG*, November 30, 1831, reprinted in *BL*, December 10, 1831.

18. Ibid.

19. Ibid.; Purvis and Whipper, *Remonstrance*, 5.

20. Purvis and Whipper, *Remonstrance*, 2.

21. Bacon, *But One Race*.

22. McCormick, "William Whipper."

23. *Easton Republican Star*, April 17, 1832; Winch, *Philadelphia's Black Elite*, 131–33.

24. Coffin, *To the Honourable the Senate and House of Representatives*; Weiner, *Race and Rights*, 42–43.

25. *USG*, November 30, 1831, reprinted in *BL*, December 10, 1831. These editorial comments led Garrison to term the *Gazette*'s editor "intelligent" and "magnanimous."

26. Whitman, *Price of Freedom*; Phillips, *Freedom's Port*, 194–96; Moses Sheppard to George F. McGill, October 10, 1833, Sheppard Papers, Series 2, Box 2.

27. Freehling, *Prelude to Civil War*, 111–15; Freehling, *Road to Disunion*, 1:254–59. On nullification as both a solution to and defense against disunion, see Varon, *Disunion!*, 57–60.

28. Remini, *Henry Clay*, 394–95.

29. Lightner, *Slavery and the Commerce Power*, 37–64; Remini, *Henry Clay*, 394. For Clay's major speech on the bill, see *Register of Debates*, Senate, 22nd Cong., 1st sess., 1096–1118. For an example of the Senate opposition to the bill based both on its perceived unfairness to the West and its support for the "visionary" colonization scheme, see Thomas Hart Benton's speech, *Register of Debates*, Senate, 22nd Cong., 1st sess., 1156.

30. Varon, *Disunion!*, 89–90; Andrew Jackson, "Nullification Proclamation," in Watson, *Andrew Jackson vs. Henry Clay*, 208.

31. Henry C. Carey to Henry Clay, December 3, 1831, in Clay, *Papers*, 8:426; Remini, *Henry Clay*, 419–36; Varon, *Disunion!*, 90.

32. *Register of Debates*, Senate, 22nd Cong., 2nd sess., 84; Remini, *Henry Clay*, 433–36; Henry Clay to Francis Brooke, February 28, 1833, quoted in Remini, *Henry Clay*, 434. As Howe notes, "Whether the Distribution Bill was an integral part of the com-

promise settlement depended on whom one asked" (*What Hath God Wrought*, 409). Among the recent major antebellum syntheses, Wilentz goes the furthest in emphasizing Clay's antagonism toward the abolitionists and downplays his antislavery tendencies (*Rise of American Democracy*, 331, 495, 569). Freehling depicts Clay as a continuation of "Jefferson's apologetic tradition" on the slavery issue. Though he notes Clay's dramatic shift from his somewhat radical early position to a much more conservative position later in life, Freehling notes that Clay "spent a career troubling slaveholding perpetualists" because of his continued backing of conditional emancipation (*Road to Disunion*, 1:494–98). Howe's take resembles Freehling's (*What Hath God Wrought*, 586–88).

33. *PADA*, August 24, 1831.
34. Carey, *Should the Nullifiers Succeed*, 1.
35. Howard, Harper, and Maryland, Board of Managers, *Report*, 8.
36. Ibid.; Campbell, *Maryland in Africa*, 61–62.
37. Howard, Harper, and Maryland, Board of Managers, *Report*, 1; Moses Sheppard to Robert S. Finley, May 4, 1833, Sheppard Papers, Series 2, Box 2; McKenney, *Brief Statement of Facts*.
38. *NWR*, October 3, 1835; William Watkins to William Lloyd Garrison, September 31, 1835, in Graham, *Baltimore*, 119; Howard, Harper, and Maryland, Board of Managers, *Report*.
39. Moses Sheppard to Robert S. Finley, April 27, 1833, Sheppard Papers, Series 2, Box 2.
40. *BL*, January 25, February 1, 1834.
41. Ibid., August 18, 1832.
42. Frederick Douglass, *My Bondage and My Freedom*, 109–20.
43. Ibid., 121–24.
44. Frederick Douglass, *Narrative*, 64, 75; Preston, *Young Frederick Douglass*, 149–51; Frederick Douglass, *My Bondage and My Freedom*, 233–35.
45. On the political implications of running away, see Hahn, *Political Worlds*, especially 1–53. See also Oakes, "Political Significance."
46. I believe that Watkins's writings particularly influenced Douglass, who was living in Baltimore at the time the letters from "A Colored Baltimorean" were published. Oakes does an excellent job of capturing Douglass's political mind (*Radical and the Republican*, 6).
47. McFeely, *Frederick Douglass*, 72.
48. Hahn, *Political Worlds*, 24–37. Hahn argues that northern free black communities can often best be understood as maroon communities, but this viewpoint overlooks the ways in which free blacks sought to exploit the latent antislavery sentiments of many northern whites.

CHAPTER 5. BLACK CITIZENSHIP AND REFORM

1. John Greenleaf Whittier to Harriet Minot, March 18, 1838, in Whittier, *Letters*, 1:289–90; Reinhard O. Johnson, *Liberty Party*, 151–59.

2. "Address to the Free People of Colour of These United States," in Bell, *Minutes*, 9–12.

3. Richard S. Newman, *Freedom's Prophet*, 209–10.

4. Litwack, *North of Slavery*, 72–73.

5. "Constitution of the American Society of Free Persons of Color," in Bell, *Minutes*, iv–8. On Grice and the origins of the convention movement, see *Anglo-African Magazine*, October 1859, in Bell, *Minutes*.

6. Bell, *Minutes*, 9–12.

7. "Minutes and Proceedings of the First Annual Convention of the People of Colour," in Bell, *Minutes*, 12–15. Though some historians have labeled the September 1830 organizational meeting the first annual meeting of the American Society for Persons of Colour, participants considered the 1831 gathering their first annual convention (Winch, *Philadelphia's Black Elite*, 195 n. 7).

8. "Minutes and Proceedings of the First Annual Convention of the People of Colour," in Bell, *Minutes*, 4, 10–11. On African Americans and the Fourth of July, see Quarles, "Free Blacks"; Sweet, "Fourth of July"; McDaniel, "Fourth and the First."

9. "Minutes and Proceedings of the First Annual Convention of the People of Colour," in Bell, *Minutes*, 4–5, 12.

10. *BL*, December 29, 1832.

11. Kraditor, *Means and Ends*, 118–40. On Garrisonian attitudes toward democracy more broadly, see McDaniel, *Problem of Democracy*.

12. *BL*, December 20, 1834.

13. Goodman, *Towards a Christian Republic*, 239–40.

14. *Boston Universalist Magazine*, October 13, 1827; Benson, *Concept of Jacksonian Democracy*, 194–95; Formisano, *For the People*, 132.

15. Vaughn, *Antimasonic Party*, 92–94; Formisano, *For the People*, 132–34, 137–38, 155.

16. John Sergeant to Henry Clay, May 25, 1832, Josiah Johnston to Henry Clay, September 10, 1832, both in Clay, *Papers*, 8:522, 573; Vaughn, *Antimasonic Party*, 92; *Pennsylvania Election Statistics*.

17. Whipper, *Eulogy on William Wilberforce*, iii–iv, 6. Including these sort of organizational details at the beginning of a printed address was not uncommon, but the eulogy delivered at the request of the Pennsylvania Abolition Society by David Paul Brown, for example, included no such information.

18. Whipper, *Eulogy on William Wilberforce*, 8; Wyatt-Brown, "Prelude to Abolitionism."

19. Whipper, *Eulogy on William Wilberforce*, 32.

20. "Minutes of the Fourth Annual Convention for the Improvement of the Free People of Colour," in Bell, *Minutes*, 18, 29.

21. "Minutes and Proceedings of the First Annual Convention of the People of Colour," in ibid., 5; Tyrrell, *Sobering Up*, 79; Abzug, *Cosmos Crumbling*, 81–104. On black temperance, see Yacovone, "Transformation."

22. "Minutes and Proceedings of the Third Annual Convention," in Bell, *Minutes*,

15–19. Here I disagree somewhat with Yacovone, who argues that early black temperance was constrained by its adoption of a white moral reform agenda that "prevented black reformers from understanding how intemperance, racism and slavery worked systematically to prevent black advancement and limit black freedom" ("Transformation," 285). Stewart similarly sees a clear distinction between the strategy of "respectability" and later, more radical black strategies ("Emergence of Racial Modernity").

23. Abzug, *Cosmos Crumbling*, 84–90; Tyrrell, *Sobering Up*, 54–86; Walters, *American Reformers*, 125–29.

24. Charles McCarthy, *Antimasonic Party*, 449; Vaughn, *Antimasonic Party*, 92. On the connections between temperance and antimasonry, see Formisano, *For the People*, 118–20.

25. See Walters, *American Reformers*, 123–43. Walters notes, "Many Southerners were disgusted by the antislavery activities of American Temperance Union leaders like Arthur Tappan and Gerrit Smith; they often pursued an independent course or else responded more enthusiastically to the organizations created in the 1840s," which were less intimately connected to northeastern evangelical reform.

26. *BL*, June 15, 1833.

27. Beecher, *Six Sermons*, 72; Abzug, *Cosmos Crumbling*, 86–96. Beecher's sermons were delivered in 1827 and were quickly and frequently reprinted.

28. "Minutes of the Second Annual Convention of the People of Colour," in Bell, *Minutes*, 28; Yacovone, "Transformation," 285; *BL*, June 21, 28, July 5, 1834; Whipper, "Slavery of Intemperance."

29. Whipper, "Slavery of Intemperance," 149; Yacovone, "Transformation," 285. On the importance of "respectability" in antebellum social thought, see Rael, *Black Identity and Black Protest*, 118–56.

30. Whipper, "Slavery of Intemperance," 149.

31. Ibid.

32. Ibid.

33. According to historian David Grimsted, the northern antiabolition riots of this period provoked extensive debate but produced surprisingly little damage. However, that fact would have offered little comfort to the black Philadelphians who suffered from the violence (*American Mobbing*, 33–38).

34. *Philadelphia Chronicle*, November 23, 1829, reprinted in *BGDA*, November 25, 1829; Scharf and Westcott, *History of Philadelphia*, 1:624; Nash, *Forging Freedom*, 275; Lapsansky, "Since They Got Those Separate Churches," 63.

35. *GUE*, July 1834; Runcie, "Hunting the Nigs," 187–218; Winch, *Philadelphia's Black Elite*, 144–45.

36. Runcie, "Hunting the Nigs," 190–91; Nash, *Forging Freedom*, 274.

37. *Philadelphia Hazard's Register of Pennsylvania*, September 1834, 200–203; Runcie, "Hunting the Nigs," 201; Lapsansky, "Since They Got Those Separate Churches," especially 76–77. See also Ignatiev, *How the Irish Became White*. The committee also suggested that free blacks' efforts to impede the recovery of fugitives also contributed to the riots.

38. *Philadelphia Pennsylvanian*, August 15, 18, September 27, October 8, 1833.
39. "Minutes of the Fifth Annual Convention," in Bell, *Minutes*, 19.
40. On citizenship generally, see Novak, "Legal Transformation."
41. *Philadelphia Hazard's Register of Pennsylvania*, February 4, 1832. For a Pennsylvania abolitionist's earlier discussion of and argument for a fugitive slave's right to a trial by jury, see *New York African Observer*, December 1827, 269–74.
42. *PF*, November 12, December 3, 1836. On the role of black Philadelphians in the Young Men's Anti-Slavery Society, see Winch, *Philadelphia's Black Elite*, 85.
43. *PF*, December 17, 24, 31, 1836; Minutes of the General Meeting, January 5, 1837, PAS Papers, Series 1, Reel 2; John Greenleaf Whittier to Joshua Leavitt, January 30, 1837, in Whittier, *Letters*, 1:211–214.
44. *PI*, December 10, 1836; Minutes of the General Meeting, January 12, 1837, PAS Papers, Series 1, Reel 2.
45. *PI*, December 10, 1836; *PF*, January 14, 1837; *BL*, December 17, 1836.
46. John Greenleaf Whittier to Joshua Leavitt, January 30, 1837, John Greenleaf Whittier to William Lloyd Garrison, February 2, 1837, both in Whittier, *Letters*, 1:211–14, 215–16.
47. George M. Baker to William Morris Meredith, March 4, 1837, Meredith Family Papers, Series 7, Box 57, Folder 10.
48. *PF*, January 14, 1837; *Emancipator*, January 26, 1837; *NWR*, March 18, 1837; John Greenleaf Whittier to William Lloyd Garrison, April 14, 1837, in Whittier, *Letters*, 1:231–32.
49. Snyder, *Jacksonian Heritage*, 96–103.
50. *CA*, June 10, 1837; Winch, *A Gentleman of Color*, 296.
51. Agg, *Proceedings and Debates*, 2:472, 477–79, 3:30.
52. Ibid., 3:83–92. William Fogg had sued the Luzerne County election inspector, claiming that in 1835 he had been turned away from the polls because of his race. Fogg won, but the decision was immediately appealed to the state supreme court. As the convention opened, the case was awaiting a hearing; however, the court decided to wait for the convention's outcome (Malone, *Between Freedom and Bondage*, 90–91).
53. Agg, *Proceedings and Debates*, 3:688, 694, 701. My thinking regarding the significance of the national discussion and the threat of disunion to the Pennsylvania debates has been influenced by Wood, "Sacrifice."
54. For the local and state context, see Malone, *Between Freedom and Bondage*, 92–94. For the national context, see Wood, "Sacrifice," 84–87; Eric Ledell Smith, "End of Black Voting Rights," 293–94.
55. *PF*, March 1, 1838; Winch, *Philadelphia's Black Elite*, 137–38.
56. Malone, *Between Freedom and Bondage*, 57–99.
57. Agg, *Proceedings and Debates*, 9:378, 356, 10:19–20.
58. Ibid., 9:353, 367, 10:59, 21.
59. On Democrats, see Richards, *Slave Power*. On Whigs, see Wilentz, *Rise of American Democracy*, esp. 482–518.
60. Agg, *Proceedings and Debates*, 9:375, 10:13.

NOTES TO CHAPTER 5   211

61. *PF*, January 25, 1838; Agg, *Proceedings and Debates*, 10:106.
62. Agg, *Proceedings and Debates*, 10:93–100.
63. *PF*, March 1, 1838.
64. Agg, *Proceedings and Debates*, 11:310–13; *CA*, January 27, 1838.
65. The two cases were the Fogg decision in Luzerne County and the Bucks County election decision of Judge John Fox (Malone, *Between Freedom and Bondage*, 92–95, 97–98).
66. *PF*, March 15, 1838; Eric Ledell Smith, "End of Black Voting Rights," 295; Purvis, *Appeal of Forty Thousand Citizens*. The "Appeal" was reprinted in the *CA*, May 3, June 2, 1838, and elsewhere.
67. Purvis, *Appeal of Forty Thousand Citizens*.
68. *CA*, January 27, 1838; Purvis, *Appeal of Forty Thousand Citizens*; Agg, *Proceedings and Debates*, 10:7.
69. *History of Pennsylvania Hall*; Winch, *Philadelphia's Black Elite*, 146; Tomek, *Pennsylvania Hall*.
70. *History of Pennsylvania Hall*, 136–43; Winch, *Philadelphia's Black Elite*, 147–48.
71. *History of Pennsylvania Hall*, 142–43; *Philadelphia Pennsylvanian*, May 18, 1838.
72. *PADA*, October 27, 1838. Cresson, a wealthy Quaker and seemingly sincere opponent of slavery, had been active in local colonization efforts since the 1820s. He engaged in rhetorical confrontations with William Lloyd Garrison while promoting the cause of colonization in the British Isles (Staudenraus, *African Colonization Movement*, 216–19).
73. *Philadelphia Pennsylvanian*, August 24, 1838; *PADA*, September 25, 1838.
74. *PADA*, October 1, 3, 1838; *Philadelphia Pennsylvanian*, October 8, 1838.
75. Agg, *Proceedings and Debates*, 13:260–61; *Pennsylvania Election Statistics*. Fewer votes were cast on the ratification question than in the gubernatorial race.
76. "Minutes of the Fifth Annual Convention for the Improvement of the Free People of Colour," in Bell, *Minutes*, 255–31; *BL*, July 2, 1836; *CA*, August 26, September 2, 1837.
77. See Rael, *Black Identity and Black Protest*, 82–117; Stuckey, *Slave Culture*, 193–244. Stuckey offers a useful reminder about not overstating the extent to which leaders spoke for the rest of the free black community.
78. *CA*, September 9, 1837; Winch, *Gentleman of Color*, 308–9.
79. Bell, "American Moral Reform Society"; Winch, *Philadelphia's Black Elite*, 108–29.
80. *CA*, June 24, 1837, June 9, September 8, 1838; Winch, *Philadelphia's Black Elite*, 114–17.
81. *CA*, September 15, 1838; *Philadelphia National Reformer*, October 1838.
82. *Philadelphia National Reformer*, October 1838; Winch, *Philadelphia's Black Elite*, 117. On Garrisonian attitudes toward American churches and their connection with slavery, see McKivigan, *War against Proslavery Religion*, 56–73. The AMRS continued to meet at Gloucester's Second African Presbyterian Church.
83. *CA*, June 24, 1837, June 16, 1838; *Emancipator*, May 29, 1840.

84. Sewell, *Ballots for Freedom*, 24–42; McKivigan, *War against Proslavery Religion*, 75–76.

85. Sewell, *Ballots for Freedom*, 51–54; *Philadelphia National Reformer*, November 1839; *Emancipator*, May 29, 1840.

86. For another crucial proponent of "practical abolition," especially with regard to the defense of fugitives, see Hodges, *David Ruggles*. Hodges uses the term "practical abolitionism" to describe Ruggles's actions (4). See also Washington, *Sojourner Truth's America*.

87. Boromé, "Vigilant Committee of Philadelphia," 320–25; Minute Book of the Vigilant Committee of Philadelphia, Vigilant Committee of Philadelphia Records.

88. Mathews, *Slavery and Methodism*, 194–211, 213–15; *Philadelphia National Enquirer*, June 4, 1840.

89. *CA*, July 4, 1840; *Emancipator*, August 20, 1840.

90. Mathews, *Slavery and Methodism*, 195, 246–82.

CHAPTER 6. WHITE IMMIGRANTS, BLACK NATIVES

1. *PI*, October 17, 1838; *Philadelphia National Gazette and Literary Register*, October 20, 1838.

2. *Philadelphia National Reformer*, December 1839.

3. *BL*, May 8, 1840.

4. *PF*, July 16, 1840.

5. *CA*, July 25, 1840; *NASS*, September 10, 1840; Hodges, *David Ruggles*, 159–61.

6. *CA*, November 7, 14, 1840; Winch, *Philadelphia's Black Elite*, 122.

7. Remini, *Henry Clay*, 525–27; "Report of the Executive Committee, Third Annual Meeting, May 1840," Pennsylvania Anti-Slavery Society Records.

8. John Greenleaf Whittier to Elizur Wright, March 25, 1840, in Whittier, *Letters*, 1:400–401; James Buchanan, "Democratic Convention Speech," James Buchanan to Martin Van Buren, September 25, 1840, both in Buchanan, *Works*, 4:294–96, 322–23.

9. Reinhard O. Johnson, *Liberty Party*, 244–48; *CA*, November 14, 1840.

10. *CA*, January 30, March 6, 1840.

11. Philip S. Foner and Walker, *Proceedings*, 1:108–13; *CA*, May 8, September 25, 1841.

12. Philip S. Foner and Walker, *Proceedings*, 1:113; *CA*, March 13, 1841.

13. *Baltimore Maryland Colonization Journal*, June 15, 1841, 15. This resolution was later reprinted by northern abolitionists as an anticolonization pamphlet.

14. *CA*, July 10, 1841.

15. *BS*, January 14, 15, 1842.

16. Ibid., January 17, 1842; Harrold, "On the Borders," 280.

17. *BL*, January 28, 1842; *PI*, January 17, 1842; *PL*, January 17, 1842.

18. *BL*, February 11, April 15, 1842; Berlin, *Slaves without Masters*, 210–11. For Methodist opposition, see *BS*, February 4, 9, 18, 22, March 3, 17, 1842.

19. *CA*, December 12, 1840.

20. Boromé, "Vigilant Committee of Philadelphia," 323–25; Blockson, *Underground Railroad in Pennsylvania*, 9–32.

21. Nogee, "Prigg Case," 185; Morris, *Free Men All*, 94. For the larger context of the case, see H. Robert Baker, *Prigg v. Pennsylvania*.

22. Morris, *Free Men All*, 94–95; *Philadelphia National Enquirer*, January 18, 1838, January 17, 1839.

23. Morris, *Free Men All*, 96–99.

24. *Emancipator*, March 10, 1842; *NASS*, August 18, 1842.

25. Minute Book of the Vigilant Committee of Philadelphia, December 28, 1843, Vigilant Committee of Philadelphia Records; Minutes, Sixth Annual Meeting, August 14, 1843, Pennsylvania Anti-Slavery Society Records.

26. Staudenraus, *African Colonization Movement*, 224–39; Kocher, "Duty to America and Africa," 129; *Washington African Repository and Colonial Journal*, October 1838.

27. "Joseph Reed Ingersoll," *Biographical Directory of the United States Congress*, http://bioguide.congress.gov/scripts/biodisplay.pl?index=I000019; Ingersoll, *Address*, 6–10. Ingersoll did not stand for reelection in 1836 but returned to the House in 1841. His brother, Charles, was a prominent Democrat who had been among the leading critics of black suffrage at the 1837–38 Pennsylvania Constitutional Convention.

28. Ingersoll, *Address*, 20. On immigration in this period, especially Irish immigration, see Clark, "Philadelphia Irish"; Kerby A. Miller, *Emigrants and Exiles*, 193–279.

29. Ingersoll, *Address*, 20. I do not mean to imply that this parallel was not severely flawed or that colonizationists' depictions of European immigration matched reality.

30. *Washington African Repository and Colonial Journal*, February 1838.

31. *CA*, June 16, 1838.

32. Ibid., July 28, 1838.

33. Ibid.

34. Ibid.

35. Waldstreicher, *In the Midst*, 201–7. For parties and antipartisanship, see Formisano, "Party Period Revisited"; Holt, "Primacy of Party Reasserted"; Altschuler and Blumin, *Rude Republic*; Voss-Hubbard, *Beyond Party*; Howe, *Political Culture*, esp. 43–68.

36. *Philadelphia National Reformer*, October 1838.

37. McDaniel, "Repealing Unions," 261; Rolston and Shannon, *Encounters*, 74.

38. *BL*, March 25, 1842.

39. *Philadelphia Pennsylvanian*, March 8, 1842; *BL*, April 22, 1842.

40. See Jacobson, *Whiteness of a Different Color*; Ignatiev, *How the Irish Became White*; Roediger, *Wages of Whiteness*. Angela F. Murphy argues that the denunciation of O'Connell's address reflected the fears that association with abolition would undermine the cause of Irish Repeal and splinter the national movement in support of it (*American Slavery, Irish Freedom*, 84–100).

41. Ignatiev, *How the Irish Became White*, 124–44; Winch, *Philadelphia's Black Elite*, 130–51.

42. Purvis, *Remarks*, 6.

43. Ibid., 16, 17.

44. Stephen H. Gloucester, *Discourse*. William Douglass, pastor of St. Thomas, delivered the eulogy, which was generally more in line with Gloucester's address (Winch, *Gentleman of Color*, 328–29). On black "respectability" more broadly, see Rael, *Black Identity and Black Protest*, 157–208.

45. *BL*, August 26, 1842; *USG*, August 2, 1842, reprinted in *BL*, August 12, 1842; Ignatiev, *How the Irish Became White*, 137.

46. *USG*, August 2, 1842, reprinted in *BL*, August 12, 1842; Winch, *Philadelphia's Black Elite*, 149.

47. *BL*, August 12, 1842; Winch, *Philadelphia's Black Elite*, 149. The *Liberator* reprinted a large number of pieces on the riots from various newspapers to recount the events of the riot and to show Philadelphians' responses to it.

48. *Philadelphia North American and Daily Advertiser*, August 11, 1842.

49. *BL*, August 12, 1842; *NASS*, August 11, 1842.

50. Robert Purvis to Henry Clarke Wright, August 22, 1842, in Ripley et al., *Black Abolitionist Papers*, 3:389–90; Bacon, *But One Race*, 99–101.

51. *Philadelphia Pennsylvanian*, August 3, 1842, *PL*, August 10, 1842.

52. *PL*, August 6, 1842. The letter was printed as a paid advertisement.

53. *PL*, August 6, 1842. Although the *Emancipator* reprinted Gloucester's letter approvingly on September 1, 1842, the *Liberator* (August 19, 1842) hinted at disapproval of Gloucester's position, and the letter was later cited as evidence of Gloucester's "treachery," most prominently by Frederick Douglass. For an example of another letter noting more respectable commemorations of the occasion, see *BL*, August 19, 1842.

54. *Emancipator*, September 1, 1842.

55. Feldberg, *Philadelphia Riots of 1844*, 78–98.

56. Ibid.

57. Ibid., 99–116.

58. *Philadelphia Riots*.

59. Annual Report, Pennsylvania Anti-Slavery Society, August 12, 1844, Pennsylvania Anti-Slavery Society Records.

60. Annual Report, Pennsylvania Anti-Slavery Society, August 12, 1844, Pennsylvania Anti-Slavery Society Records.

61. *Philadelphia North American and Daily Advertiser*, October 21, 26, November 1, 1844; *Pennsylvania Election Statistics*.

62. Holt, *Rise and Fall*, 156–57; Richards, *Slave Power*, 163–89.

63. *PL*, October 10, 1844.

64. *NE*, June 24, 1847. Both Eric Foner and Anbinder note that many opponents of slavery voted for Know-Nothings not because they were concerned about immigrants per se but specifically because they worried about immigrant support for the Democratic Party and the Slave Power. Foner and Anbinder are referring specifically to the 1850s, but the insight applies to the 1840s as well (Eric Foner, *Free Soil, Free Labor, Free Men*, 230–31; Anbinder, *Nativism and Slavery*, 53–68).

65. *Baltimore Maryland Colonization Journal*, October 1846. The fact that this publication reprinted the piece illustrates the catch-22 faced by free African Americans: any attempt to illustrate white Americans' prejudice provided evidence that blacks were better off in Africa, away from American prejudice.

66. Bacon, *But One Race*, 103-4.

CHAPTER 7. THE TUMULTUOUS POLITICS OF THE EARLY 1850S

1. *NS*, October 31, 1850; *BS*, October 15, 1850.

2. *NS*, October 31, 1850; Ripley et al., *Black Abolitionist Papers*, 4:68-72.

3. Tomek, *Colonization and Its Discontents*, 199-201; LaRoche, *Geography of Resistance*, 120-21.

4. Maltz, *Fugitive Slave on Trial*, 62-63; Salafia, *Slavery's Borderland*, 218-19; Hahn, *Political Worlds*, 30-44.

5. For an account of the reaction to the Fugitive Slave Law in Pennsylvania that is complementary to the one given here, see Blackett, *Making Freedom*, 32-67.

6. Morris, *Free Men All*, 117-18; Minutes of the Anti-Slavery Society of Eastern Pennsylvania, February 8, March 9, 1847, Pennsylvania Anti-Slavery Society Records.

7. Morris, *Free Men All*, 118-19; *Philadelphia North American*, February 8, 1847; *NE*, July 1, 1847.

8. *BL*, June 11, 1847; *London Anti-Slavery Reporter*, June 1, 1847; Winch, *Philadelphia's Black Elite*, 212 n. 15.

9. McFeely, *Frederick Douglass*, 127-30.

10. *BL*, October 29, 1847; *PF*, September 23, 1847.

11. *NS*, March 3, August 25, September 1, 1848.

12. Ibid., September 1, 1848.

13. Ibid., October 13, 1848.

14. Ibid.

15. *NS*, October 13, 1848. On Wears, see Silcox, "Black 'Better Class' Dilemma," 47. On Bowers, see Winch, *Philadelphia's Black Elite*, 156. The pastor of St. Thomas, William Douglass, also defended the three churches against Frederick Douglass's attacks with letters published in the *NS* (October 27, November 24, 1848).

16. *NS*, December 8, 1848.

17. Philip S. Foner and Walker, *Proceedings*, 1:119-31. Black Philadelphians had earlier in the year rallied in Independence Square in support of the French Republic (*NS*, May 4, 1848). On Americans' use of European revolutions to reassert U.S. exceptionalism, see Timothy Mason Roberts, *Distant Revolutions*.

18. *BL*, July 24, 1843; William Douglass, *Annals*, 139-54.

19. William Douglass, *Annals*, 154-66.

20. Scharf, *History of Baltimore*, 584; *NS*, November 23, 1849.

21. *NS*, July 6, 1849. Many historians have echoed this criticism. Julie Winch, for one, has argued that Philadelphia's black elite divided into a small cadre of motivated

men and women who embraced Douglass's form of activism and a larger group whose members "limited the scope of their activism and abandoned any cause which they believed would provoke a hostile reaction from whites" (*Philadelphia's Black Elite*, 169).

22. See Kantrowitz, "Intended for the Better Government." For an expansion of the idea that black associations helped foster a "citizenship of the heart," see Kantrowitz, *More Than Freedom*, 6.

23. *NE*, February 24, 1848.

24. Blockson, *Underground Railroad in Pennsylvania*, 12–15; Phillips, *Freedom's Port*, 230; *NS*, October 27, 1848.

25. Harrold, *Border War*, 138–43.

26. *Congressional Globe*, 31st Cong., 1st sess., Appendix, 123; Morris, *Free Men All*, 132–34.

27. Morris, *Free Men All*, 135–47; *PI*, August 23, 1850.

28. *Washington Southern Press*, n.d., quoted in *PI*, August 29, 1850.

29. *BS*, October 5, October 15, 17, 1850.

30. *Albany Evening Journal*, October 19, 1850; *BS*, October 19, 1850; *New Orleans Daily Picayune*, October 24, 1850.

31. Language is an especially important ground for political conflict in the realm of law and Constitution. See for example, Wong, *Neither Fugitive nor Free*, which is situated in the context of historians who have focused on slavery and the law, especially Paul Finkelman and Don Fehrenbacher (6).

32. *PI*, November 4, 5, 1850.

33. *PL*, November 14, 1850; *PI*, November 16, 1850; *Proceedings of the Great Union Meeting*, 3–4.

34. *Proceedings of the Great Union Meeting*, 7.

35. Ibid., 6–11.

36. *Philadelphia North American*, November 4, 1850; *Proceedings of the Great Union Meeting*, 12–20.

37. *BS*, December 5, 1850, April 4, May 14, 1851; Fields, *Slavery and Freedom*, 79–80. Freehling holds up Jacobs as the sort of Border South slaveholder who could have abandoned the border and moved to the Lower South but who instead dug in and defended slavery in Maryland (*Road to Disunion*, 2:195–96).

38. *Proceedings of the Maryland State Convention*, 127-29, quote on 128.

39. Slaughter, *Bloody Dawn*, 18–19, 52–57.

40. Ibid., 54–58.

41. Ibid., 59–75.

42. Ibid., 76–77, 87–88. The network involved in the Christiana riot suggests the limits of seeing northern free black communities as maroon settlements (Hahn, *Political Worlds*, 38–41).

43. Henry M. Phillips to William Bigler, March 15, 1851, Bigler Papers, Box 1; *NE*, July 31, 1851; *BS*, September 16, 1851; Slaughter, *Bloody Dawn*, 96–101.

44. *BS*, September 16, 24, 1851; *NE*, October 23, 1851; Slaughter, *Bloody Dawn*, 93.

Slaughter suggests that southerners wanted to see white men convicted to demonstrate the North's willingness to deal with those who were perceived as instigating black resistance.

45. Slaughter, *Bloody Dawn*, 112–38; *FDP*, November 13, 1851; *BS*, November 25, 1851.

46. Slaughter, *Bloody Dawn*, 45–46, 131–32; *PF*, November 6, 1851. The signers of the printed resolution passed by the meeting included individuals active in the clandestine operations of the Vigilant Committee, including William Still, J. J. G. Bias, and James McCrummell.

47. Maryland, Attorney General's Office, *Report*; Slaughter, *Bloody Dawn*, 135. Participants at the 1850 meeting in Philadelphia had also attempted to downplay concerns about kidnapping. Most prominently, James Buchanan had scoffed at such concerns, implying that they simply masked attempts to prevent the return of fugitives (*Proceedings of the Great Union Meeting*, 48–50).

48. *Voice of the Fugitive*, January 1, 1852.

49. Still, *Underground Railroad*, vii.

50. Tomek, *Colonization and Its Discontents*, 187–218; Floyd Miller, *Search for a Black Nationality*, 105–33. On *Condition*, see Levine, *Martin Delany*, 58–69.

51. Lapsansky-Werner and Bacon, *Back to Africa*, 30–31; Tomek, *Colonization and Its Discontents*, 163–86.

52. *NS*, January 16, 1851.

53. *NS*, October 30, 1851, March 11, 1852; Tomek, *Colonization and Its Discontents*, 176–77. While Tomek emphasizes the antislavery, humanitarian spirit of colonizationists like Coates, she notes that all Pennsylvania colonizationists walked a fine line between humanitarianism and political realities.

54. Pettit, *Addresses*; Burin, "Rethinking Northern White Support," 218–19.

55. *FDP*, April 29, 1852.

56. Levine, *Martin Delany*, 61–69; Delany, *Condition*, 219.

57. *PF*, November 6, 1851; *Voice of the Fugitive*, August 27, 1851.

58. *Voice of the Fugitive*, April 9, May 21, 1851.

59. Moses Sheppard to Samuel Ford McGill, January 18, 1850, Sheppard Papers, Series 2, Box 2.

60. John H. B. Latrobe to Moses Sheppard, February 7, 1851, ibid.

61. *Baltimore Maryland Colonization Journal*, October 1851.

62. *BS*, July 7, July 21, 22, 1852; "Address to the Free Colored People of the State of Maryland," *ARCJ*, July 1852.

63. *Baltimore Daily Times*, n.d., reprinted in *ARCJ*, July 1852; *FDP*, August 6, 1852.

64. "Typical Colonization Convention," 323; *BS*, July 29, 1852.

65. *BS*, July 28, 1852.

66. Ibid., July 27, 1852.

67. Ibid., July 29, 1852.

68. *FDP*, August 6, 1852.

69. *PF*, December 9, 1852.
70. Numbers drawn from the McGowan Index, which compiles the cases recorded by Still and later published (http://guides.temple.edu/c.php?g=77805&p=515005).
71. *NE*, January 2, 1851; Wilson, *Freedom at Risk*, 55.
72. Morris, *Free Men All*, 154–55.

CHAPTER 8. AFRICAN AMERICANS AND "POLITICAL INSUBORDINATION"

1. Mayo, "Charles Lewis Reason"; Biddle and Dubin, *Tasting Freedom*, 156–57; Still, *Underground Railroad*, 439; *FDP*, February 10, 1854; Still, Journal C, 3.
2. *PF*, November 25, 1852.
3. Mueller, *Whig Party in Pennsylvania*, 200; *Pennsylvania Election Statistics*.
4. James Buchanan to William Bigler, March 24, 1852, Bigler Papers, Box 1; Holt, *Rise and Fall*, 744–45; George Plitt to William Bigler, September 2, 1852, William G. Crans to William Bigler, September 29, 1852, both in Bigler Papers, Box 2.
5. Holt, *Rise and Fall*, 789–790; Mueller, *Whig Party in Pennsylvania*, 202–6; *Philadelphia Inquirer*, October 3, 1853; *PL*, October 13, 1853; *Philadelphia North American*, October 21, 1853.
6. *PF*, October 13, 1853.
7. Wilentz, *Rise of American Democracy*, 671–72.
8. *FDP*, April 7, 1854. For an account of the response of free blacks throughout the North to the Kansas-Nebraska crisis, see Lechner, "Black Abolitionist Response."
9. *CR*, July 13, 1854.
10. *NASS*, July 15, 1854.
11. Billington, *Protestant Crusade*, 380–89. Anbinder argues that voters in general supported the Know-Nothings as a means of expressing opposition to slavery but notes that the appeal of the party varied locally. According to Anbinder, "In the Philadelphia area, Know Nothingism effectively capitalized on anti-immigrant sentiment; in Harrisburg, the Order stressed anti-Catholicism, temperance, and anti-slavery; and in northern and western Pennsylvania Know Nothingism focused on anti-slavery and temperance issues." Most important, these issues overlapped and reinforced each other (*Nativism and Slavery*, 68).
12. Warner, *Private City*, 95.
13. Holt, *Rise and Fall*, 880–81.
14. *PF*, April 27, 1854; *NASS*, September 2, 9, 1854; Holt, *Rise and Fall*, 881–82.
15. Holt, *Rise and Fall*, 883–86; Anbinder, *Nativism and Slavery*, 55–68; *NASS*, October 21, 1854. In June 1854, the Pennsylvania Anti-Slavery Society had agreed to merge the *Pennsylvania Freeman* with the *National Anti-Slavery Standard*. The *Standard* subsequently contained significantly more material on Philadelphia and Pennsylvania (Minutes of the Anti-Slavery Society of Eastern Pennsylvania, New Jersey, and Delaware, June 14, 1854, Pennsylvania Anti-Slavery Society Records).
16. Jacob C. White Jr., "What Rum Is Doing for the Colored People," in Ripley et al., *Black Abolitionist Papers*, 4:210–11.

17. *FDP*, February 2, 1855; James Pollock to John M. Clayton, October 30, 1854, quoted in Holt, *Rise and Fall*, 884–85. For pro–Know-Nothing sentiment, see William Watkins in *FDP*, June 30, December 1, 1854.

18. Jacob C. White Jr., "Address Read at the Reception of Governor Pollock at the Institute for Colored Youth," Gardiner Collection; *NASS*, June 2, 1855. White's address appeared in the *Toronto Provincial Freeman*, June 9, 1855, with a few errors in transcription.

19. Still, *Underground Railroad*, 54.

20. Brandt with Brandt, *In the Shadow*, 34–39.

21. Ibid., 51–86.

22. Ibid., 96–112; Holt, *Rise and Fall*, 943; *NASS*, September 29, 1855; *NE*, October 4, 1855; *Pennsylvania Election Statistics*.

23. "Proceedings of the Colored National Convention, October 17th, 18th and 19th, 1855," in Bell, *Minutes*, 25, 29; *Toronto Provincial Freeman*, September 8, 1855.

24. *Toronto Provincial Freeman*, February 9, 1856; *NASS*, November 17, 1855. Sewell notes the importance of this aspect of fears of slavery expansion among Pennsylvanians (*Ballots for Freedom*, 299).

25. Gienapp, *Origins*, 415–16; *Pennsylvania Election Statistics*; *Toronto Provincial Freeman*, June 28, 1856. Gienapp asserts that anti-Catholicism was more damaging to the Frémont campaign than were fears of disunion. Whether or not this assessment is correct, both were important elements of Fillmore's appeal.

26. *Toronto Provincial Freeman*, February 28, 1857; *NE*, April 9, 1857.

27. Finkelman, *Imperfect Union*, 255–65, 274–84; Finkelman, *Dred Scott v. Sandford*, 43.

28. *BL*, April 10, 1857.

29. *Toronto Provincial Freeman*, April 18, 1857.

30. *BL*, April 10, 1857.

31. *Toronto Provincial Freeman*, March 28, 1857; *Pennsylvania Election Statistics*.

32. *Toronto Provincial Freeman*, April 27, 1855; *Liberty Bell*, 1857, reprinted in *BL*, February 5, 1858. For the public dimension of the Vigilant Committee, see Varon, "Beautiful Providences." On McKim, see Ira V. Brown, "Miller McKim."

33. Lapsansky-Werner and Bacon, *Back to Africa*, 32–33, 116–17, 122–23; Tomek, *Colonization and Its Discontents*, 163–86.

34. Moses, *Golden Age*, 15–55.

35. *Philadelphia Inquirer*, September 11, 1858.

36. *ARCJ*, May 1858.

37. Burin, "Rethinking Northern White Support," 228.

38. Collins, "Democrats' Loss of Pennsylvania."

39. Jean H. Baker, *Ambivalent Americans*, 1–7, 50, 94; Towers, *Urban South*, 15–36.

40. Berlin, *Slaves without Masters*, 346–47.

41. *BS*, February 3, 1858; *New York Herald*, February 12, 1858; *Philadelphia Inquirer*, July 22, September 11, 1858.

42. *New York Herald*, November 6, 1858; Freehling, *Road to Disunion*, 2:194–95.

43. Phillips, *Freedom's Port*, 205–6; Freehling, *Road to Disunion*, 2:195–97.
44. Freehling, *Road to Disunion*, 2:209–15.
45. *BS*, November 9, 1857, November 6, 7, 1859.
46. Ibid., December 14, 1859.
47. Phillips, *Freedom's Port*, 207–8; Freehling, *Road to Disunion*, 2:197–98.
48. Phillips, *Freedom's Port*, 232–34; Cross, *To Mr. Jacobs*.
49. Stowe, *Uncle Tom's Cabin*, 425–26.
50. *PF*, April 29, 1852.
51. *FDP*, May 20, 27, 1852; *PF*, September 16, 1853. Purvis denied that his father, a Charleston cotton merchant, had ever owned slaves, but Purvis's biographer, Margaret Bacon, disagrees (*But One Race*, 7–12).
52. *BS*, August 25, 1853; *PF*, September 29, 1953; *BL*, October 7, 1853.
53. *PF*, November 25, 1852. In his introduction to one edition of a similar Nell work, Wendell Phillips offered a similar reading, even including a quote from an old anticolonization speech: "We are NATIVES of this country: we ask only to be treated as well as FOREIGNERS. Not a few of our fathers suffered and bled to purchase its independence; we ask only to be treated as well as those who fought against it" (Nell, *Colored Patriots*, 8). Nell offered his own reading along these lines, explicitly placing it in the context of the political nativism of his Boston home: "The Boston Bee and Post have been lately discussing Irish valor and antecedents. This compilation will show the world Colored American valor and antecedents" (in Ripley et al., *Black Abolitionist Papers*, 4:298–301).
54. *BL*, May 19, 1854. Mitchel's words are reprinted in *NE*, January 26, 1854, among other places. Perhaps just as critical of northern society as he was of the British government, Mitchel moved to Knoxville, Tennessee, soon after making this declaration. There he published a newspaper, the *Southern Citizen*, and ultimately became a staunch advocate of the Confederacy (McGovern, *John Mitchel*, 129–54).
55. *BL*, May 19, 1854.
56. Payne, *History*, 278–79; *CR*, September 16, October 18, 1854.
57. *CR*, August 17, September 16, 1854.
58. *NASS*, October 28, 1854; "Speech by William Wells Brown, Delivered at the Horticultural Hall, West Chester, Pennsylvania, 23 October, 1854," in Ripley et al., *Black Abolitionist Papers*, 4:245–55.
59. "Speech by William Wells Brown," 248.
60. Gardiner, "Gentleman of Superior Cultivation." See also Otter, *Philadelphia Stories*, esp. 211–78.
61. Webb, *Garies and Their Friends*, 144–232.
62. Gardiner, "Gentleman of Superior Cultivation," 300. On this aspect of the Know-Nothing movement, see Voss-Hubbard, *Beyond Party*.
63. *Washington Daily Globe*, January 17, 1855; *BS*, January 17, 1855; *FDP*, January 26, 1855; *Memorial of Thirty Thousand Disfranchised Citizens*. Benjamin Quarles (and those who have drawn on his pathbreaking work) described this memorial as addressed to the U.S. Senate and House rather than the Senate and House of Pennsylvania (*Black Aboli-*

tionists, 174–75). Douglass comments on the memorial and its context in *FDP*, March 24, 1855.

64. *Memorial of Thirty Thousand Disfranchised Citizens*, 13; Kantrowitz, "Place for 'Colored Patriots'"; Katchun, "From Forgotten Founder to Indispensable Icon"; Price, "Black Voting Rights Issue," 364.

CHAPTER 9. THE END OF THE BORDER

1. Gara, "William Still," 38; *BL*, December 23, 1859; *BS*, December 5, 17, 1859.
2. *BL*, April 15, 1859.
3. *NASS*, August 18, 1860.
4. Ibid.; Still, *Underground Railroad*, 384–85.
5. Oakes, *Freedom National*, 171–74.
6. Ibid., 169–70, 176–81; Wagandt, *Mighty Revolution*, 116–18.
7. Stephens, *Voice of Thunder*, 167.
8. "Report by William Still," May 22, 1862, in Ripley et al., *Black Abolitionist Papers*, 5:140–41.
9. Wagandt, *Mighty Revolution*, 55–70.
10. *Philadelphia North American*, August 31, 1859.
11. Philip S. Foner, "Battle to End Discrimination (Part I)"; Philip S. Foner, "Battle to End Discrimination (Part II)." See also Diemer, "Reconstructing Philadelphia."
12. *New York Weekly Anglo-African*, March 17, 1860.
13. Bacon, *But One Race*, 135–36.
14. *BL*, May 18, 1860.
15. Ibid.; *New York Herald*, October 30, 1860; Bacon, *But One Race*, 136–38.
16. McPherson, *Struggle for Equality*, 192–93; Green, "Let Us Take Up the Sword," 357–59.
17. "R.H.V. to Robert Hamilton," September 1861, in Ripley et al., *Black Abolitionist Papers*, 5:117–21. According to Ripley, the author is probably Robert H. Vandyne.
18. Alfred M. Green to Robert Hamilton, October 1861, in ibid., 121–24.
19. *CR*, August 23, 1862. On this incident as an example of Lincoln's "strategic racism," see Oakes, *Radical and the Republican*, 125–30.
20. *BL*, September 12, 1862.
21. Eric Foner, "Lincoln and Colonization"; *BL*, March 6, 1863.
22. Fields, *Slavery and Freedom*, 123–27.
23. *CR*, May 30, 1863; Fields, *Slavery and Freedom*, 129; Phillips, *Freedom's Port*, 240–41.
24. *BL*, May 22, 1863.
25. Ibid.
26. Ibid.
27. Diemer, "Reconstructing Philadelphia"; Countryman, *Up South*.
28. Fields, *Slavery and Freedom*, 131–66.
29. Fredrickson, *Black Image*, 228–55; Blight, *Race and Reunion*, esp. 192–98.

BIBLIOGRAPHY

PRIMARY SOURCES

Archival Material

American Colonization Society Papers, Microfilm Edition, Library of Congress.
William Bigler Papers, Historical Society of Pennsylvania, Philadelphia.
Leon Gardiner Collection of American Negro Historical Society Records, Historical Society of Pennsylvania, Philadelphia.
Benjamin Chew Howard Papers, Maryland Historical Society, Baltimore.
Charles Jared Ingersoll Papers, Historical Society of Pennsylvania, Philadelphia.
Francis Scott Key Papers, Maryland Historical Society, Baltimore.
Meredith Family Papers, Historical Society of Pennsylvania, Philadelphia.
Pennsylvania Abolition Society Papers, Microfilm Edition, Historical Society of Pennsylvania, Philadelphia.
Pennsylvania Anti-Slavery Society Records, Historical Society of Pennsylvania, Philadelphia.
Rawle Family Papers, Historical Society of Pennsylvania, Philadelphia.
Jonathan Roberts Papers, Historical Society of Pennsylvania, Philadelphia.
Moses Sheppard Papers, Friends Historical Library, Swarthmore College, Swarthmore, Pa.
William Still, Journal C of Station no. 2, Vigilance Committee of Philadelphia, Historical Society of Pennsylvania, Philadelphia.
Roger Brooke Taney Papers, Maryland Historical Society, Baltimore.
Vaux Family Papers, Historical Society of Pennsylvania, Philadelphia.
Vigilant Committee of Philadelphia Records, 1839–1844, Historical Society of Pennsylvania, Philadelphia.

Periodicals

Albany (New York) Evening Journal
Alexandria (Virginia) Gazette

BIBLIOGRAPHY

Amherst (New Hampshire) Hillsboro Telegraph
Annapolis Maryland Gazette
Augusta Chronicle and Georgia Advertiser
Baltimore American Commercial Daily Advertiser
Baltimore Gazette and Daily Advertiser
Baltimore Genius of Universal Emancipation
Baltimore Genius of Universal Emancipation and Baltimore Courier
Baltimore Maryland Colonization Journal
Baltimore Niles Weekly Register
Baltimore Patriot
Baltimore Sun
Boston Emancipator and Republican
Boston Liberator
Boston Missionary Herald
Boston Recorder
Boston Universalist Magazine
Chillicothe (Ohio) Weekly Recorder
Cincinnati Philanthropist
Concord New Hampshire Observer
Easton (Maryland) Gazette
Easton (Maryland) Republican Star and General Advertiser
Independent Chronicle and Boston Patriot
Ithaca (New York) Journal
Leesburg (Virginia) Genius of Liberty
Lexington (Kentucky) Western Monitor
London Anti-Slavery Reporter
New Bedford (Massachusetts) Mercury
New Orleans Daily Picayune
Newport (Rhode Island) Mercury
New York African Observer
New York Christian Herald
New York Colored American
New York Emancipator
New York Freedom's Journal
New York Herald
New York National Advocate
New York National Anti-Slavery Standard
New York Weekly Anglo-African
Ontario Voice of the Fugitive
Philadelphia Aurora and Pennsylvania Gazette
Philadelphia Catholic Herald
Philadelphia Christian Recorder
Philadelphia Democratic Press

Philadelphia Franklin Gazette
Philadelphia Hazard's Register of Pennsylvania
Philadelphia National Enquirer
Philadelphia National Gazette
Philadelphia National Recorder
Philadelphia National Reformer
Philadelphia North American and Daily Advertiser
Philadelphia Pennsylvania Freeman
Philadelphia Pennsylvania Inquirer
Philadelphia Pennsylvanian
Philadelphia Poulson's American Daily Advertiser
Philadelphia Public Ledger
Philadelphia United States Gazette
Philadelphia Weekly Aurora
Portsmouth New Hampshire Gazette
Providence (Rhode Island) Religious Intelligencer
Richmond (Virginia) Enquirer
Rochester (New York) Frederick Douglass' Paper
Rochester (New York) North Star
Salem (Massachusetts) Essex Register
Salem (Massachusetts) Gazette
St. Louis Enquirer
Toronto Provincial Freeman
Trenton (New Jersey) Federalist
Washington African Repository and Colonial Journal
Washington Daily Globe
Washington Daily National Intelligencer
Washington Daily National Journal
Washington National Era
West Chester (Pennsylvania) Village Record
Wilmington (Delaware) American Watchman
Windsor Vermont Journal

Books, Pamphlets and Other Printed Materials

Address to the People of Maryland: With the Constitution. Baltimore: Maryland State Colonization Society, 1831.

Agg, John, ed. *Proceedings and Debates of the Convention of the Commonwealth of Pennsylvania*. Harrisburg: Packer, Barrett, and Parks, 1837–38.

American Colonization Society. *Annual Reports of the American Society for Colonizing Free People of Color of the United States*. New York: Negro Universities Press, 1969.

Annals of Congress. Washington, D.C.: Gales and Seaton, 1834–56.

Beecher, Lyman. *Six Sermons on the Nature, Occasions, Signs, Evils, and Remedy of Intemperance*. New York: American Tract Society, 1833.

Bell, Howard Holman, ed. *Minutes of the Proceedings of the National Negro Conventions, 1830–1864.* New York: Arno, 1969.
Breck, Samuel. "Diary of Samuel Breck, 1814–1822." Ed. Nicholas B. Wainwright. *Pennsylvania Magazine of History and Biography* 102, no. 4 (October 1978): 469–508.
Brown, Isaac V. *Biography of the Rev. Robert Finley.* 1819. New York: Arno, 1969.
Buchanan, James. *The Works of James Buchanan, Comprising His Speeches, State Papers, and Private Correspondence.* Ed. John Bassett Moore. New York: Antiquarian, 1960.
Carey, Matthew. *Should the Nullifiers Succeed in Their Views of Separation, and the Union Be in Consequence Dissolved, the Following Will Be an Appropriate Epitaph.* Philadelphia: n.p., 1832.
Child, Lydia Maria Francis. *Isaac T. Hopper: A True Life.* Boston: Jewett, 1854.
Clay, Henry. *The Papers of Henry Clay.* Ed. James F. Hopkins. Lexington: University of Kentucky Press, 1959–92.
Coffin, Joshua. *To the Honourable the Senate and House of Representatives of the Commonwealth of Pennsylvania, in General Assembly Met: The Memorial of the Subscribers, Free People of Colour, Residing in the County of Philadelphia.* Philadelphia: n.p., 1832.
Coker, Daniel. "A Dialogue between a Virginian and an African Minister." In *Pamphlets of Protest: An Anthology of Early African American Protest Literature, 1790–1860*, ed. Richard S. Newman, Patrick Rael, and Philip Lapsansky, 53–65. New York: Routledge, 2001.
———. *Journal of Daniel Coker, a Descendent of Africa.* Baltimore: Coale, 1820.
Congressional Globe. Washington, D.C.: Blair and Rives, 1834–73.
Cross, Andrew B. *To Mr. Jacobs, Chairman of the Committee on the Colored Population.* Baltimore: n.p., 1860.
Cuffe, Paul. *Captain Paul Cuffe's Logs and Letters, 1808–1817: A Black Quaker's "Voice from Within the Veil."* Ed. Rosalind Cobb Wiggins. Washington, D.C.: Howard University Press, 1996.
Cunningham, Noble, ed. *Circular Letters of Congressmen to Their Constituents, 1789–1829.* Chapel Hill: University of North Carolina Press, 1978.
Delany, Martin R. *The Condition, Elevation, Emigration and Destiny of the Colored People of the United States and Official Report of the Niger Valley Exploring Party.* Intro. Toyin Falola. Amherst, N.Y.: Humanity, 2004.
Dewey, Loring L. *Correspondence Relative to the Emigration to Hayti of the Free People of Color of the United States.* New York: Day, 1824.
Douglass, Frederick. *My Bondage and My Freedom.* Intro. Brent Hayes Edwards. New York: Barnes and Noble Classics, 2005.
———. *Narrative of the Life of Frederick Douglass, an American Slave, Written by Himself.* Ed. David W. Blight. New York: Bedford/St. Martin's, 2003.
Douglass, William. *Annals of the First African Church, in the United States of America, Now Styled the African Episcopal Church of St. Thomas, Philadelphia.* Philadelphia: King and Baird, 1862.

Foner, Philip S., and Robert J. Branham, eds. *Lift Every Voice: African American Oratory, 1787–1900*. Tuscaloosa: University of Alabama Press, 1998.

Foner, Philip S., and George E. Walker, eds. *Proceedings of the Black State Conventions, 1840–1865*. Philadelphia: Temple University Press, 1979.

Forten, James. "Series of Letters by a Man of Color." In *Pamphlets of Protest: An Anthology of Early African American Protest Literature, 1790–1860*, ed. Richard S. Newman, Patrick Rael, and Philip Lapsansky, 67–72. New York: Routledge, 2001.

Freehling, William W., and Craig M. Simpson, eds. *Secession Debated: Georgia's Showdown in 1860*. New York: Oxford University Press, 1992.

Garrison, William Lloyd. *The Letters of William Lloyd Garrison*. Ed. Walter M. Merrill. Cambridge: Belknap Press of Harvard University Press, 1971–81.

———. *Thoughts on African Colonization*. 1832. New York: Arno, 1968.

Gloucester, Jeremiah. *An Oration Delivered on January 1, 1823 in Bethel Church on the Abolition of the Slave Trade*. Philadelphia: Young, 1823.

Gloucester, Stephen H. *A Discourse Delivered on the Occasion of the Death of Mr. James Forten, Sr.* Philadelphia: Ashmead, 1843.

Green, Alfred M. "Let Us Take Up the Sword." In *Lift Every Voice: African American Oratory, 1787–1900*, ed. Philip S. Foner and Robert J. Branham, 357–59. Tuscaloosa: University of Alabama Press, 1998.

Greenberg, Kenneth S., ed. *The Confessions of Nat Turner and Related Documents*. New York: Bedford/St. Martin's, 1996.

Harris, Alex. *A Biographical History of Lancaster County: Being a History of Early Settlers and Eminent Men of the County*. Lancaster, Pa.: Barr, 1872.

History of Pennsylvania Hall Which Was Destroyed by a Mob, May 17th, 1838. Philadelphia: Merrihew and Gunn, 1838.

Howard, Charles, Charles C. Harper, and Maryland, Board of Managers for Removing the Free People of Color. *Report of the Board of Managers for the Removal of the People of Colour, Enclosing a Communication from Charles Howard, Esquire, to the Governor of Maryland*. Baltimore: n.p., 1834.

Ingersoll, Joseph Reed. *Address of Joseph R. Ingersoll at the Annual Meeting of the Pennsylvania Colonization Society, October 25, 1838*. Philadelphia: Stavely, 1838.

Jackson, Andrew. *The Papers of Andrew Jackson*. Ed. Sam B. Smith et al. Knoxville: University of Tennessee Press, 1980–2013.

Jones, Absalom. "A Thanksgiving Sermon Preached January 1, 1808 in St. Thomas's, or the African Episcopal Church, Philadelphia." In *Early Negro Writing, 1760–1837*, ed. Dorothy Porter, 335–42. Boston: Beacon, 1971.

Journal of the Proceedings of the Senate of the State of Maryland. Annapolis: McNeir, 1831.

Lundy, Benjamin. *The Life, Travels, and Opinions of Benjamin Lundy*. 1847. New York: Negro Universities Press, 1969.

Maryland, Attorney General's Office. *Report of Attorney General Brent to His Excellency, Gov. Lowe, in Relation to the Christiana Treason Trials in the Circuit Court of the United States, Held at Philadelphia*. Annapolis: Martin, 1852.

Maryland, Board of Managers for Removing the Free People of Color. *News from Africa: A Collection of Facts, Relating to the Colony in Liberia, for the Information of the Free People of Color in Maryland*. Baltimore: Colonization Managers, 1832.

McKenney, William. *A Brief Statement of Facts: Shewing the Origin, Progress, and Necessity of African Colonization, Addressed to the Citizens of Maryland*. Baltimore: Toy, 1836.

Memorial of Thirty Thousand Disfranchised Citizens of Philadelphia. Philadelphia: for the Memorialists, 1855.

Minutes, Constitution Addresses, Memorials, Resolutions, Reports, Committees and Anti-Slavery Tracts. New York: Bergman, 1969.

Nell, William C. *The Colored Patriots of the American Revolution*. 1855. New York: Arno and New York Times, 1968.

Newman, Richard S., Patrick Rael, and Philip Lapsansky, eds. *Pamphlets of Protest: An Anthology of Early African American Protest Literature, 1790–1860*. New York: Routledge, 2001.

Parrott, Russell. "An Oration on the Abolition of the Slave Trade" (1814). In *Pamphlets of Protest: An Anthology of Early African American Protest Literature, 1790–1860*, ed. Richard S. Newman, Patrick Rael, and Philip Lapsansky, 75–79. New York: Routledge, 2001.

———. *Two Orations on the Abolition of the Slave Trade Delivered in Philadelphia in 1812 and 1816*. Philadelphia: Rhistoric, 1969.

Payne, Daniel Alexander. *History of the African Methodist Episcopal Church* Nashville, Tenn.: AME Sunday School Union, 1891.

———. *Recollections of Seventy Years*. New York: Arno, 1968.

Peck, Nathaniel. *Report of Messrs. Peck and Price Who Were Appointed at the Meeting of the Free People of Baltimore*. Baltimore: Woods and Crane, 1840.

Pennsylvania Election Statistics, 1682–2006. Wilkes University Election Statistics Project, Dr. Harold E. Cox, Director. http://staffweb.wilkes.edu/harold.cox/index.html.

Pettit, William V. *Addresses Delivered in the Hall of the House of Representatives, Harrisburg Pa., on Tuesday Evening April 6, 1852, by William V. Pettit, Esq. and Rev. John P. Durbin, D.D*. Philadelphia: Geddes, 1852.

De Philadelphia Riots; or, I Guess It Wan't de Niggas Dis Time. Philadelphia: Torr, 1844.

Proceedings of the Great Union Meeting. Philadelphia: Mifflin, 1850.

Proceedings of the Maryland State Convention to Frame a New Constitution. Annapolis: Riley and Davis, 1850.

Purvis, Robert. *Appeal of Forty Thousand Citizens, Threatened with Disfranchisement, to the People of Pennsylvania*. Philadelphia: Merrihew and Gunn, 1838.

———. *Remarks on the Life and Character of James Forten*. Philadelphia: Merrihew and Thompson, 1842.

Purvis, Robert, and William Whipper. *A Remonstrance against the Proceedings of a Meeting, Held November 23d, 1831, at Upton's, in Dock Street*. Philadelphia: n.p., 1832.

Register of Debates. Washington, D.C.: Gales and Seaton, 1825–37.
Report of the Committee of the Maryland Reform Convention on the Late Acts of Congress Forming the Compromise, etc. Annapolis: Riley and Davis, 1850.
"Resolution by Philadelphia Select Council, February 8, 1827." In Eric Ledell Smith, "Rescuing African American Kidnapping Victims in Philadelphia as Documented in the Joseph Watson Papers at the Historical Society of Pennsylvania." *Pennsylvania Magazine of History and Biography* 129, no. 3 (July 2005): 340–41.
Ripley, C. Peter, et al., eds. *Black Abolitionist Papers*. Chapel Hill: University of North Carolina Press, 1985–92.
Saunders, Prince. "An Address before the Pennsylvania Augustine Society." In *Pamphlets of Protest: An Anthology of Early African American Protest Literature, 1790–1860*, ed. Richard S. Newman, Patrick Rael, and Philip Lapsansky, 81–83. New York: Routledge, 2001.
Sergeant, John. "Speech on the Missouri Question, Delivered in the House of Representatives of the United States, on the Eighth and Ninth of February 1820." In *Selected Speeches of John Sergeant*, 185–256. Philadelphia: Carey and Hart, 1832.
Stephens, George E. *A Voice of Thunder: The Civil War Letters of George E. Stephens*. Ed. Donald Yacovone. Urbana: University of Illinois Press, 1997.
Still, William. *The Underground Railroad: A Record of Facts, Authentic Narratives, Letters, &c.* 1872. Medford, N.J.: Plexus, 2005.
Stowe, Harriet Beecher. *Uncle Tom's Cabin; or, Life among the Lowly*. Intro. Amanda Claybaugh. 1852. New York: Barnes and Noble Classics, 2003.
Turnbull, Robert James. *The Crisis; or, Essays on the Usurpations of the Federal Government, by Brutus*. Charleston: Miller, 1827.
"A Typical Colonization Convention." *Journal of Negro History* 1, no. 3 (June 1916): 318–38.
Van Buren, Martin. "Autobiography of Martin Van Buren." Ed. John C. Fitzpatrick. In *Annual Report of the American Historical Association for the Year 1918*, 2:55–56. Washington, D.C.: U.S. Government Printing Office, 1920.
Walker, David. *David Walker's Appeal, in Four Articles; Together with a Preamble, to the Colored Citizens of the World*. 1830. Intro. Sean Wilentz. New York: Hill and Wang, 1995.
Webb, Frank J. *The Garies and Their Friends*. 1857. New York: Arno, 1969.
Whipper, William. *Eulogy on William Wilberforce, Esq.: Delivered at the Request of the People of Colour of the City of Philadelphia, in the Second African Presbyterian Church, on the Sixth Day of December, 1833*. Philadelphia: Gibbons, 1833.
———. "The Slavery of Intemperance." In *Lift Every Voice: African American Oratory, 1787–1900*, ed. Philip S. Foner and Robert J. Branham, 145–54. Tuscaloosa: University of Alabama Press, 1998.
Whittier, John Greenleaf. *The Letters of John Greenleaf Whittier*. Ed. John B. Pickard. Cambridge: Harvard University Press, 1975.

SECONDARY SOURCES

Abzug, Robert H. *Cosmos Crumbling: American Reform and the Religious Imagination*. New York: Oxford University Press, 1994.

Adelman, Jeremy, and Stephan Aron. "From Borderlands to Borders: Empires, Nation-States, and the Peoples in between in North American History." *American Historical Review* 104, no. 3 (June 1999): 814–41.Alexander, Leslie M. *African or American?: Black Identity and Political Activism in New York City, 1784–1861*. Urbana: University of Illinois Press, 2008.

Altschuler, Glenn C., and Stuart M. Blumin. *Rude Republic: Americans and Their Politics in the Nineteenth Century*. Princeton: Princeton University Press, 2000.

American National Biography Online. www.anb.org.

Anbinder, Tyler. *Nativism and Slavery: The Northern Know Nothings and the Politics of the 1850s*. New York: Oxford University Press, 1992.

Ayers, Edward, *In the Presence of Mine Enemies: War in the Heart of America, 1859–1863*. New York: Norton, 2003.

Bacon, Margaret Hope. *But One Race: The Life of Robert Purvis*. Albany: State University of New York Press, 2007.

Baker, H. Robert. *Prigg v. Pennsylvania: Slavery, the Supreme Court, and the Ambivalent Constitution*. Lawrence: University Press of Kansas, 2012.

Baker, Jean H. *Affairs of Party: The Political Culture of Northern Democrats in the Mid-Nineteenth Century*. Ithaca: Cornell University Press, 1983.

———. *Ambivalent Americans: The Know-Nothing Party in Maryland*. Baltimore: Johns Hopkins University Press, 1977.

Baxter, Maurice G. *Henry Clay and the American System*. Lexington: University Press of Kentucky, 1995.

Bay, Mia. "See Your Declaration Americans!!!: Abolitionism, Americanism, and the Revolutionary Tradition in Free Black Politics." In *Americanism: New Perspectives on the History of an Ideal*, ed. Michael Kazin and Joseph A. McCartin, 25–52. Chapel Hill: University of North Carolina Press, 2006.

———. *The White Image in the Black Mind: African American Ideas about White People, 1830–1925*. New York: Oxford University Press, 1999.

Bell, Howard H. "The American Moral Reform Society, 1836–1841." *Journal of Negro Education* 27, no. 1 (Winter 1858): 34–40.

Bennett, David H. *The Party of Fear: From Nativist Movements to the New Right in American History*. Chapel Hill: University of North Carolina Press, 1988.

Benson, Lee. *The Concept of Jacksonian Democracy: New York as a Test Case*. Princeton: Princeton University Press, 1961.

Berlin, Ira. *Generations of Captivity: A History of African-American Slaves*. Cambridge: Harvard University Press, 2003.

———. *Slaves without Masters: The Free Negro in the Antebellum South*. New York: Pantheon, 1975.

Biddle, Daniel R., and Murray Dubin. *Tasting Freedom: Octavius Catto and the Battle for Equality in Civil War America*. Philadelphia: Temple University Press, 2010.
Billington, Ray Allen. *The Protestant Crusade, 1800–1860*. New York: Macmillan, 1938.
Blackett, Richard J. M. *Making Freedom: The Underground Railroad and the Politics of Slavery*. Chapel Hill: University of North Carolina Press, 2013.
Blight, David W. *Race and Reunion: The Civil War in American Memory*. Cambridge: Harvard University Press, 2001.
Blockson, Charles. *The Underground Railroad in Pennsylvania*. Jacksonville, N.C.: Flame, 1981.
Bolster, W. Jeffrey. *Black Jacks: African American Seamen in the Age of Sail*. Cambridge: Harvard University Press, 1997.
Bordewich, Fergus M. *Bound for Canaan: The Epic Story of the Underground Railroad, America's First Civil Rights Movement*. New York: Harper Collins, 2005.
Boromé, Joseph A. "The Vigilant Committee of Philadelphia." *Pennsylvania Magazine of History and Biography* 92, no. 3 (July 1968): 320–51.
Bowman, Shearer Davis. *At the Precipice: Americans North and South during the Secession Crisis*. Chapel Hill: University of North Carolina Press, 2010.
Bradburn, Douglas. *The Citizenship Revolution: Politics and the Creation of the American Union, 1774–1804*. Charlottesville: University of Virginia Press, 2009.
Brandt, Nat, with Yanna Kroyt Brandt. *In the Shadow of the Civil War: Passmore Williamson and the Rescue of Jane Johnson*. Columbia: University of South Carolina Press, 2007.
Brown, Ira V. "Miller McKim and Pennsylvania Abolitionism." *Pennsylvania History* 30, no. 1 (January 1963): 56–72.
Browne, Gary Lawson. *Baltimore in the Nation, 1789–1861*. Chapel Hill: University of North Carolina Press, 1980.
Burin, Eric. "Rethinking Northern White Support for the African Colonization Movement: The Pennsylvania Colonization Society as an Agent of Emancipation." *Pennsylvania Magazine of History and Biography* 127, no. 2 (April 2003): 197–229.
———. *Slavery and the Peculiar Solution: A History of the American Colonization Society*. Gainesville: University Press of Florida, 2005.
Campbell, Penelope. *Maryland in Africa: The Maryland State Colonization Society, 1831–1857*. Urbana: University of Illinois Press, 1971.
Clark, Dennis J. "The Philadelphia Irish: Persistent Presence." In *The Peoples of Philadelphia: A History of Ethnic Groups and Lower Class Life, 1790–1940*, ed. Allen F. Davis and Mark H. Haller, 135–54. Philadelphia: Temple University Press, 1973.
Cole, Donald B. *Vindicating Andrew Jackson: The 1828 Election and the Rise of the Two-Party System*. Lawrence: University Press of Kansas, 2009.
Collins, Bruce. "The Democrats' Loss of Pennsylvania in 1858." *Pennsylvania Magazine of History and Biography* 109, no. 4 (October 1985): 499–536.
Cotlar, Seth. "The Federalists' Transatlantic Cultural Offensive of 1798 and the Moderation of American Democratic Discourse." In *Beyond the Founders: New*

Approaches to the Political History of the Early American Republic, ed. Jeffrey L. Pasley, Andrew W. Robertson and David Waldstreicher, 274–99. Chapel Hill: University of North Carolina Press, 2004.

Countryman, Matthew J. *Up South: Civil Rights and Black Power in Philadelphia*. Philadelphia: University of Pennsylvania Press, 2006.

Crofts, Daniel W. *Reluctant Confederates: Upper South Unionists in the Secession Crisis*. Chapel Hill: University of North Carolina Press, 1989.

Curry, Leonard P. *The Free Black in Urban America, 1800–1850: The Shadow of the Dream*. Chicago: University of Chicago Press, 1981.

Dain, Bruce R. *A Hideous Monster of the Mind: American Race Theory in the Early Republic*. Cambridge: Harvard University Press, 2002.

Davis, Susan G. *Parades and Power: Street Theatre in Nineteenth-Century Philadelphia*. Philadelphia: Temple University Press, 1986.

Davison, Nancy Reynolds. "E. W. Clay: American Political Caricaturist of the Jacksonian Era." PhD diss., University of Michigan, 1980.

Dew, Charles. *Apostles of Disunion: Southern Secession Commissioners and the Causes of the Civil War*. Charlottesville: University Press of Virginia, 2001.

Diemer, Andrew. "Reconstructing Philadelphia: African Americans and Politics in the Post–Civil War North." *Pennsylvania Magazine of History and Biography* 133, no. 1 (January 2009): 29–58.

Du Bois, W. E. B. *Black Reconstruction in America, 1860–1880*. 1935. New York: Free Press, 1992.

———. *The Philadelphia Negro*. New York: Lippincott, 1899.

Dunbar, Erica Armstrong. *A Fragile Freedom: African American Women and Emancipation in the Antebellum City*. New Haven: Yale University Press, 2008.

Dusinberre, William. *Civil War Issues in Philadelphia, 1856–1865*. Philadelphia: University of Pennsylvania Press, 1965.

Earle, Jonathan H. *Jacksonian Antislavery and the Politics of Free Soil, 1824–1854*. Chapel Hill: University of North Carolina Press, 2004.

Egerton, Douglas R. *He Shall Go Out Free: The Lives of Denmark Vesey*. Madison, Wis.: Madison House, 1999.

———. "'Its Origin Not a Little Curious': A New Look at the American Colonization Society." *Journal of the Early Republic* 5, no. 4 (Winter 1985): 463–80.

Ernest, John. *Liberation Historiography: African American Writers and the Challenge of History, 1794–1861*. Chapel Hill: University of North Carolina Press, 2004.

Evitts, William J. *A Matter of Allegiances: Maryland from 1850 to 1861*. Baltimore: Johns Hopkins University Press, 1974.

Feldberg, Michael. *The Philadelphia Riots of 1844: A Study of Ethnic Conflict*. Westport, Conn.: Greenwood, 1975.

Ferrer, Ada. *Freedom's Mirror: Cuba and Haiti in the Age of Revolution*. New York: Cambridge University Press, 2014.

Fields, Barbara Jeanne. *Slavery and Freedom on the Middle Ground: Maryland during the Nineteenth Century*. New Haven: Yale University Press, 1985.

Finkelman, Paul. *Dred Scott v. Sandford: A Brief History with Documents.* Boston: Bedford, 1997.

———. *An Imperfect Union: Slavery, Federalism, and Comity.* Chapel Hill: University of North Carolina Press, 1981.

———. "The Problem of Slavery in the Age of Federalism." In *Federalists Reconsidered*, ed. Doron Ben-Atar and Barbara Oberg, 135–56. Charlottesville: University Press of Virginia, 1998.

Foner, Eric. *The Fiery Trial: Abraham Lincoln and American Slavery.* New York: Norton, 2010.

———. *Free Soil, Free Labor, Free Men: The Ideology of the Republican Party before the Civil War.* New York: Oxford University Press, 1970.

———. *Gateway to Freedom: The Hidden History of the Underground Railroad.* New York: Norton, 2015.

———. "Lincoln and Colonization." In *Our Lincoln: New Perspectives on Lincoln and His World*, ed. Eric Foner, 135–66. New York: Norton, 2008.

Foner, Philip S. "The Battle to End Discrimination against Negroes on Philadelphia Streetcars: (Part I) Background and Beginning of the Battle." *Pennsylvania History* 40, no. 3 (July 1973): 260–90.

———. "The Battle to End Discrimination against Negroes on Philadelphia Streetcars: (Part II) The Victory." *Pennsylvania History* 40, no. 3 (October 1973): 354–79.

Forbes, Robert Pierce. *The Missouri Compromise and Its Aftermath: Slavery and the Meaning of America.* Chapel Hill: University of North Carolina Press, 2007.

Ford, Lacy K. *Deliver Us from Evil: The Slavery Question in the Old South.* New York: Oxford University Press, 2009.

Formisano, Ronald P. "The Concept of Political Culture." *Journal of Interdisciplinary History* 31, no. 3 (Winter 2001): 393–426.

———. *For the People: American Populist Movements from the Revolution to the 1850s.* Chapel Hill: University of North Carolina Press, 2008.

———. "The Party Period Revisited." *Journal of American History* 86, no. 1 (June 1999): 93–120.

———. *The Transformation of Political Culture: Massachusetts Parties, 1790s–1840s.* New York: Oxford University Press, 1983.

Fortenbaugh, Robert. "American Lutheran Synods and Slavery, 1830–60." *Journal of Religion* 13, no. 1 (January 1933): 72–92.

Franchot, Jenny. *Roads to Rome: The Antebellum Protestant Encounter with Catholicism.* Berkeley: University of California Press, 1994.

Fredrickson, George M. *The Black Image in the White Mind: The Debate on Afro-American Character and Destiny, 1817–1914.* New York: Harper and Row, 1971.

Freehling, William W. *Prelude to Civil War: The Nullification Controversy in South Carolina, 1816–1836.* New York: Harper and Row, 1966.

———. *The Reintegration of American History: Slavery and the Civil War Era.* New York: Oxford University Press, 1994.

———. *The Road to Disunion*. Vol. 1, *Secessionists at Bay, 1776–1854*. New York: Oxford University Press, 1990.

———. *The Road to Disunion*. Vol. 2, *Secessionists Triumphant, 1854–1861*. New York: Oxford University Press, 2007.

———. *The South vs. the South: How Anti-Confederate Southerners Shaped the Course of the Civil War*. New York: Oxford University Press, 2001.

Furstenberg, François. *In the Name of the Father: Washington's Legacy, Slavery, and the Making of a Nation*. New York: Penguin, 2006.

Gara, Larry. "William Still and the Underground Railroad." *Pennsylvania History* 28, no. 1 (January 1961): 33–44.

Gardiner, Eric. "'A Gentleman of Superior Cultivation and Refinement': Recovering the Biography of Frank J. Webb." *African American Review* 35, no. 2 (Summer 2001): 297–308.

Gienapp, William. *The Origins of the Republican Party, 1852–1856*. New York: Oxford University Press, 1987.

Glaude, Eddie S. *Exodus!: Religion, Race, and Nation in Early Nineteenth-Century Black America*. Chicago: University of Chicago Press, 2000.

Goodman, Paul. *Of One Blood: Abolitionism and the Origins of Racial Equality*. Berkley: University of California Press, 1998.

———. *Towards a Christian Republic: Antimasonry and the Great Transition in New England, 1826–1836*. New York: Oxford University Press, 1988.

Gosse, Van. "'As a Nation the English Are Our Friends': The Emergence of African American Politics in the British Atlantic World, 1772–1861." *American Historical Review* 113, no. 4 (October 2008): 1003–28.

Graham, Leroy. *Baltimore: The Nineteenth Century Black Capital*. Lanham, Md.: University Press of America, 1982.

Gravely, William B. "The Dialectic of Double-Consciousness in Black American Freedom Celebrations, 1808–1863." *Journal of Negro History* 67, no. 4 (Winter 1982): 302–15.

Grimsted, David. *American Mobbing, 1828–1861: Toward Civil War*. New York: Oxford University Press, 1998.

Guyatt, Nicholas. *Providence and the Invention of the United States*. New York: Cambridge University Press, 2007.

Hahn, Steven. *The Political Worlds of Slavery and Freedom*. Cambridge: Harvard University Press, 2009.

Haller, Mark H. "The Rise of the Jackson Party in Maryland, 1820–1829." *Journal of Southern History* 28, no. 3 (August 1962): 307–26.

Hämäläinen, Pekka, and Benjamin H. Johnson, eds. *Major Problems in the History of North American Borderlands: Documents and Essays*. Boston: Wadsworth, 2012.

Hämäläinen, Pekka, and Samuel Truett. "On Borderlands." *Journal of American History* 98 (September 2011): 338–61.

Hammond, John Craig. *Slavery, Freedom, and Expansion in the Early American West*. Charlottesville: University of Virginia Press, 2007.

Hammond, John Craig, and Matthew Mason, eds. *Contesting Slavery: The Politics of Bondage and Freedom in the New American Nation*. Charlottesville: University of Virginia Press, 2011.

Hardack, Richard. "The Slavery of Romanism: The Casting Out of the Irish in the Work of Frederick Douglass." In *Liberating Sojourn: Frederick Douglass and Transatlantic Reform*, ed. Alan J. Rice and Martin Crawford, 115–40. Athens: University of Georgia Press, 1999.

Harris, Leslie M. *In the Shadow of Slavery: African Americans in New York City, 1626–1863*. Chicago: University of Chicago Press, 2003.

Harrold, Stanley. *Border War: Fighting over Slavery before the Civil War*. Chapel Hill: University of North Carolina Press, 2010.

———. "On the Borders of Slavery and Race: Charles T. Torrey and the Underground Railroad." *Journal of the Early Republic* 20, no. 2 (Summer 2000): 273–92.

Heale, M. J. *The Presidential Quest*. New York: Longman, 1982.

Hellwig, David J. "Strangers in their Own Land: Patterns of Black Nativism, 1830–1930." *American Studies* 23, no. 1 (Spring 1982): 85–98.

Henig, Gerald S. *Henry Winter Davis: Antebellum and Civil War Congressman from Maryland*. New York: Twayne, 1973.

Hickey, Donald R. *The War of 1812: A Forgotten Conflict*. Urbana: University of Illinois Press, 1989.

Higham, John. *Strangers in the Land: Patterns of American Nativism*. New Brunswick, N.J.: Rutgers University Press, 1955.

Hine, Darlene Clark, and Jaqueline McCloud, eds. *Crossing Boundaries: Comparative History of Black People in Diaspora*. Bloomington: Indiana University Press, 2001.

Hodges, Graham Russell Gao. *David Ruggles: A Radical Black Abolitionist and the Underground Railroad in New York City*. Chapel Hill: University of North Carolina Press, 2010.

———. *Root and Branch: African Americans in New York and East Jersey, 1613–1863*. Chapel Hill: University of North Carolina Press, 1999.

———. *Slavery and Freedom in the Rural North: African Americans in Monmouth County, New Jersey, 1665–1865*. Madison, Wis.: Madison House, 1997.

Holt, Michael F. *The Political Crisis of the 1850s*. New York: Wiley, 1978.

———. "The Primacy of Party Reasserted." *Journal of American History* vol. 86, no. 1 (June 1999): 151–57.

———. *The Rise and Fall of the American Whig Party: Jacksonian Politics and the Onset of the Civil War*. New York: Oxford University Press.

Horton, James Oliver, and Lois E. Horton. *Black Bostonians: Family Life and Community Struggle in the Antebellum North*. New York: Holmes and Meier, 1979.

———. *In Hope of Liberty: Culture Community and Protest among Northern Free Blacks, 1700–1860*. New York: Oxford University Press, 1997.

Howe, Daniel Walker. *The Political Culture of the American Whigs*. Chicago: University of Chicago Press, 1979.

———. *What Hath God Wrought: The Transformation of America, 1815 to 1848*. New York: Oxford University Press, 2007.

Hunt, Alfred N. *Haiti's Influence on Antebellum America: Slumbering Volcano in the Caribbean*. Baton Rouge: Louisiana State University Press, 1988.

Ignatiev, Noel. *How the Irish Became White*. New York: Routledge, 1995.

Isenberg, Nancy. *Sex and Citizenship in Antebellum America*. Chapel Hill: University of North Carolina Press, 1998.

Jacobson, Matthew Frye. *Whiteness of a Different Color: European Immigrants and the Alchemy of Race*. Cambridge: Harvard University Press, 1998.

Johnson, Reinhard O. *The Liberty Party, 1840–1848*. Baton Rouge: Louisiana State University Press, 2009.

Johnson, Ronald Angelo. *Diplomacy in Black and White: John Adams, Toussaint Louverture, and Their Atlantic World Alliance*. Athens: University of Georgia Press, 2014.

Johnson, Walter. "On Agency." *Journal of Social History* 37, no. 1 (Autumn 2003): 113–24.

Jones, Martha S. "Leave of Court: African American Claims-Making in the Era of *Dred Scott v. Sanford*." In *Contested Democracy: Freedom, Race, and Power in American History*, ed. Manisha Sinha and Penny Von Eschen, 54–74. New York: Columbia University Press, 2007.

Kachun, Mitch. *Festivals of Freedom: Memory and Meaning in African American Emancipation Celebrations, 1808–1915*. Amherst: University of Massachusetts Press, 2003.

———. "From Forgotten Founder to Indispensable Icon: Crispus Attucks, Black Citizenship, and Collective Memory, 1770–1865." *Journal of the Early Republic* 29, no. 2 (Summer 2009): 249–86.

Kantrowitz, Stephen. "'Intended for the Better Government of Man': The Political History of African American Freemasonry in the Era of Emancipation." *Journal of American History* 96, no. 4 (March 2010): 1001–26.

———. *More Than Freedom: Fighting for Black Citizenship in a White Republic, 1829–1889*. New York: Penguin, 2012.

———. "A Place for 'Colored Patriots': Crispus Attucks among the Abolitionists, 1842–1863." *Massachusetts Historical Review* 11 (2009): 96–117.

Kerr-Ritchie, J. R. *Rites of August First: Emancipation Day in the Black Atlantic World*. Baton Rouge: Louisiana State University Press, 2007.

Kettner, James H. *The Development of American Citizenship, 1608–1870*. Chapel Hill: University of North Carolina Press, 1978.

Keyssar, Alexander. *The Right to Vote: The Contested History of Democracy in the United States*. New York: Basic Books, 2000.

Klein, Phillip Shriver. *Pennsylvania Politics, 1817–1832: A Game without Rules*. Philadelphia: Historical Society of Pennsylvania, 1940.

Knobel, Dale T. "'Native Soil': Nativists, Colonizationists, and the Rhetoric of Nationality." *Civil War History* 27, no. 4 (December 1981): 314–37.

———. *Paddy and the Republic: Ethnicity and Nationality in Antebellum America.* Middletown, Conn.: Wesleyan University Press, 1986.

Kocher, Kurt Lee. "A Duty to America and Africa: A History of the Independent African Colonization Movement in Pennsylvania." *Pennsylvania History* 51, no. 2 (April 1984): 118–53.

Kolchin, Peter. "Whiteness Studies: The New History of Race in America." *Journal of American History* 89, no. 1 (June 2002): 154–73.

Kraditor, Aileen S. *Means and Ends in American Abolitionism: Garrison and His Critics on Strategy and Tactics, 1834–1850.* New York: Random House, 1967.

Lapsansky, Emma Jones. "'Since They Got Those Separate Churches': Afro-Americans and Racism in Jacksonian Philadelphia." *American Quarterly* 32, no. 1 (Spring 1980): 54–78.

Lapsansky-Werner, Emma, and Margaret Bacon, eds. *Back to Africa: Benjamin Coates and the Colonization Movement in America, 1848–1880.* University Park: Pennsylvania State University Press, 2005.

LaRoche, Cheryl Janifer. *The Geography of Resistance: Free Black Communities and the Underground Railroad.* Urbana: University of Illinois Press, 2013.

Larson, John Lauritz. *Internal Improvements: National Public Works and the Promise of Popular Government in the Early United States.* Chapel Hill: University of North Carolina Press, 2001.

Laurie, Bruce. *Beyond Garrison: Antislavery and Social Reform.* New York: Cambridge University Press, 2005.

Lechner, Zachary J. "Black Abolitionist Response to the Kansas Crisis, 1854–1856." *Kansas History: A Journal of the Central Plains* 31, no. 1 (Spring 2008): 14–31.

Leslie, William R. "The Pennsylvania Fugitive Slave Act of 1826." *Journal of Southern History* 18, no. 4 (November 1952): 429–45.

Levesque, George A. *Black Boston: African American Life and Culture in Urban America, 1750–1860.* New York: Garland, 1994.

Levine, Robert S. *Martin Delany, Frederick Douglass, and the Politics of Representative Identity.* Chapel Hill: University of North Carolina Press, 1997.

Lightner, David L. *Slavery and the Commerce Power: How the Struggle against the Interstate Slave Trade Led to the Civil War.* New Haven: Yale University Press, 2006.

Linebaugh, Peter, and Marcus Rediker. *The Many-Headed Hydra: Sailors, Slaves, Commoners, and the Hidden History of the Revolutionary Atlantic.* Boston: Beacon, 2000.

Litwack, Leon F. "The Emancipation of the Negro Abolitionist." In *The Antislavery Vanguard*, ed. Martin Duberman, 137–55. Princeton: Princeton University Press, 1965.

———. *North of Slavery: The Negro in the Free States.* Chicago: University of Chicago Press, 1961.

Livingwood, James Weston. *The Philadelphia-Baltimore Trade Rivalry, 1780–1860.* Harrisburg: Pennsylvania Historical and Museum Commission, 1947.

Lubet, Steven. *Fugitive Justice: Runaways, Rescuers, and Slavery on Trial*. Cambridge: Belknap Press of Harvard University Press, 2010.

Malone, Christopher. *Between Freedom and Bondage: Race, Party, and Voting Rights in the Antebellum North*. New York: Routledge, 2007.

Maltz, Earl M. *Fugitive Slave on Trial: The Anthony Burns Case and Abolitionist Outrage*. Lawrence: University Press of Kansas, 2010.

Mason, Matthew. *Slavery and Politics in the Early American Republic*. Chapel Hill: University of North Carolina Press, 2006.

Mathews, Donald. *Slavery and Methodism: A Chapter in American Morality, 1780–1845*. Princeton: Princeton University Press, 1965.

Mayer, Henry. *All on Fire: William Lloyd Garrison and the Abolition of Slavery*. New York: St. Martin's, 1998.

Mayo, Anthony R. "Charles Lewis Reason." *Negro History Bulletin* 5, no. 9 (June 1942): 212–15.

McCarthy, Charles. *The Antimasonic Party: A Study of Political Antimasonry in the United States, 1827–1840*. 1903. Le Vergne, Tenn.: Kessinger, 2009.

McCarthy, Timothy Patrick. "'To Plead Our Own Cause': Black Print Culture and the Origins of American Abolitionism." In *Prophets of Protest: Reconsidering the History of American Abolitionism*, ed. Timothy Patrick McCarthy and John Stauffer, 114–44. New York: New Press, 2006.

McCormick, Richard P. "William Whipper: Moral Reformer." *Pennsylvania History* 43, no. 1 (January 1976): 23–46.

McDaniel, W. Caleb. "The Fourth and the First: Abolitionist Holidays, Respectability, and Radical Interracial Reform." *American Quarterly* 57, no. 1 (March 2005): 129–51.

———. *The Problem of Democracy in the Age of Slavery: Garrisonian Abolitionists and Transatlantic Reform*. Baton Rouge: Louisiana State University Press, 2013.

———. "Repealing Unions: American Abolitionists, Irish Repeal, and the Origins of Garrisonian Disunionism." *Journal of the Early Republic* 28, no. 2 (Summer 2008): 243–69.

McFeely, William S. *Frederick Douglass*. New York: Norton, 1991.

McGovern, Bryan P. *John Mitchel: Irish Nationalist, Southern Secessionist*. Knoxville: University of Tennessee Press, 2009.

McKivigan, John R. *The War against Proslavery Religion: Abolitionism and the Northern Churches, 1830–1865*. Ithaca: Cornell University Press, 1984.

McPherson, James M. *The Struggle for Equality: Abolitionists and the Negro in the Civil War and Reconstruction*. Princeton: Princeton University Press, 1964.

Meaders, Daniel. "Kidnapping Blacks in Philadelphia: Isaac Hopper's Tales of Oppression." *Journal of Negro History* 80, no. 2 (Spring 1995): 47–65.

Miller, Floyd. *The Search for a Black Nationality: Black Emigration and Colonization, 1787–1863*. Urbana: University of Illinois Press, 1975.

Miller, Kerby A. *Emigrants and Exiles: Ireland and the Irish Exodus to North America*. New York: Oxford University Press, 1985.

Morris, Thomas D. *Free Men All: The Personal Liberty Laws of the North, 1780–1861.* Baltimore: Johns Hopkins University Press, 1974.

Morrison, Michael A. *Slavery and the American West: The Eclipse of Manifest Destiny and the Coming of the Civil War.* Chapel Hill: University of North Carolina Press, 1997.

Moses, Wilson Jeremiah. *The Golden Age of Black Nationalism, 1850–1925.* New York: Oxford University Press, 1978.

Mouser, Bruce L. "Baltimore's African Experiment, 1822–1827." *Journal of Negro History* 80, no. 3 (Summer 1995): 113–30.

Mueller, Henry Richard. *The Whig Party in Pennsylvania.* New York: Columbia University Press, 1922.

Murphy, Angela F. *American Slavery, Irish Freedom: Abolition, Immigrant Citizenship, and the Transatlantic Movement for Irish Repeal.* Baton Rouge: Louisiana State University Press, 2010.

Nash, Gary B. *Forging Freedom: The Formation of Philadelphia's Black Community, 1720–1840.* Cambridge: Harvard University Press, 1988.

Newman, Richard S. *Freedom's Prophet: Bishop Richard Allen, the AME Church, and the Black Founding Fathers.* New York: New York University Press, 2008.

———. "Protest in Black and White: The Formation and Transformation of an African American Political Community during the Early Republic." In *Beyond the Founders: New Approaches to the Political History of the Early American Republic,* ed. Jeffrey L. Pasley, Andrew W. Robertson and David Waldstreicher, 180–206. Chapel Hill: University of North Carolina Press, 2004.

———. *The Transformation of American Abolitionism: Fighting Slavery in the Early Republic.* Chapel Hill: University of North Carolina Press, 2002.

Newman, Richard S., and James Mueller, eds. *Antislavery and Abolition in Philadelphia: Emancipation and the Long Struggle for Racial Justice in the City of Brotherly Love.* Baton Rouge: Louisiana State University Press, 2011.

Newman, Simon Peter. *Parades and the Politics of the Street: Festive Culture in the Early American Republic.* Philadelphia: University of Pennsylvania Press, 1997.

Nogee, Joseph. "The Prigg Case and Fugitive Slavery, 1842–1850: Part I." *Journal of Negro History* 39, no. 3 (July 1954): 185–205.

Novak, William J. "The Legal Transformation of Citizenship in Nineteenth-Century America." In *The Democratic Experiment: New Directions in American Political History,* ed. Meg Jacobs, William J. Novak, and Julian E. Zelizer, 85–119. Princeton: Princeton University Press, 2003.

Nwankwo, Ifeoma. *Black Cosmopolitanism: Racial Consciousness and Transnational Identity in the Nineteenth-Century Americas.* Philadelphia: University of Pennsylvania Press, 2005.

Oakes, James. *Freedom National: The Destruction of Slavery in the United States, 1861–1865.* New York: Norton, 2013.

———. "Natural Rights, Citizenship Rights, States' Rights, and Black Rights: Another

Look at Lincoln and Slavery." In *Our Lincoln: New Perspectives on Lincoln and His World*, ed. Eric Foner, 109–34. New York: Norton, 2008.

———. "The Political Significance of Slave Resistance." In *African-American Activism before the Civil War: The Freedom Struggle in the Antebellum North*, ed. Patrick Rael, 188–205. New York: Routledge, 2008.

———. *The Radical and the Republican: Frederick Douglass, Abraham Lincoln, and the Triumph of Antislavery Politics*. New York: Norton, 2007.

Onuf, Peter. *Jefferson's Empire: The Language of American Nationhood*. Charlottesville: University of Virginia Press, 2000.

Otter, Samuel. *Philadelphia Stories: America's Literature of Race and Freedom*. New York: Oxford University Press, 2010.

Parsons, Lynn Hudson. *The Birth of Modern Politics: Andrew Jackson, John Quincy Adams, and the Election of 1828*. New York: Oxford University Press, 2009.

Pease, Jane H., and William H. Pease. *They Who Would Be Free: Blacks' Search for Freedom, 1830–1861*. New York: Atheneum, 1974.

Phillips, Christopher. *Freedom's Port: The African American Community in Baltimore, 1790–1860*. Urbana: University of Illinois Press, 1997.

———. "Resistance to Colonization in Antebellum Baltimore." *Maryland Historical Magazine* 91, no. 2 (Summer 1996): 181–202.

Power-Greene, Ousmane K. *Against Wind and Tide: The African American Struggle against the Colonization Movement*. New York: New York University Press, 2014.

Preston, Dickson J. *Young Frederick Douglass: The Maryland Years*. Baltimore: Johns Hopkins University Press, 1980.

Price, Edward. "The Black Voting Rights Issue in Pennsylvania, 1780–1900." *Pennsylvania Magazine of History and Biography* 100, no. 3 (July 1976): 356–73.

Quarles, Benjamin. *Black Abolitionists*. New York: Oxford University Press, 1969.

———. "Free Blacks and the 'Spirit of '76.'" *Journal of Negro History* 61, no. 3 (July 1976): 229–42.

Rael, Patrick, ed. *African-American Activism before the Civil War: The Freedom Struggle in the Antebellum North*. New York: Routledge, 2008.

———. *Black Identity and Black Protest in the Antebellum North*. Chapel Hill: University of North Carolina Press, 2002.

———. "A Common Nature, a United Destiny: African American Responses to Racial Science from the Revolution to the Civil War." In *Prophets of Protest: Reconsidering the History of American Abolitionism*, ed. Timothy Patrick McCarthy and John Stauffer, 183–99. New York: New Press, 2006.

Remini, Robert V. *Henry Clay: Statesman for the Union*. New York: Norton, 1991.

Reséndez, Andrés. "National Identity on a Shifting Border: Texas and New Mexico in the Age of Transition, 1821–1848." *Journal of American History* 86, no. 2 (September 1999): 668–88.

Richards, Leonard L. *The Slave Power: The Free North and Southern Domination, 1780–1860*. Baton Rouge: Louisiana State University Press, 2000.

Roberts, Jonathan, and Philip Shriver Klein. "Notes and Documents: Memoirs of a Senator from Pennsylvania: Jonathan Roberts, 1771–1854." *Pennsylvania Magazine of History and Biography* 61, no. 4 (October 1937): 446–74.

Roberts, Rita. *Evangelicalism and Politics of Reform in Northern Black Thought, 1776–1863*. Baton Rouge: Louisiana State University Press, 2010.

Roberts, Timothy Mason. *Distant Revolutions: 1848 and the Challenge to American Exceptionalism*. Charlottesville: University of Virginia Press, 2009.

Rockman, Seth. *Scraping By: Wage Labor, Slavery, and Survival in Early Baltimore*. Baltimore: Johns Hopkins University Press, 2009.

Roediger, David. *The Wages of Whiteness: Race and the Making of the American Working Class*. New York: Verso, 1991.

Rolston, Bill, and Michael Shannon. *Encounters: How Racism Came to Ireland*. Belfast: Beyond the Pale, 2002.

Rubin, Jay. "Black Nativism: The European Immigrant in Negro Thought, 1830–1860." *Phylon* 39, no. 3 (Third Quarter 1978): 193–202.

Runcie, John. "'Hunting the Nigs' in Philadelphia: The Race Riot of August 1834." *Pennsylvania History* 39, no. 2 (April 1972): 187–218.

Salafia, Matthew. *Slavery's Borderland: Freedom and Bondage along the Ohio River*. Philadelphia: University of Pennsylvania Press, 2013.

Saxton, Alexander. *The Rise and Fall of the White Republic: Class, Politics and Mass Culture in Nineteenth Century America*. New York: Verso, 1990.

Scharf, John Thomas. *History of Baltimore City and County, from the Earliest Period to the Present Day*. Philadelphia: Lippincott, 1881.

Scharf, John Thomas, and Thompson Westcott. *History of Philadelphia, 1609–1884*. Philadelphia: Everts, 1884.

Sewell, Richard H. *Ballots for Freedom: Antislavery Politics in the United States, 1837–1860*. New York: Oxford University Press, 1976.

Sidbury, James. *Becoming African in America: Race and Nation in the Early Black Atlantic*. New York: Oxford University Press, 2007.

Silcox, Harry C. "The Black 'Better Class' Dilemma: Philadelphia Prototype Isaiah C. Wears." *Pennsylvania Magazine of History and Biography* 113, no. 1 (January 1989): 45–66.

Sinha, Manisha. "An Alternative Tradition of Radicalism: African American Abolitionists and the Metaphor of Revolution." In *Contested Democracy: Freedom, Race, and Power in American History*, ed. Manisha Sinha and Penny Von Eschen, 9–30. New York: Columbia University Press, 2007.

Slaughter, Thomas P. *Bloody Dawn: The Christiana Riot and Racial Violence in the Antebellum North*. New York: Oxford University Press, 1991.

Smith, Eric Ledell. "The End of Black Voting Rights in Pennsylvania: African American and the Pennsylvania Constitutional Convention of 1837–1838." *Pennsylvania History* 65, no. 3 (Summer 1998): 279–99.

Smith, Rogers M. *Civic Ideals: Conflicting Visions of Citizenship in U.S. History*. New Haven: Yale University Press, 1997.

———. *Stories of Peoplehood: The Politics and Morals of Political Membership*. New York: Cambridge University Press, 2003.
Snyder, Charles McCool. *The Jacksonian Heritage: Pennsylvania Politics, 1833–1848*. Harrisburg: Pennsylvania Historical and Museum Commission, 1958.
Staudenraus, Phillip. *The African Colonization Movement, 1816–1865*. New York: Columbia University Press, 1961.
Stauffer, John. *The Black Hearts of Men: Radical Abolitionists and the Transformation of Race*. Cambridge: Harvard University Press, 2002.
Stewart, James Brewer. "The Emergence of Racial Modernity and the Rise of the White North, 1790–1840." *Journal of the Early Republic* 18, no. 2 (Summer 1998): 181–217.
———. *Holy Warriors: The Abolitionists and American Slavery*. New York: Hill and Wang, 1976.
———. "Modernizing 'Difference': The Political Meanings of Color in the Free States, 1776–1840." *Journal of the Early Republic* 19, no. 4 (Winter 1999): 691–712.
Stuckey, Sterling. *Slave Culture: Nationalist Theory and the Foundations of Black America*. New York: Oxford University Press, 1987.
Sweet, Leonard I. "The Fourth of July and Black Americans in the Nineteenth Century: Northern Leadership Opinion within the Context of the Black Experience." *Journal of Negro History* 61, no. 3 (July 1976): 256–75.
Taylor, George Rogers. *The Transportation Revolution, 1815–1860*. New York: Rinehart, 1951.
Teilhac, Earnest. *Pioneers of American Economic Thought in the Nineteenth Century*. Trans. E. A. J. Johnson. New York: Macmillan, 1936.
Tomek, Beverly C. *Colonization and Its Discontents: Emancipation, Emigration, and Antislavery in Antebellum Pennsylvania*. New York: New York University Press, 2011.
———. *Pennsylvania Hall: A "Legal Lynching" in the Shadow of the Liberty Bell*. New York: Oxford University Press, 2014.
Towers, Frank. *The Urban South and the Coming of the Civil War*. Charlottesville: University of Virginia Press, 2004.
Travers, Len. *Celebrating the Fourth: Independence Day and the Rites of Nationalism in the Early Republic*. Amherst: University of Massachusetts Press, 1997.
Truett, Samuel. *Fugitive Landscapes: The Forgotten History of the U.S.-Mexico Borderlands*. New Haven: Yale University Press, 2006.
Tyrrell, Ian R. *Sobering Up: From Temperance to Prohibition in Antebellum America, 1800–1860*. Westport, Conn.: Greenwood, 1979.
Varon, Elizabeth R. "'Beautiful Providences': William Still, the Vigilance Committee, and Abolitionists in the Age of Sectionalism." In *Antislavery and Abolition in Philadelphia: Emancipation and the Long Struggle for Racial Justice in the City of Brotherly Love*, ed. Richard Newman and James Mueller, 229–45. Baton Rouge: Louisiana State University Press, 2011.
———. *Disunion!: The Coming of the American Civil War, 1789–1859*. Chapel Hill: University of North Carolina Press, 2008.

Vaughn, William Preston. *The Antimasonic Party in the United States, 1826–1843*. Lexington: University Press of Kentucky, 1983.

Voss-Hubbard, Mark. *Beyond Party: Cultures of Antipartisanship in Northern Politics before the Civil War*. Baltimore: Johns Hopkins University Press, 2002.

Wagandt, Charles Lewis. *The Mighty Revolution: Negro Emancipation in Maryland, 1862–1864*. 1964. Baltimore: Maryland Historical Society, 2004.

Waldstreicher, David. *In the Midst of Perpetual Fêtes: The Making of American Nationalism, 1776–1820*. Chapel Hill: University of North Carolina Press, 1997.

Walters, Ronald G. *American Reformers, 1815–1860*. New York: Hill and Wang, 1978.

Warner, Sam Bass, Jr. *The Private City: Philadelphia in Three Periods of Its Growth*. Philadelphia: University of Pennsylvania Press, 1968.

Washington, Margaret. *Sojourner Truth's America*. Urbana: University of Illinois Press, 2009.

Watson, Harry L. *Andrew Jackson vs. Henry Clay: Democracy and Development in Antebellum America*. New York: Bedford/St. Martin's, 1998.

Weiner, Dana Elizabeth. *Race and Rights: Fighting Slavery and Prejudice in the Old Northwest, 1830–1870*. DeKalb: Northern Illinois University Press, 2013.

White, Arthur O. "Prince Saunders: An Instance of Social Mobility among Antebellum Free Blacks." *Journal of Negro History* 60, no. 4 (October 1975): 526–35.

White, Shane. "'It Was a Proud Day': African Americans, Festivals, and Parades in the North, 1741–1834." *Journal of American History* 81, no. 1 (June 1994): 13–50.

White, Shane, and Graham White. *Stylin': African American Expressive Culture from Its Beginnings to the Zoot Suit*. Ithaca: Cornell University Press, 1998.

Whitman, T. Stephen. *The Price of Freedom: Slavery and Manumission in Baltimore and Early National Maryland*. Lexington: University Press of Kentucky, 1997.

Wilentz, Sean. *The Rise of American Democracy: Jefferson to Lincoln*. New York: Norton, 2005.

Wilson, Carol. *Freedom at Risk: The Kidnapping of Free Blacks in America, 1780–1865*. Lexington: University Press of Kentucky, 1994.

Winch, Julie. *A Gentleman of Color: The Life of James Forten*. New York: Oxford University Press, 2002.

———. "Philadelphia and the Other Underground Railroad." *Pennsylvania Magazine of History and Biography* 111, no. 1 (January 1987): 3–25.

———. *Philadelphia's Black Elite: Activism, Accommodation and the Struggle for Autonomy, 1787–1848*. Philadelphia: Temple University Press, 1988.

Wolf, Eva Sheppard. *Race and Liberty in the New Nation: Emancipation in Virginia from the Revolution to Nat Turner's Rebellion*. Baton Rouge: Louisiana State University Press, 2006.

Wong, Edlie L. *Neither Fugitive nor Free: Atlantic Slavery, Freedom Suits, and the Legal Culture of Travel*. New York: New York University Press, 2009.

Wood, Nicholas. "'A Sacrifice on the Altar of Slavery': Doughface Politics and Black Disfranchisement in Pennsylvania, 1837–1838." *Journal of the Early Republic* 31, no. 1 (Spring 2011): 75–106.

Wyatt-Brown, Bertram. "Prelude to Abolitionism: Sabbatarian Politics and the Rise of the Second Party System." *Journal of American History* 58, no. 2 (September 1971): 316–41.

Yacovone, Donald. "The Transformation of the Black Temperance Movement, 1827–1854: An Interpretation." *Journal of the Early Republic* 8, no. 3 (Autumn 1988): 281–97.

INDEX

Illustrations are denoted by italics

abolition: and Anti-Masons, 88; as antipartisan, 124; and black churches, 140–41, 144; and black citizenship, 102, 105–11; and black suffrage, 98, 113; critics of, 141, 144; Gag Rule for, 98, 102; and Irish immigrants, 124–25; Irish-nativist riots, 131; and moral reform, 105–11; in Philadelphia politics, 113; and political insubordination, 163; practical, 109, 138–44, 196n15; and Slave Power, 113–14; *and Uncle Tom's Cabin*, 177–78; and Vigilant Committee, 118; Whig views of, 115, 149

Adams, John Quincy, 54, 59–60, 87

African Americans: and ACS, 18–26; and antislavery politics, 88–89; and Brawner Report, 65–66, 68; colonization rhetoric of, 13–18; and emigration to Canada, 69, 84–85, 154–55; to Haiti, 35–36; and Homestead Bill, 164; and Maryland legislation, 65–66; moral reform and tactical disagreements of, 105–11; and national convention movement, 84–90; as native-born Americans, 18–23; as political actors, 3, 5–6, 8, 20, 33, 57, 62; political coalitions of, 84–87; religious-political divisions of, 33; as socioeconomic danger, 24–25; solidarity of, 22–23; and Turner rebellion, 64–72. *See also* black citizenship; free blacks

African Civilization Society, 188

African colonization movement: and abolitionists, 102–3; and ACS, 4, 14, 102; after Dred Scott decision, 170–74; and Baltimore convention, 155–56; and Brawner Report, 65–66; as civilizing/evangelizing effort, 15–16, 33–34; and Clay's American System, 13, 41–43, 74; of Coates, 172–73; as consensual, 15, 121–22, 198n9; vs. cosmopolitan worldview, 85; debated in *Niles Weekly Register*, 24; denounced in *Colored American*, 122–23; and economic development, 13, 42–45; and forcible removal threat, 117; free black attitudes to, 4, 28, 102, 199n23; and Fugitive Slave Law, 152–60; and Haiti, 33–39; and Kansas-Nebraska Bill, 164; Lincoln's view of, 190–91; in Maryland, 66–67, 72, 114; and Missouri Crisis, 26–30; northern motives for, 15; Pennsylvania appropriations for, 153; Philadelphian views of, 25; proposed financial support of, 74; proposed in Princeton, NJ, 11; protests against, 20; and public lands bill, 74–75; resurgence of, 173; and state power, 72–80; and Turner rebellion, 68–69, 72–79; in *Uncle Tom's Cabin*, 177–78; as undermining slave trade, 34; and white immigration, 121–23

African Episcopal Church of St. Thomas, 16–17, 116, 118, 125–26, 140–42, 144

African Institution of Philadelphia, 16

African Methodist Episcopal (AME) Church: 16–17, 18, 33, 39, 53, 164

African Presbyterian Church, 93

African Repository and Colonial Journal, 39–40, 45

Albany Convention, 109

Alberti, George, 159

alcoholism, 90–92, 187

Alien and Sedition Acts (1798), 21

Allen, Richard: engraving of, *2*; founder of AME church, 33, 53; and Fugitive Slave Bill, 1–4; on Haitian emigration, 35–36, 40; hosts black convention, 84; and lawsuit vs. Bethel Church,

Allen, Richard: (*continued*) 50; leadership skills of, 1–4, 57; as Philadelphian elite, 21, 34–35, 37; and southern refugees, 53
amalgamation, 102–3, 181–82
American and Foreign Anti-Slavery Society, 108
American Anti-Slavery Society, 86, 108, 178–79
American Colonization Society (ACS): auxiliaries of, 23, 25, 44; on black citizenship, 40–41, 45, 102; on consensual emancipation, 13–14, 19, 43, 121; constitution of, 13; denounced, 31, 152–54, 178; domestic threats to and colonial revolt, 39–40; financial support for, 45; free black opposition to, 4, 12–13, 18–26, 33–34, 114; on Haitian emigration, 35, 37, 39; on Missouri slavery, 29; reorganization of, 120–21
American Moral Reform Society (AMRS), 105–7, 109, 116
American Party, 169, 172, 174, 176
American Society for the Promotion of Temperance, 90
American Society of Free People of Color, 85–87
American System economic plan, 13, 41–44, 57–59, 73
American Temperance Union, 90, 209n25
antikidnapping bill/law, 138, 149, 159
Anti-Masonry, 87–88, 90–91, 100
Anti-Slavery Convention of American Women, 102
antislavery politics: and Kansas-Nebraska Bill, 164; and nativists, 133; and patriotism, 179–80; in Pennsylvania, 83, 105–11, 130–33, 170–74; and Republican Party, 169; and Whig Party, 161–62, 165
Anti-Slavery Society for Eastern Pennsylvania, 108–9
arson, 102–3, 127, 130
Asbury Methodist Church (Baltimore), 110
Ashmore, Margaret, 119
Attucks, Crispus, 183
Augusta, Alexander T., 191
Aurora periodical, 56

Bailey, Frederick. *See* Douglass, Frederick
Ballard, John, 169
Baltimore, 5, 12, 23, 50, 72
Baltimore American, 79
Baltimore Clipper, 191
Baltimore Emigration Society, 37
Baltimore Patriot, 55
Baltimore Sun, 1, 137, 143, 150, 156, 176
banking, as part of American System, 43
Beecher, Lyman, 91

Benezet, Anthony, 17
Bensalem Horse Company, 133
Bethel African Methodist Church, 12, 79, 84–85, 118
Bias, James J. Gould, 140, 164
Bibb, Henry, *Voice of the Fugitive,* 154
Bible (KJV), 130
Biddle, James C., 98
Bigler, William, 159, 163, 165
Binns, John, 60
Birney, James G., 115, 132
black activism: in 1860s, 185; and cultural conflict, 128–30; after Dred Scott decision, 170–74; in fiction, 181; and Fugitive Slave Law, 138, 147; and Missouri Compromise, 28; and political activity, 84, 161–62; varieties of, 215–16n21
black citizenship: and ACS views of, 40–41, 45, 102; and American Society of Free People of Color, 85–86; and AMRS, 105–11; attainment of, 192–93; as birthright and ACS views of, 4, 13, 19–22, 37–39; and black institutions, 50, 79; and the border, 56–62, 71–80, 112–20; and border politics, 112–13; fighting for, in Pennsylvania, 162–65; as *Christian Recorder* mission, 180; and civic engagement, 143; concepts of, 52, 54, 69–72, 76–77, 198n9; denial of, 4, 24, 45, 182, 197n21; denounced with violence, 116; Douglass's view of, 157; and Dred Scott case, 170; failure of in Pennsylvania legislature, 182–83; and foreigners, 177–83; and Fugitive Slave Law, 50–57, 138, 152–60; and Maryland politics, 174–77; and Missouri Compromise, 29–30; and political parties, 161–62; and political temperance, 166; and politics of union, 5, 61–63, 144–48; post-war resistance to, 193–94; and protection of the law, 94–105; rights of, 3–4, 13, 29, 32, 54–55, 196n19, 197n18; and white immigrants, 120–34; Wilberforce's support of, 88–89. *See also* suffrage for African Americans
Black Codes, 55–56, 84, 194
black nationalism concept, 173
blacks. *See* African Americans
black uplift movement, 105, 185–86, 1887
border/borderland, 6, 64–80, 112–20, 129
Boston Liberator, 63, 67, 69
Bowers, John C., 141
Boyer, Jean-Pierre, 35–36, 54
Brawner, Henry, 65
Brawner Report, 65–66, 68, 71
Breck, Samuel, 49, 62
Brick Wesley Church, 137, 141, 178

British-American Commercial Convention (1815), 54
British West Indies. *See* West Indies
Brown, David Paul, 102, 147
Brown, John, 140, 176
Brown, William Wells, 140, 180–81
Buchanan, James, 115, 162–63
Burr, John, 107
Burton, Belfast, 86

Calhoun, John C., 60, 73–74
Campbell, James, 164
Canada, as emigration destination, 69, 84–85, 154–55, 170–71, 187
Cary, Mary Ann Shad, 171
Catholic Church, arson against, 130
Catholicism, depicted in *Christian Recorder*, 180
Catholics, 36, 129–30, 164
Catto, William, 164
Chalmers, Thomas, 139
Chambers, Ezekiel, 4, 45, 56
Chesapeake and Delaware Canal, 58–59
Chinese Museum meeting, 146
Christiana town, 148–51, 216n42
Christianity, 15–16, 20, 87–89, 139
Christian Recorder, 180, 191
churches (in general): attack against, 102; black, criticized by Purvis, 140; denounced by Garrison, 1–8, 139; and electoral politics, 116; integration and disfranchisement, 109–10; moral reform and black abolition, 105–11; as racist, 107, 142; status of black members, 109–10
churches (specific): African Methodist Episcopal, 12, 16–17, 33, 39, 44, 50, 53; African Presbyterian, 93; Asbury Methodist, 110; Episcopal, 17; First African Presbyterian, 31–32, 87; First Presbyterian (Philadelphia), 101; Light Street Methodist Church, 118; Methodist, 23, 40, 44–45; Methodist Episcopal, 110–11; Methodist Episcopal Wesley, 115; Mother Bethel AME, 12, 44, 50, 53, 79, 84–85, 97, 116; Protestants, and black citizenship rights, 142; Second African Presbyterian, 107; Sharp Street Methodist, 23, 40, 44–45, 79, 110; St. Thomas (Philadelphia), 16–17; Third Presbyterian, 87; Wharton Street Methodist, 93; Zion Methodists, 143
Cincinnati, threats/riots in, 84–85
citizenship, 124–26, 142. *See also* black citizenship
civic institutions, 50, 79, 130, 143
Clarkson, Thomas, 17
Clay, Cassius, 132
Clay, Edward Williams, 61, 61–62

Clay, Henry: ACS rhetoric of, 26–27, 42–43; American System rhetoric of, 13, 73; and antimasonry, 88; and colonization, 11, 26–27, 41, 61; and Congressional legislation, 74–75; defends tariff, 43; on emancipation, 14–15; on Fugitive Slave Law, 144; as presidential candidate, 115; Public Lands Bill of, 73–74; as Whig, 132; and Whig Party, 86–87. *See also* American System economic plan
Coates, Benjamin, 152–53, 172–73
Coker, Daniel, 33–34, 46
colonization. *See* African colonization movement
Colored American, 101, 105–7, 115, 118, 122
A Colored Baltimorean (pseud.), 4
Colored Protestant Methodist Churches, 142
Compromise of 1850, 146–48, 161–62. *See also* Missouri Compromise
Conrad, Robert, 164
constitutional convention, of Pennsylvania, 95–97, 101–5
Copperhead Democrats, 193
Cornish, Samuel, 105–6
cosmopolitan worldview, vs. colonization, 21, 85, 199n28
Cotlar, Seth, 21
cotton cultivation, proposed for Africa, 172
Countryman, Matthew, 193
Crawford, William, 13, 41
Cresson, Elliott, 103, 211n72
Cuffe, Paul, 15–16, 18–19, 21, 33

Dallas, George M., 146–47
Dangerfield, Daniel (Daniel Webster), 185
Davis, Henry Winter, 174
Declaration of Independence, 99
Deists, 123–24
Delany, Martin, 133, 152, 154
Delaware, and fugitive slave laws, 56
Democratic Party: as antipartisan, 123–24; and black citizenship, 96, 98, 193; defeated in Pennsylvania, 174; and Democratic Free Soilers, 163; denounces Williamson, 168; endorsed by Know-Nothings, 166; on fugitive slave laws, 52; and Irish voters, 133; and Maryland legislature, 176; as northern defenders of slavery, 132–33; in Pennsylvania legislature, 168–70, 172; on Philadelphia riots, 128; on ratification of constitution, 104; on slavery issue, 100, 132, 149; on suffrage restriction, 99; and vote to repeal Fugitive Slave Law, 159
Democratic Press (Philadelphia), 41, 53, 56, 60
Devany, Francis, 67–68

248 INDEX

Dewey, Loring, 35, 37–38
Douglas, Stephen, 163–64
Douglass, Frederick (Frederick Bailey), 79; on Baltimore convention, 157; cross-border movement of, 5; denunciations of colonization,
Douglass, Frederick (Frederick Bailey) (*continued*) 117, 153; forced removal from Maryland, 117; Gloucester and churches, 140; slaveholder money, 139; split from Purvis, 178
Douglass, William, 141–42, 144, 215n15
Dred Scott v. Sandford, 170–74
Dupee, N. W., *158*, 159

Earle, Thomas, 101
East Baltimore Mental Improvement Society, 79
Eastern Pennsylvania Anti-Slavery Society, 138
economic development, 42, 58–59
economic nationalism, 13
education, 24, 167
elections, 98
Elizabeth sailing ship, 33
Ely, Ezra Stiles, 87, 89
emancipation: and colonization proposal, 14–15; as consensual, 13–14, 19, 43; and Fugitive Slave Law, 186; prohibited in Missouri Constitution, 38–39; and Turner rebellion, 65
Emancipation Proclamation, 190
Emancipator. See *Boston Liberator*
emigration: after Fugitive Slave Law, 137–38, 152–60; to Canada, 69, 84–85; of Coker, 33; focus on Canada/British West Indies, 154; and Haiti, 35–40; and immigration to U.S., 153

Federalists, 21–22, 37, 49, 52, 59–60
Few, Ignatius, 110
Fields, Barbara Jeanne, 193
Fillmore, Millard, 169, 174
Finley, Robert, 18, 22
First African Presbyterian Church, 31
First Presbyterian Church (Philadelphia), 101
Forbes, Robert, 29
"foreigner," as audience for citizenship claims, 178–79
Formisano, Ronald P., 88
Forten, James: activism of, 126; "A Series of Letters by a Man of Color," 17; on colonization, 19–22, 25, 28, 35, 62–63; as freeborn Philadelphian, 16; funeral of, 125; supports Breck, 49; violence against son of, 93
Forten, James Jr., 93, 100
Fortie, John, 77–79
Forward, Walter, 100, 102

Fourth of July celebrations, 17–18, 40, 52, 67, 86–87
Franklin Gazette, 27
Frederick Douglass's Paper, 166
free banking bill, as Whig issue, 163
free blacks: and ACS, 18–26; activism of, 127–28, 138; "A guard of colored soldiers," *192*; and AMRS, 106; Anti-Colonization and Anti-Nebraska Meeting of, 164; Baltimorean status of, 23, 55; and Christiana trial, 150–51; civic institutions of, 50, 79; on colonization movement, 4, 12, 14–15, 19–20, 25–26, 44–46, 153–54; and cross-border movement, 53, 170; and emigration to Canada, 69, 154–55; and fugitive slave laws, 1–2, 50–58, 94–95; and Haiti-Africa debates, 39–46; and Haitian colonization, 33–39; as inciting riots, 127–28; institutional support of, 50, 79; and Irish Americans, 124–25; kidnapping of, 50–56; of Maryland, 55, 65–66, 117, 176–77; military service of, 99, 126, 178–79, 189–90; and Negro Seaman Act, 53–54; patriotism of, 16, 39; and political maneuvering, 169–70; and politics of vigilance, 152–60; politics/political rights of, 2–8, 20, 24, 33, 57–58, 61–62, 174–75; and practical antislavery, 109–10; reconsideration of emigration, 152–60; and suffrage in Pennsylvania, 49–50, 86, 97–98, 210n52, 211n65; as threat to slaveholders, 11, 37–40, 54–55, 63, 65–66; and Turner rebellion, 64–72; and Vigilant Committee's work, 119; and Whig Party, 162; white support of, 138. See also black citizenship
Free Church of Scotland, 139
Freedmen's Relief Association, 187
Freedom's Journal, 4, 39, 61
Freehling, William, 73
Freemasonry. See Anti-Masonry
Free Soil Party, 161–62, 165
Frémont, John C., 169
Fugitive Slave Law: and AMRS goals, 109; black activism against, 112, 137, 185; and black citizenship, 94–95, 137–38, 159–60; and citizenship/protection of, under law, 94–95; and colonization goals, 157–58; and Compromise of 1850, 161–62; development of, 50–56; and free blacks, 1–2, 57–58, 94–95, 154; legal arguments/resolutions against, 137; opposed by Pennsylvania, 75, 148; and political rights, 57–58; political support for, 146–47; and practical abolition, 138–44; and *Prigg v. Pennsylvania*, 119; and slave catchers, 148–51; 185; and Slave Power, 137–38; and trial by jury,

95, 101, 116–17, 145, 147, 165; and U.S. Congress, 51, 144–45, 148; and U.S. Supreme Court rulings, 119–20; and Vigilant Committee of Philadelphia, 109, 159

Gardner, Charles, 78, 97–98, 114
Garrett, Thomas, *158*
Garrison, William Lloyd, 67, 77, 86–87, 108, 139
Garrisonianism, 108, 113, 131
General Paez privateer ship, 34
Genius of Universal Emancipation (Lundy), 37–38, 44–46, 60, 66, 93
German immigrants, 155
Gibson, Adam, 159
Gloucester, Jeremiah, 31, *32*
Gloucester, Stephen, 32, 106–8, 122, 126–30, 139–40
Goldsborough, Robert, 56
Gordon, Robert C., Jr., 116
Gorsuch, Dickinson, 148
Gorsuch, Edward, 148–49
Granville, Jonathan, 35–37
Great Britain, 88–89
Green, Alfred M., 189–90
Green, Duff, 60
Greener, Jacob, 44
Grice, Hezekiah, 84
Gurley, Ralph, 37, 40, 44

Haiti, 31, 33–46, 77
Hale, John P., 162
Hanway, Caster, 149, 151
Harper, Charles C., 44, 46
Harper, Robert Goodloe, 28, 37
Harpers Ferry raid, 176
Harrison, William Henry, 115
Hayne, Robert Y., 41, 45
Hemphill, Joseph, 27, 41–42, 58
Henry, Alexander, 174
Hiester, Joseph, 52
Hinks, Samuel, 174
Hinton, Frederick, 97–98, 105
Homestead Bill, 164
Hopkinson, Joseph, 20, 100
Horn, Henry, 59
Howard, Benjamin, 59
Howard, John E., 24, 59
Hugo, Victor, 155

immigrants/immigration, 112–32, 154–56, 180–82
Independence Day. *See* Fourth of July celebrations
Ingersoll, Charles Jared, 97, 104, 122

Ingersoll, Joseph, 121
Institute for Colored Youth, 161, 167
internationalism, 16–17, 31, 40
Ireland, "An Address" to abolitionists, 124
Irish Americans, 124–25
Irish immigrants, 124–25, 126–30, 133, 179, 181–82
Israel Colored Protestant Methodist Church, 142, 170

Jackson, Andrew, 13, 42–43, 60, 74
Jackson-Calhoun election, 60
Jacobs, Curtis W., 147–48, 175–76, 184
Jefferson, Thomas, 14
Jesuits, 123–24
Johnson, William, 54, 118
Johnson, Jane, 168–69
Johnson, Oliver, 177–78
Johnston, Gov. William, 149–50, 159, 163
Jones, Absalom, 16–17
Judah, Harriet, 69
jurisprudence. *See* Fugitive Slave Law

Kane, John, 168–70
Kansas-Nebraska Act, 164–65
Kantrowitz, Stephen, 6
Kenrick, Bp. Joseph, 130
Key, Francis Scott, 23
kidnapping: engraving of, *3*; of free blacks, 50–56; and fugitive slave bill, 1, 3, 51–52, 94, 112; as imminent threat, 159; and Maryland Colonization Society, 114; and personal liberty laws, 138–39; *Prigg v. Pennsylvania* case, 119; in southeast Pennsylvania, 150–51
Kittera, Thomas, 59
Kline, Henry, 148–49
Know-Nothing movement: as antislavery, 180; in Baltimore, 174; concerns of, 214n64; and political corruption, 182; Pollock's goals for, 166–67; varieties of, 218n11. *See also* Native American Party

language, use of *colored*, 106–7
Latrobe, John H. B., 44, 46, 122, 155
Leavitt, Joshua, 108
Leavitt Anti-Slavery Society, 108
Levine, Robert S., 154
Levington, William, 77–78
Liberator periodical, 63, 67, 69, 86, 96, 117–18
Liberia, 66–68, 152–53, 155–56, 173–74, 177
Liberty Party, 115, 132, 139
Light Street Methodist Church, 118
Lincoln, Abraham, 186, 190

literacy, 78–79
literature, 177, 181
Little Wesley Church, Gloucester-Remond debate, 140
Lundy, Benjamin, 37–38, 40, 56, 60, 93

Maine, and Missouri Compromise, 28
Maine Law Party, 166
Maine Liquor Law, 166
Maryland: and ACS, 45; Black Codes of, 55–56, 194; Black Law of, 114; Constitutional Convention of, 147–48, 155, 175; free black convention in, 155–57; on free black immigration, 117; and Fugitive Slave Law, 1, 56; party politics in, 174–77; as Second Middle Passage, 29; slaveholders' meeting in, 17; tension with Pennsylvania, 52; and Turner rebellion, 64–72
Maryland Colonization Journal, 155
Maryland State Colonization Society, 44, 66–67, 76, 114, 122
Mason, James, fugitive slave bill of, 144
Matlock, Lucius, 129
McKim, James Miller, 158
Mercer, Charles Fenton, 14
Meredith, William Morris, 57–59, 99–100
Methodist Episcopal Church, 110–11
Methodist Episcopal Wesley Church, 115
Methodists, 142, 118. *See also* African Methodist Episcopal (AME) church; churches; Methodist Episcopal Church
military service of free blacks, 99, 126, 178–79, 189–190
Miller, Floyd, 16
Missouri Compromise, 26–29, 31, 164. *See also* Compromise of 1850
Mitchel, John, 179, 220n54
mob violence. *See* violence/riots
moral reform, and black abolition, 105–11, 116
Morel, Junius, 86
Morgan, Margaret, 119
Morris, Thomas D., 144
Moses, Wilson, 173
Mother Bethel AME Church, 12, 44, 50, 53, 79, 84–85, 97, 116, 141, 125–26
Moyamensing Prison, 168
Moyamensing Temperance Society, 126

National Anti-Slavery Standard, 120, 143, 164–67
national bank, 43
national convention movement, 84–90
National Era periodical, 177

National Intelligencer, 22
nationalism, 84–85, 123–24. *See also* economic nationalism
National Journal, 41
National Reform Convention of the Colored Inhabitants of the United States of America, 114
National Reformer (of AMRS), 107–9, 113–14
National Republican Party. *See* Republican Party
National Union League, call for black troops, 191
Native American Party, 132, 162–63, 166. *See also* Know-Nothing movement
nativism/nativists: and antislavery, 133, 180; and black citizenship appeals, 182–83; vs. Irish immigrants, 129–32; as Know-Nothing movement, 165; and Pollock, 167
Naylor, Charles, 104
Negro Seaman Act (South Carolina), 53–54, 73
Nell, William Cooper, 178–79
New Haven, Connecticut, National Reform Convention, 114
Newman, Richard S., 21, 50
New York Herald, 189
Niles, Hezekiah, 24, 29
Niles Weekly Register, 24, 76
North American periodical, 147, 187–88
North Star journal, 137, 140–41, 143, 215n15
Novak, William J., 50
Nullification Crisis, 73–75

Oakes, James, 186
O'Connell, Daniel, 124, 192
Ohio Black Codes, 84

Panama Congress, 41–42
Parker, William, 149
Parrott, Russell, 17, 19, 25
partisanship, and antipartisanship, 115, 123–24, 132
patriotism, 16, 39, 40, 69, 179–80
Payne, Daniel, 118
Peck, Nathaniel, 77–78, 142
Pennsylvania: antislavery coalitions, 83–84; constitutional convention of, 95–97, 101–5; decline of Whig Party in, 163; legal protections for free blacks, 69–72; political antislavery legislators, 96; Third Congressional District, 103
Pennsylvania Abolition Society (PAS), 29, 35, 51–53, 57, 95
Pennsylvania Anti-Slavery Society, 115, 131–32, 181, 188
Pennsylvania Colonization Society, 114, 121, 153, 173
Pennsylvania Freeman, 83, 95, 133, 143, 161, 163, 177–78

Pennsylvania Hall, destroyed by arson, 102, 108, 113, 122–23, 159
Pennsylvania Inquirer, 96, 146
Pennsylvania legislature, appropriations for colonization, 153
Pennsylvanian, 103
People's Party, 174
Philadelphia: antislavery politics of, 5, 59–60; black elites of, 22, 34–35, 37, 69–70, 105; as borderland, 50, 52, 185–86, 195n11; and free blacks, 5, 12; and Fugitive Slave Act, 1–2, 51–52, 185
Philadelphia Association for the Moral and Mental Improvement of People of Color, 107
Philadelphia Chronicle, 92–93
Philadelphia Daily News, on Fugitive Slave Law, 159
Philadelphia Democratic Press, 41
Philadelphia Inquirer, on colonization, 173
Philadelphia Institute, 140, 153
Philadelphia North American, 139
Philadelphia Pennsylvanian, 124–25, 128
Philadelphia Public Ledger, on Torrey's arrest, 117–18
Philadelphia Sun, 168–69
Philanthropic Order of Sons of Temperance, 143
Pierce, Franklin, 162, 168
political parties, 123–24, 162–67, 174–77. See also *individual parties*
political temperance movement, 166
politics of union, vs. black citizenship, 63, 144–48, 184
politics/political rights: African American strategies for, 116–17; and colonization and state power, 72–80; and corruption, 182; endorsed by *Christian Recorder,* 180; and free blacks, 2–3, 5–6, 8, 24, 57–58, 61–62; and Haiti-Africa links, 35, 39–46; vs. natural rights, 99; and religious liberties, 33, 36–37, 39–40; and slavery question, 59–60, 86
Pollock, James, 165–67
Pottstown, Pennsylvania, 124–25
Poulson's American Daily Advertiser, 11, 56, 68, 75
poverty, as argument against black citizenship, 6, 325
Presbyterians: 31, 35, 87, 139, 143
Prigg, Edward, 119
Prigg v. Pennsylvania, 119, 138
printing industry, 5
Protestant Episcopal Church, 142
Protestants, 36, 130, 180
Provincial Freeman (Toronto), 169, 171, 187
public lands bill, 74–75

Public Ledger, 128
Purvis, Robert: and AMRS, 105; as anti-colonizationist, 177–78; and Anti-Slavery Society, 138, 179; on Brown's rebellion, 184; on cause of rioting, 127–29; as a citizen, 192; and Colored National Convention, 168; criticizes black church, 140; denounces Republican Party, 188–89; on disfranchisement, 101–2; on Dred Scott case, 170–71; eulogy for Forten, 125–26; on military service, 190; optimistic for the future, 188; as Philadelphian elite, 69–70; portrait of, *70*; supports *Colored American,* 114–15; and Vigilant Committee, *158,* 159
Purvis, William, 69

Quakers, 15, 44, 143, 211n72

racism: and American citizenship, 122, 181; and black suffrage, 98–99; and colonizing factor, 121, 173, 215n65; and "complexional" concerns, 111, 114–15; and Homestead Bill, 164; as insurmountable, 15, 155; and intemperance and slavery, 92; by Irish, 129; parable of drowning men, 107; among Protestant churches, 142; and razing of temperance hall, 127; of white immigrants, 120–21, 129, 180–81. See also suffrage for African Americans; violence/riots
Ralston, Robert, 14–15
Randall, Josiah, 147, 149
Randolph, John, 11
Rawle, William, 49, 60
Raymond, Daniel, 43, 59
Read, John (fugitive slave), 52
Reason, Charles L., 161
Reed, Frank (fugitive slave), 55
refugees, 53
religious organizing, 142–43
religious-political liberties, 33, 36–39, 40, 92, 123
Remond, Charles Lenox, 124, 140
Republican Party: and Anti-Masonic party, 88; as antislavery, 169; and black citizenship, 162, 184, 188–89, 193–94; on Fugitive Slave Law, 196; and Kansas-Nebraska Bill, 164; in Pennsylvania legislature, 174; political candidate of, 168
Richards, Leonard L., 132
Richmond Enquirer, 38, 44
Rider, Alexander, "Kidnapping" engraving, *3*
rights: political, 2–3, 5–8, 24, 57–58, 61–62; religious, 33, 36–40
riots. *See* violence/riots
Ritner, Gov. Joseph, 87–88, 90, 95–96, 103–4
Roach, Isaac, 113

Roberts, Jonathan, 2–3, 27, 57
Ruggles, David, 114
Rush, Benjamin, 17, 60
Rush, Richard, 14

Saunders, Prince, 35–36
Scott, Winfield, 162, 186
Scott, Daniel, 140
Second African Presbyterian Church, 107
Second Colored Presbyterian Church, 127–30, 139
sectionalism movement, 73–74, 103
Sergeant, John, 27, 41, 49, 59, 70, 88, 96, 146
Seward, William H., 144
Shadd, Mary Ann, 178
Sharp, Granville, 17
Sharp Street Methodist Church, 23, 40, 44–45, 79, 110
Shelter for Colored Orphans, 102
Sheppard, Moses, 72, 76–77, 155
Shunk, Gov. Francis R, 138
Slaughter, Thomas P., 149
Slave Power: and black and white abolitionists, 113–14, 169; and Christiana violence/riot, 149; and Dred Scott decision, 171; as encroaching on northerners, 181; and Fugitive Slave Law, 137–38; and immigrant voters, 182; and Kansas-Nebraska Bill, 163–65; and Whigs, 132
slavery/slaveholders: and ACS, 13–14, 37–38; as election issue, 58–61; influence of, on northerners, 101–2; and Kansas-Nebraska Bill, 164; Maryland, 186–87; in Maryland, 65–66, 175, 193; Mitchel's support of, 179; and Nullification Crisis, 73–75; and partisanships, 124; and political system, 86; and proposed racist legislation, 169–70; and reenslavement campaign, 176–77; self-purchase as control measure, 55; as strengthened by colonization movement, 20, 31–32; and temperance movement, 91–92; threatened by free blacks, 11, 37–40, 54–55, 63, 65–66, 175. *See also* Fugitive Slave Law
slaves: and Black Codes, 55–56, 84, 194; city vs. rural, 79; as consensual relationship, 14, 19, 43, 198n9; Maryland's eviction of, 65–66; offer to purchase freedom, 55; and Vigilant Committee, 119
Smith, Rogers M., 22
Smith's Beneficial Hall, destroyed by arson, 127
South Carolina, 53–55, 73–74, 139
southerners, and Methodist Episcopal Church, 110
Southern power. *See* Slave Power

states' rights: and citizenship issues, 99, 122–23; and Dred Scott case, 170; invoked by Maryland, 75–76; and nullification crisis, 73–74; and political rights, 99–100
Stevens, Thaddeus, 97
Still, William: aids fugitives, 167–69; and anti-colonizing meeting, 178; call for black uplift, 185; and Dred Scott decision, 171; on emigration, 154; and Freedman's Relief Association, 187; on kidnapping, 151; officer obtaining employment for colored persons, 187; portrait of, *152, 158*; *Provincial Freeman* letter, 169; and Vigilant Committee, *158*, 159, 161
St. Louis Enquirer, 18
Story, Joseph, 119–20, 138
Stowe, Harriet Beecher, 177
St. Thomas Church, Philadelphia. *See* African Episcopal Church of St. Thomas
suffrage for African Americans: and alleged illegal votes, 97–98; as birthright, 141–42; campaigns to restore, 116; and citizenship rights, 49–50, 101, 108–9, 193; and court cases, 97, 210n51, 211n65; disfranchisement of, 99–100; and military service, 99; in Pennsylvania, 49, 97, 101, 104–5, 116; and political action, 86; and presidential election, 116; and racism, 97–99; symbolism of, 113; violence/riots against, 102–3
Swift, John, 102, 113

Tallmadge, James, 26–27
Taney, Roger B., 120, 170
tariffs, 41–43, 73–75
Taylor, John, 28
temperance movement, 90–92, 163–66, 208–9n22
Third Presbyterian Church, 87
Toronto Provincial Freeman, 169
Torrey, Charles, 117–18
Torrey, Jesse, *Portraiture of Domestic Slavery,* 3
Tubman, Harriet, 186
Turner, Nat, 63–72

Underground Railroad. *See* Vigilant Committee of Philadelphia
Union Army, and Fugitive Slave Law, 186–87
Union Baptist Church, 140
U. S. Congress: on colonization, 45, 74; and fugitive slave laws, 51, 75; Gag Rule for abolitionists, 98, 102; Missouri Compromise debate, 28–29; Senate's Public Lands Bill, 73
U. S. Constitution: and black citizenship, 85–86, 122–23, 170; First Amendment, 123–24; and

Fugitive Slave Laws, 137–38, 144–48; invoked by Clay, 75; Thirteenth Amendment, 193–94; as weapon against slavery, 95
U. S. Declaration of Independence, 85–86
United States Gazette, 72
U. S. government, 43, 171
U. S. Supreme Court, 119–20, 170
U. S. War Department, 191

Van Buren, Martin, 41
Vesey, Denmark, and Negro Seaman Act, 53–54
Vesey African Methodist Episcopal (AME) church, 53
Vigilant Committee of Philadelphia: aids fugitives, 118–20, 159, 161, 166–68, 186–87; and AMRS, 109; and black network, 154–55; and Brown, 181; and Christiana riot trial, 150–51; and Harriet Tubman, 186; members of, *158*; photo of members, *158*; and slave catchers, 148; and violence/riots, 127–28
violence/riots: after Turner rebellion, 77; in Baltimore, 23; against black reform politics, 92–94; at Christiana town, 148–51; depicted in Webb's novel, 181–82; against Forten's son, 93; and Fugitive Slave Law, 137–38, 210n37; Irish-nativist conflicts, 130–31; linked to Deists/Jesuits, 124; and Maryland urban politics, 174; nativists vs. Irish, 130–32; Pennsylvania Hall arson, 102, 108, 113; and temperance movement, 126–30
voting rights. *See* suffrage

Waldstreicher, David, 124
Walker, David, 67, 157
Washington, Bushrod, 14
Washington, George, 21
Washington Southern Press, 145
Watkins, William, 4, 40, 46, 66–67, 77–78, 107, 110
Wears, Isaiah, 141
Webb, Frank, 181

Webster, Daniel (Daniel Dangerfield), 185
Weekly Anglo-African, 189
West Indies, 35, 129, 154, 185
Wharton Street Methodist Church, 93
Wheeler, John, 168
Whig Party: and abolitionists, 115, 149; and antikidnapping bill, 138–39; and Anti-Mason coalition, 96, 104, 115; as antipartisan/nonpartisan, 115, 123–24, 132; as antislavery, 100, 132, 149, 165; on black suffrage, 99; and Christiana trial, 151; collapse of, 161–63; and free blacks, 161–62; and Fugitive Slave Law, 147; of Philadelphia, 113; platform of, 163; as proslavery, 86–87, 100; and Slave Power, 132, 163; and temperance movement, 163, 166; and U.S. Constitution, 147
Whipper, William: as abolitionist, 69–71, 86, 88–89; AMRS spokesman, 106; on black suffrage, 124; on colonization, 173; on interracial violence, 94; Philadelphian abolitionist, 69–70
White, Jacob C., *158*, 159
White, Jacob C., Jr., 166–67
white citizens, 64–65, 97–98
white immigrants, 120–34, 180–81
Whittier, John Greenleaf, 83, 96, 115
Wilberforce, William, 17, 88–89
Williams, Samuel, 148
Williamson, Passmore, *158*, 159, 167–69
Wilmot, David, 165, 172
Winch, Julie, 50
Wise, Charles, *158*
Wise, Gov. Henry, 184
Wolf, George, 88, 90–91
women's rights, supported by Garrison, 108
Woolman, John, 17

Young Men's Anti-Slavery Society (Philadelphia), 95–96
Young Men's Vigilant Association, 128

Zion Methodists, 143

RACE IN THE ATLANTIC WORLD, 1700–1900

*The Hanging of Angélique: The Untold Story of Canadian
Slavery and the Burning of Old Montréal*
    BY AFUA COOPER

Christian Ritual and the Creation of British Slave Societies, 1650–1780
    BY NICHOLAS M. BEASLEY

*African American Life in the Georgia Lowcountry:
The Atlantic World and the Gullah Geechee*
    EDITED BY PHILIP MORGAN

*The Horrible Gift of Freedom:
Atlantic Slavery and the Representation of Emancipation*
    BY MARCUS WOOD

*The Life and Letters of Philip Quaque,
the First African Anglican Missionary*
    EDITED BY VINCENT CARRETTA AND TY M. REESE

*In Search of Brightest Africa: Reimagining the Dark Continent in
American Culture, 1884–1936*
    BY JEANNETTE EILEEN JONES

*Contentious Liberties: American Abolitionists in
Post-emancipation Jamaica, 1834–1866*
    BY GALE L. KENNY

*We Are the Revolutionists: German-Speaking Immigrants and
American Abolitionists after 1848*
    BY MISCHA HONECK

The American Dreams of John B. Prentis, Slave Trader
    BY KARI J. WINTER

*Missing Links: The African and American Worlds of
R. L. Garner, Primate Collector*
    BY JEREMY RICH

Almost Free: A Story about Family and Race in Antebellum Virginia
    BY EVA SHEPPARD WOLF

*To Live an Antislavery Life: Personal Politics and the
Antebellum Black Middle Class*
    BY ERICA L. BALL

*Flush Times and Fever Dreams: A Story of Capitalism and
Slavery in the Age of Jackson*
    BY JOSHUA D. ROTHMAN

Diplomacy in Black and White: John Adams, Toussaint Louverture, and Their Atlantic World Alliance
  BY RONALD ANGELO JOHNSON

Enterprising Women: Gender, Race, and Power in the Revolutionary Atlantic
  BY KIT CANDLIN AND CASSANDRA PYBUS

Eighty-Eight Years: The Long Death of Slavery in the United States, 1777–1865
  BY PATRICK RAEL

Finding Charity's Folk: Enslaved and Free Black Women in Maryland
  BY JESSICA MILLWARD

The Mulatta Concubine: Terror, Intimacy, Freedom, and Desire in the Black Transatlantic
  BY LISA ZE WINTERS

The Politics of Black Citizenship: Free African Americans in the Mid-Atlantic Borderland, 1817–1863
  BY ANDREW K. DIEMER

Punishing the Black Body: Marking Social and Racial Structures in Barbados and Jamaica
  BY DAWN P. HARRIS

Race and Nation in the Age of Emancipations
  EDITED BY WHITNEY NELL STEWART
  AND JOHN GARRISON MARKS

www.ingramcontent.com/pod-product-compliance
Lightning Source LLC
Chambersburg PA
CBHW011749220426
43669CB00022B/2956